VALUING ACCOUNTING PRACTICES

ROBERT F. REILLY

ROBERT P. SCHWEIHS

John Wiley & Sons, Inc.

New York • Chichester • Brisbane • Toronto • Singapore • Weinheim

657
R36v

Library of Congress Cataloging in Publication Data:

Reilly, Robert F.
    Valuing accounting practices / Robert Reilly, Robert Schweihs.
        p.   cm.
    Includes index.
    ISBN 0-471-17224-3 (cloth : alk. paper)
    1. Valuation.   2. Accounting.   I. Schweihs, Robert P.   II. Title.
HF5681.V3R43   1996
657—dc20   96-34963

Printed in the United States of America

10   9   8   7   6   5   4   3   2   1

ABOUT THE AUTHORS

ROBERT F. REILLY

Robert F. Reilly is a managing director of Willamette Management Associates, a valuation consulting, economic analysis, and financial advisory services firm with offices in principal cities across the country.

Before coming to Willamette Management Associates, Robert Reilly was a partner and national director of the Deloitte & Touche Valuation Group. Prior to that he was a vice president of Arthur D. Little Valuation, Inc.; held various financial management positions with Huffy Corporation, a diversified manufacturing firm; and was a senior consultant for Booz, Allen & Hamilton.

Mr. Reilly has performed the following types of valuation and economic analyses: event analyses, merger and acquisition appraisals, divestiture and spin-off appraisals, solvency analysis, fairness opinions, ESOP feasibility and formation analysis, purchase price allocations, business and stock valuations, feasibility and investment analyses, ad valorem appraisals, intangible asset appraisals, and transfer pricing analyses.

Mr. Reilly has been accepted as an expert witness on over 150 occasions in various federal, state, and international courts and before various state boards of equalization and tribunals. These controversy engagements have related to business, stock, and asset appraisal matters and to economic-damages matters. As an appraiser and economist, he has been an expert witness in the following types of litigation: bankruptcy, breach of contract, condemnation, conservatorship, corporate dissolution, expropriation, federal income tax, gift and estate tax, infringement (value of intangible assets), marital dissolution, minority shareholder rights, property tax appeal, reasonableness of executive compensation, solvency and insolvency, stockholder suits, tortious damages, and reasonableness of royalty rates and/or transfer prices.

Mr. Reilly holds a master of business administration degree in finance from the Columbia University Graduate School of Business. He holds a bachelor of arts degree in economics from Columbia University.

He is a certified public accountant (CPA), a certified management accountant (CMA), an accredited senior appraiser (ASA), a chartered financial analyst (CFA), a certified real estate appraiser (CREA), and a certified review appraiser (CRA).

Mr. Reilly is a certified general appraiser in several states. Also, he is a state certified affiliate of the Appraisal Institute.

Mr. Reilly is coauthor of *Valuing a Business: The Analysis and Appraisal of Closely Held Companies,* 3rd edition, and *Valuing Small Businesses and Professional Practices,* 2nd edition (both published by Irwin Professional Publishing). He is also coeditor (with Robert Schweihs) of *Financial Valuation: Businesses and Business Interests—1997 Update* (published by Warren, Gorham & Lamont).

ROBERT P. SCHWEIHS

Robert P. Schweihs is a managing director of Willamette Management Associates, one of the oldest and largest independent valuation consulting, economic analysis, and financial advisory firms in the country.

Before joining Willamette Management Associates, Mr. Schweihs was a partner and a national director of valuation services for Deloitte & Touche Valuation Group. Before that he was a manager for Arthur D. Little Valuation, Inc. And prior to that, he held various engineering management positions at Westinghouse Electric Corporation.

He has performed the following types of valuation analyses: merger and acquisition appraisals, purchase price allocation appraisals, business and stock valuations, ad valorem appraisals, litigation support and expert testimony, ESOP appraisals, forensic accounting analyses, and intangible asset appraisal and transfer pricing analysis.

These analyses have been performed for the following purposes: transaction pricing and structuring (merger, acquisition, divestiture), taxation planning and compliance (federal income, gift, and estate), financing securitization and collateralization, litigation support and dispute resolution, management information and planning, and bankruptcy and reorganization.

Mr. Schweihs holds a master of business administration degree in economics and finance from the University of Chicago Graduate School of Business. He also holds a bachelor of science degree in mechanical engineering from the University of Notre Dame.

Mr. Schweihs is an accredited senior appraiser (ASA), designated in business valuation, by the American Society of Appraisers. He is a member of The ESOP Association, the Institute of Property Taxation, and the Association for Corporate Growth (ACG).

He is often called upon to offer expert testimony on valuation and financial advisory matters related to gift and estate tax, income tax, property tax, shareholder disputes, securities fraud, infringement, expropriation, marital dissolution, lender liability, bankruptcy, breach of contract, tortious damages, and ESOP securities transactions.

Mr. Schweihs is coauthor of *Valuing a Business: The Analysis and Appraisal of Closely Held Companies,* 3rd edition, and *Valuing Small Businesses and Professional Practices,* 2nd edition (both published by Irwin Professional Publishing). He is also coeditor (with Robert Reilly) of *Financial Valuation: Businesses and Business Interests—1997 Update* (published by Warren, Gorham & Lamont).

CONTENTS

FOREWORD

This is, by far, the most comprehensive book ever written specifically on valuing accounting practices. Every CPA or public accountant that has or contemplates having an interest in an accounting practice will find it an insightful and useful reference.

Accountants who may have favorite approaches to valuing accounting practices will appreciate this book's many checklists and its perspective on what drives the value of an ownership interest in an accounting practice. I regard it as an indispensable reference for a professional appraiser who is valuing accounting practices. The positions taken by the authors are totally compatible with texts of broader scope (e.g., *Valuing a Business, Valuing Small Businesses and Professional Practices,* and *Guide to Business Valuations*), but this text goes into far more detail with regard to accounting practices.

The authors are uniquely well qualified to the task of this book. Their careers span Arthur D. Little Valuation, Deloitte & Touche (including the time of the merger between Deloitte Haskins & Sells and Touche-Ross), and, most currently, over five years heading up Willamette Management Associates. During this time, they have played active roles in many important accounting practice valuations.

Readers will also appreciate the clear, straightforward writing style, the cleanly organized flow, and the many helpful illustrative examples. Finally, the book is thoroughly indexed for convenient reference to specific topics and problems.

This book is a well-crafted, worthwhile extension of the literature of valuation. Given the number of accounting practices and accounting practice owners, it will find a wide and appreciative audience.

Shannon Pratt, CFA, FASA

PREFACE

With this book, the authors have attempted to address a diverse audience, encompassing owners of accounting practices, valuation practitioners (both certified public accountant and non-CPA valuation analysts), and parties who rely upon professional practice valuations (lawyers, judges, bankers, and others). This book, then, is intended to be useful both to those who prepare practice valuation analyses and to those who use practice valuation reports to make legal, financing, and other decisions.

From the perspective of the valuation practitioner, this book provides both the theory of practice valuation (i.e., *why* does one use certain approaches, methods, and procedures) and the application of practice valuation (i.e., *how* does one use certain approaches, methods, and procedures). It explains both how the various practice valuation approaches relate to each other and how the results of these approaches can be correlated and reconciled in order to reach a well-reasoned and well-documented valuation conclusion. The numerous examples included in the text should be useful not only to less experienced practitioners but also to seasoned analysts.

This volume also includes several bibliographies and provides numerous sources of industry data regarding accounting practice results of operations, practice management, and practice sale transactional data. These supplemental research sources and industry data sources should be useful to practitioners at all levels of experience.

Professional practice valuation methodology is based on the technical disciplines of applied micro-economic analysis and of investment analysis and portfolio management. These technical disciplines have been around for a long time. Therefore, during the past decade the most significant advancements in practice valuation have not been in the domain of analysis; rather, the most significant advancements have been in the area of professional standards.

The topic of professional standards is of direct interest both to analysts and to all parties who rely upon (or otherwise use) practice valuations. During the last decade, the American Society of Appraisers, the Institute of Business Appraisers, and the National Association of Certified Valuation Analysts have all promulgated professional standards for their members. The Appraisal Foundation has promulgated, and regularly updates, the *Uniform Standards of Professional Appraisal Practice* (USPAP). The American Institute of Certified Public Accountants has implemented a series of training courses for its members who practice in the valuation disciplines; these courses teach the professional standards of these various standards-setting organizations.

In this book these standards are described in great detail. Many of the promulgated standards are included as appendixes. These promulgated professional standards have caused considerable standardization in the valuation profession in such important areas as:

Terminology and vocabulary

Defining the valuation assignment

General methodology

Analytical documentation

Valuation reporting

The authors recommend that all valuation analysts—and also all who rely upon practice valuations—become familiar with these professional standards. Our recommendation is particularly emphatic when parties are reviewing and relying upon practice valuations within transactions, financing, or litigation or other controversy contexts.

We also recommend compliance with these professional standards on the part of accounting practice owners who perform valuation analyses for internal use only (e.g., buy-sell agreements, estate planning, management information, etc.). These professional standards simply make good business sense.

The organization of the book, described in the Introduction, is intended to be user-friendly to practice owners, valuation analysts, and those who rely on practice valuations. We welcome questions, comments, and suggestions from readers. We would hope to incorporate these comments in the form of improvements to subsequent editions of this book. Please feel free to write to us or to call either of us at (312) 399-4300.

8600 West Bryn Mawr Avenue   Robert F. Reilly
Suite 950   Robert P. Schweihs
Chicago, Illinois 60631
September 1996

ACKNOWLEDGMENTS

We would like to recognize several individuals who were instrumental in the preparation of, and production of, this book.

First, we would like to acknowledge three of our colleagues at Willamette Management Associates, who significantly contributed to the text. James Rabe and Charles Wilhoite contributed greatly to the writing of several of the practice valuation methodology chapters. Also, they were the principal authors of the comprehensive practice valuation case study chapter. Jim and Charles are principals of Willamette Management Associates and co-directors of the firm's Portland, Oregon, practice office. Jeffrey Tarbell was the principal author of the practice valuation discounts and premiums chapter. Jeff is a senior associate in the Chicago practice office of Willamette Management Associates.

Second, we would like to acknowledge the assistance of two members of the Willamette Management Associates research staff. Jan Tudor, director of information services, assembled the various bibliographies included in the text. Jan also helped to research and review the various court cases that are referenced in the text. Charlene Blalock, research associate, performed numerous tasks related to this book, including researching several sources of accounting industry data, obtaining permissions to reprint data source materials and appraisal industry professional standards, formatting and reformatting the text, and proofreading and editing the manuscript. In general, Charlene brought the entire project together.

Third, we would like to thank all of the Willamette Management Associates partners and staff members who provided their moral support and understanding during this project. In particular, we would like to thank Dr. Shannon Pratt, our colleague and co-managing director of Willamette Management Associates, who contributed the foreword for this book.

Fourth, we wish to express our appreciation to Irwin Professional Publishing, publishers of two other text books that we have contributed to: *Valuing a Business* and *Valuing Small Businesses and Professional Practices*. In particular, Irwin Professional Publishing allowed us to condense and to adapt certain sections of these two texts for use in this book.

Fifth, we would like to thank the following organizations that allowed us to use their materials:

The Appraisal Foundation
The American Society of Appraisers

The Institute of Business Appraisers
The National Association of Certified Valuation Analysts
The California Society of Certified Public Accountants
Mergerstat Review

Sixth, we would like to acknowledge Armanda Squadrilli, the John Wiley & Sons editor for this project. Armanda was very supportive of this project from the time we first submitted the original manuscript to John Wiley & Sons. We would also like to express our appreciation to Robin Sarantos, the John Wiley & Sons assistant managing editor for this project.

Lastly, we would like to thank the staff at Impressions Book and Journal Services, Inc. Their copyediting suggestions enhanced the layout of the text and the readability of the manuscript.

Robert F. Reilly
Robert P. Schweihs

INTRODUCTION

PURPOSE AND OBJECTIVE OF THIS BOOK

This book provides a solid conceptual and theoretical foundation—and presents practical applications and illustrations—with regard to the analysis and appraisal of accounting practices. The principal topics covered include the following:

- Fundamental valuation concepts and approaches related to accounting practices
- Income, market, and asset-based valuation methods
- Preparation of the overall accounting practice valuation synthesis and conclusion
- Identification and quantification of accounting practice valuation discounts and premiums—and other special topics—related to the valuation of fractional ownership interests (i.e., partial ownership interests in accounting practices)
- Special topics related to the valuation of accounting practices
- Reporting the results of the accounting practice appraisal

The purpose of this book is twofold:

1. To provide a practical introduction to the principles of accounting practice valuation for the novice analyst
2. To provide a comprehensive review of the principles of accounting practice valuation for the experienced analyst

We will discuss the procedural and analytical steps in the accounting practice appraisal, and we will review all the procedures, data, analyses, and appraiser inputs needed to reach the final value estimate. The reader can expect to learn the following:

1. How to conduct a thorough and effective review of the appraisal analyses and of the appraisal work product

2. How to reconcile different value estimates developed from the different valuation approaches into one estimate of the single, most probable, price the subject accounting practice will bring—under the market conditions at the time of the appraisal and in conformance with a client's instructions, legal considerations, and the contingent and limiting conditions applied by the analyst

3. Why much of the accepted dogma concerning the applicability or appropriateness of the various valuation approaches is not necessarily true for every situation. We will consider the limitations of practice valuation rules of thumb, nevertheless conceding that they sometimes have valid bases in economic theory. Understanding those bases helps the appraiser articulate the process for the client. The economic theory, as well as the market in which the appraiser is working, must point up that these rules should not be stated as universal truths.

4. How to develop a supportable and defensive estimate of the most probable price that the accounting practice will bring, using knowledge of the subject practice being appraised, of the data being used, and of the theory behind the various valuation approaches

OVERVIEW

The first several chapters of this book discuss the planning stages of an accounting practice valuation, which involve recognizing the various reasons to conduct an accounting practice appraisal, delineating the purpose and objective of the appraisal, considering the promulgated professional standards related to professional practice appraisals, selecting among the basic accounting practice valuation approaches, and gathering data and conducting the due diligence related to the accounting practice appraisal.

The next several chapters discuss—and illustrate—specific accounting practice valuation methods, including market-based, income-based, and asset-based methods. This section also describes the process of reaching a synthesis and conclusion with respect to the total value of an overall accounting practice.

Next we are concerned with the valuation of fractional business interests related to accounting practices. These fractional interests—often called *partial interests*—typically involve the analysis and appraisal of a less-than-100 percent ownership interest in the overall accounting practice. The third section, therefore, includes topics related to the identification and valuation of valuation discounts and premiums (e.g., discounts for minority ownership interest, discounts for lack of marketability, etc.). This section closes with a discussion of the process of reaching a valuation synthesis and conclusion with regard to a fractional ownership interest in an accounting practice.

From there we turn to the professional standards and other relevant issues related to the reporting of the results of the accounting practice valuation.

Finally, the appendixes present important reference topics related to the valuation of accounting practices.

A FEW CAVEATS

The valuation of professional practices, and particularly of accounting practices, is a complex subject. This book is introductory in nature. Accordingly, although all the essential topics are introduced, they are not examined in the level of detail that would be appropriate for an advanced text. Rather, we provide a general discussion of the theoretical underpinnings and practical applications of accounting practice valuation methods, and we introduce all of the essential concepts, analyses, and processes involved in an accounting practice valuation. However, this is not a cookbook; that is, we do not provide a step-by-step template that would enable a novice to perform a thorough accounting practice valuation. The subject matter does not lend itself to such an approach.

We assume that the reader has rigorous training in the principles of accounting and has a reasonable background in the principles of finance. The reader should also have more than a passing familiarity with the basic operations of and administration of accounting practices.

Also, this book focuses specifically on the application of basic valuation principles to accounting practices. It is not intended to be a general text on business valuation or, for that matter, a general text that treats the valuation of all professional practices. We assume that readers are familiar with the fundamentals of business valuation and security analysis. For readers who want a refresher course—or more background—on the general valuation of small businesses and professional practices, we recommend the following texts:

- Jay E. Fishman et al., *Guide to Business Valuations,* 6th ed. (Fort Worth, Tex.: Practitioners Publishing Company, 1996)
- Shannon P. Pratt et al., *Valuing Small Businesses and Professional Practices,* 2d ed. (Burr Ridge, Ill.: Irwin Professional Publishing, 1993)
- James Horvath, *Valuing Professional Practices* (Chicago: Commerce Clearing House, 1990)

Of course, the American Institute of Certified Public Accountants (AICPA) publication *Conducting a Valuation of a Closely Held Business* provides valuation-related technical consulting practice guidance and is available directly through the AICPA (Harborside Financial Center, 201 Plaza Three, Jersey City, NJ 07311-3881; phone: (201) 938-3000, fax: (201) 938-3329).

Finally, most of the illustrative examples in this book relate to small (i.e., one- to ten-partner) accounting firms. Such examples were used in order to maintain reasonable simplicity in the presentation. However, generally speaking, the same analytical principles and valuation methods illustrated in these examples apply to regional and national accounting firms.

TERMINOLOGY

For purposes of stylistic simplicity only, we have adopted certain conventions and assumed certain synonyms. For example, we use the terms *appraisal* and *valuation* interchangeably. Likewise, we treat the terms *partner* and *equityholder, accounting practice* and *accounting firm,* and *accountant* and *CPA* as synonyms. Also, we use the terms *appraiser, analyst,* and *valuation expert* interchangeably.

1

REASONS TO CONDUCT AN ACCOUNTING PRACTICE VALUATION

In this chapter we introduce some of the reasons to conduct a comprehensive valuation of an accounting practice. Although many are presented, this is not a comprehensive list of all of the reasons to perform a practice valuation.

Accounting practice valuations are performed for transactional as well as notational purposes. In transactional appraisals, clients rely on the analyst's advice and opinions to negotiate, structure, and consummate actual economic transactions. For example, a transactional appraisal would be an analysis performed to (1) negotiate the purchase or sale of a practice or (2) set a buy-sell agreement price between partners in an accounting firm.

Transactional appraisals are distinguished from notational appraisals in that notational appraisals are performed for purely accounting, recording, or informational reasons—with no actual cash changing hands as a result of the valuation conclusion. An example of a notational appraisal would be an analysis of the value of a sole practitioner's practice for estate-planning purposes.

Because their clients have many different motivations and needs, experienced analysts are accustomed to performing professional practice valuations and fractional ownership interest valuations under a variety of alternative definitions of value and under a variety of alternative premises of value.

MOTIVATIONS FOR CONDUCTING AN ACCOUNTING PRACTICE APPRAISAL

Although there are numerous individual reasons for conducting an accounting practice appraisal, typically the individual reasons can be grouped into a few categories of client motivations:

1. Transaction pricing and structuring, either for the sale or for purchase of the accounting practice

2. Financing securitization and collateralization, for both cash-flow-based financing and asset-based financing

3. Taxation planning and compliance, with regard to asset amortization, abandonment, charitable contribution, and other federal income taxation matters, as well as federal estate-tax compliance and estate planning

4. Management information and planning, including practice value enhancement purposes, estate planning, and other long-range strategic issues

5. Bankruptcy and reorganization analysis, including the value of the estate in bankruptcy, debtor in possession financing, traditional refinancing, restructuring, and assessment of the impact of proposed reorganization plans

6. Litigation support and dispute resolution, including marital dissolution infringement, fraud, lender liability, and a wide range of deprivation-related purposes (e.g., breach of contract, shareholder appraisal rights matters, shareholder oppression matters)

There are many requirements for, and opportunities related to, accounting practice appraisals. The following list briefly describes some of the specific reasons for conducting such an appraisal:

1. Purchase price allocation for financial accounting purposes—the recording of the acquisition of a practice, accounted for as a purchase transaction, requires the valuation of all of the acquired tangible and intangible assets of the practice.

2. Purchase price allocation for tax accounting purposes—Internal Revenue Code Section 1060 dictates the tax accounting for purchased assets that are acquired as part of the purchase of the assets of a going-concern accounting practice. As an important aside, Internal Revenue Code Section 197 allows for the amortization of most intangible assets acquired as part of the purchase of the assets of a going-concern practice.

3. Preacquisition assessment of value—after the question "Should I buy this practice?" the questions "How much should I pay?" and "How should I structure the deal?" raise the key issues in accounting practice acquisition planning and execution. An accounting practice valuation should be instrumental in objectively answering these questions.

4. Purchase of selected assets—the strategy for acquiring and/or expanding the accounting practice may involve only the purchase of particular intangible assets such as client relationships. In this case, the accounting practice intangible assets should be appraised within the context of an overall going-concern practice valuation.

5. Obtaining financing—many financial institutions are willing to consider in their lending decisions the capacity of the accounting practice to generate cash flow. If so, these institutions may require an independent appraisal of the

practice for asset-based financing and for cash-flow-based financing or for accounting practice ownership interests pledged as collateral against loan commitments or lines of credit.

6. Bankruptcy and reorganization analysis—an appraisal of the practice of a debtor may be necessary in the assessment of a proposed plan of reorganization, the quantification of a secured creditor collateral position, the identification of any cancellation of debt income, or for other bankruptcy-related accounting and taxation considerations.

7. Federal income tax reasons—when an accounting practice converts from one form of ownership to another (e.g., from a partnership to a corporation), a practice appraisal is often useful to establish the equityholders' basis in the practice equity and the practice's basis in the practice assets.

8. Litigation support and dispute resolution—accounting practice appraisals are often required in breach-of-contract matters, tortious damages cases, breach-of–noncompete-covenant cases, and other types of commercial litigation.

9. The valuation of an accounting practice—or a fractional interest in an accounting practice—is particularly relevant when one of the spouses in a marital dissolution is a partner in the firm. Then, typically, the value of the equity interest becomes part of the marital estate, subject to distribution between the parties in the marital dissolution.

10. The value of an accounting practice—or of a fractional interest in an accounting practice—is a relevant concern in practice equityholder disputes. An example of a common dispute is an equityholder who is squeezed out of the practice and who demands the fair value of his partnership or other equity interest.

11. Practice formation and dissolution—when professional practices merge, the owners' equity allocation is often a function of the relative contribution of the values of the merging practices.

12. When professional practices dissolve, the settlement payments—or other dissolution terms—often relate to the value of the portion of the practice that is transferred away from the remaining practice.

13. Other purposes—accounting practice valuations are often useful, if not necessary, in the negotiation, structuring, or execution of buy-sell agreements between practice equityholders. Practice valuations are also useful in the structuring and pricing of equity interests to allow new partners to buy into the firm, and to allow old partners to sell out their equity interests in the firm.

SUMMARY

There are numerous reasons to conduct an accounting practice valuation. Typically, all of these reasons may be grouped into common categories such as taxation, financing, transaction pricing and structuring, succession planning, and litigation.

2

PROFESSIONAL STANDARDS FOR ACCOUNTING PRACTICE VALUATIONS

In recent years the existence and efficacy of business valuation standards have become better known. Today this awareness is growing apace—in fact, it is accelerating—and importantly, the courts are now recognizing promulgated business valuation standards.

Those responsible for preparing, reviewing, and using professional practice valuations must be aware both of the existing standards and also of new standards as they evolve. CPAs, too, obviously need to be cognizant of both. Moreover, analysts should keep in mind that these professional standards cover both accounting practice valuations and valuations of fractional ownership interest in accounting practices.

Business valuation standards have been promulgated by The Appraisal Foundation, by the Business Valuation Committee of the American Society of Appraisers, by the Institute of Business Appraisers, and by the National Association of Certified Valuation Analysts. These organizations—and their current work—are described briefly in this chapter. The promulgated business valuation standards of these organizations (except The Appraisal Foundation) are provided in the appendixes.

We will also briefly discuss the activities of the Appraisal Institute and of the Canadian Institute of Chartered Business Valuators in setting professional standards.

The American Institute of Certified Public Accountants (AICPA) has established professional standards that generally apply to all services provided by CPAs. Some of the AICPA professional standards relate to business valuation engagements. AICPA professional standards such as those relating to prospective financial information—including forecasts and projections—and those relating to reports on historical financial statements may or may not be applicable to a particular engagement, depending on the type of information contained in the practice valuation report.

In 1992 the AICPA Management Consulting Services Executive Committee (MCSEC) formed an MCS Business Valuations and Appraisals Subcommittee in recognition of the role of CPAs as valuation consultants. The subcommittee is expected to develop:

1. An exposure draft of a consulting standard that addresses the CPA's responsibilities in a business valuation engagement
2. An education and testing program that will lead to accreditation of participating CPAs as business valuation specialists

At the present time this subcommittee has not completed either of these projects, nor has it announced a timetable for completion.

THE APPRAISAL FOUNDATION

Background

In 1987 nine of the leading U.S. professional appraisal organizations formed The Appraisal Foundation, which in turn established the Appraisal Standards Board and the Appraiser Qualifications Board. The Appraisal Foundation developed and adopted a landmark document entitled *Uniform Standards of Professional Appraisal Practice,* updated and reissued annually. Eight of the founding member organizations of The Appraisal Foundation are composed entirely of real estate appraisers. The ninth, the American Society of Appraisers, is multidisciplinary, awarding designations in real estate appraisal, machinery and equipment appraisal, personal property appraisal, business valuation, and technical valuation.

Content of *Uniform Standards of Professional Appraisal Practice (USPAP)*

Prefatory material of *USPAP* contains, among other things, an Ethics Provision, a Competency Provision, and a Departure Provision. These provisions apply to all appraisers.

Standards 1 through 6 deal with real estate appraisal. Standard 3 is oriented toward the review of real estate appraisals, but it applies with only minor modification to the review of a business valuation or an accounting practice appraisal.

Standards 7 and 8 deal with personal property appraisal. Standards 9 and 10 deal with business appraisal and with intangible asset appraisal. Accordingly, Standards 9 and 10 encompass the valuation of an accounting practice or of a fractional ownership interest in an accounting practice.

The title page and table of contents of the 1996 edition of *USPAP* are provided in Appendix E. Copies of these standards may be ordered directly from The Appraisal Foundation at the following address:

The Appraisal Foundation
1029 Vermont Avenue, N.W., Suite 900
Washington, DC 20005
(202) 347-7722

The current cost for a complete set of *USPAP*, which is updated annually in November, is $25.

USPAP is widely recognized and accepted. At least five federal agencies have adopted USPAP as requirements for the real estate appraisals over which they have jurisdiction; it is generally expected that other agencies will likewise adopt these standards as mandatory for real estate appraisals.

Through its Standards 9 and 10, *USPAP* provides nationally recognized standards and promulgated authority for the conduct and the reporting of business valuations and professional practice valuations.

AMERICAN SOCIETY OF APPRAISERS

Background

The American Society of Appraisers (ASA), formed in 1936, is an important appraisal testing/certifying organization representing all major disciplines of appraisal specialists, including those who specialize in business and professional practice valuation.

To ensure that professional appraisers adhere to the highest technical and ethical standards in performing valuation projects, the ASA has prepared a comprehensive set of *Principles of Appraisal Practice and Code of Ethics* for its members. These standards are appropriate for business valuation specialists as well as for appraisers of real estate, machinery and equipment, personal property, and other valuation disciplines.

Professional Standards

In addition to the general ASA Principles of Appraisal Practice and Code of Ethics, the Business Valuation Committee of the ASA has promulgated eight standards for the business valuation profession.

1. General Requirements for Developing a Business Valuation
2. Financial Statement Adjustments
3. Asset-based Approach to Business Valuation
4. Income Approach to Business Valuation
5. Market Approach to Business Valuation
6. Reaching a Conclusion of Value
7. Discounts and Premiums
8. Comprehensive, Written Business Valuation Report

The eight Business Valuation Standards are reproduced in full in Appendix F. Copies of these standards are also available from:

American Society of Appraisers
P.O. Box 17265
Washington, DC 20041
(703) 478-2228

Compliance with both *USPAP* and the ASA Business Valuation Standards is mandatory for all members of the American Society of Appraisers.

INSTITUTE OF BUSINESS APPRAISERS

Background

The Institute of Business Appraisers (IBA) is a national professional society of persons whose activities include the appraisal of businesses and of major business assets. Founded in 1978, more than two-thirds of the IBA's 2000-plus members are CPAs. As a testing and certifying organization, the IBA awards the professional designation *CBA,* or Certified Business Appraiser.

Professional Standards

The IBA Business Appraisal Standards are reproduced in Appendix G. Copies of these standards are available from the IBA (ask for publication P-311*a*):

The Institute of Business Appraisers, Inc.
P.O. Box 1447
Boynton Beach, FL 33425
(407) 732-3202

NATIONAL ASSOCIATION OF CERTIFIED VALUATION ANALYSTS

Background

The purpose of the National Association of Certified Valuation Analysts (NACVA) is to promulgate the member's status, credentials, and esteem in the field of performing valuations of business enterprises. To further this purpose, NACVA strives to advance valuation services as an art and science, foster standards for admission to the association, promote professional development and education, advance standards of ethical and professional practice, enhance public awareness of valuation analysts, and promote working relationships with other professional organizations.

To achieve these purposes, NACVA

- Advances, communicates, and enforces standards of ethical and professional practice
- Develops and presents quality education and training programs
- Certifies professionals on the basis of their competence, ethical behavior, independence, and objectivity and establishes criteria for certification as a Certified Valuation Analyst (CVA)
- Fosters public awareness that a Certified Valuation Analyst has met and continues to abide by standards of ethical conduct, objectivity, independence, and performs his or her services at the highest level of professional competence
- Promotes and enhances collegial and professional relationships between members of the association and between the association and other professional organizations

Professional Standards

The NACVA professional standards are reproduced in Appendix H. Copies of these standards are available from the NACVA:

National Association of Certified Valuation Analysts
Brickyard Towers, Suite 110
1245 East Brickyard Road
Salt Lake City, UT 84106
(801) 486-0600

APPRAISAL INSTITUTE

Background

The real estate appraisal profession has evolved over the years. And like all truly professional occupations, it has formal national organizations that oversee the education and conduct of its members. While there are many such appraisal organizations, the largest is the Appraisal Institute, which resulted from the 1991 merger of the American Institute of Real Estate Appraisers and the Society of Real Estate Appraisers.

As with any professional group, the Appraisal Institute has promulgated professional standards (adopted from its two merging organizations) in the areas of education, conduct, and reporting requirements.

In addition to the Appraisal Institute professional standards, the Financial Institutions Reform, Recovery, and Enforcement Act (FIRREA) requires all real estate appraisers to be either licensed or certified by the state in which they do business (to conduct real estate appraisals).

Professional Standards

Professionally designated real estate appraisers follow standards of practice that are essentially the work product guidelines of their appraisal work. In general terms, these standards cover the development, communication, and review of valuation assignments for real estate, personal property, and business entities. They extend to special analysis studies and mass appraisal assignments as well.

Basically, the Appraisal Institute professional standards outline the minimum requirements for conducting an appraisal. These standards include the following:

- Proper definition of terms
- Identification of the property and nature of the assignment
- Identification of assumptions and limiting conditions
- Explanation of appraisal techniques used in the assignment
- Highest and best uses of the property
- Certification by the appraiser
- Types of data to be considered
- Prohibition of committing substantial error or a series of errors
- Clearly communicating the analysis and conclusions of the assignment

CANADIAN INSTITUTE
OF CHARTERED BUSINESS VALUATORS

Background

In 1970 The Canadian Association of Business Valuators began as a federally chartered, nonprofit, professional association. The organization grew quickly after Canada imposed a capital gains tax requiring businesses and investors to establish a "base value" for all of their assets as of December 31, 1971.

In 1985 the association became the Canadian Institute of Chartered Business Valuators (CICBV). The CICBV offers services in English and in French and grants members the designation CBV (Chartered Business Valuator) or EEE (d'Expert en Evaluation d'Enterprises).

The CICBV, now the largest professional valuation organization in Canada, trains and certifies individuals in business valuation. It continues to develop and update its education program; it develops and issues valuation Practice Standards; it enforces adherence by its members to its Code of Ethics and Practice Standards; and, through its conferences and publications, it provides continuing education of its members.

Professional Standards

The CICBV considers it essential to develop and issue Practice Standards in the field of business valuation. While the field continues to evolve, the Canadian courts and regulatory bodies look to the institute to establish and codify Practice Standards and to ensure competent and thoroughly documented valuations (especially when litigation is or may be involved).

In 1991 the CICBV formed a Practice Standards Committee to develop standards that would set out the minimum requirements expected of all members. In 1992 the first valuation Practice Standard was introduced; other standards are being developed and issued on a regular basis.

SUMMARY

Accounting practice appraisers should be familiar with four principal sets of professional standards:

1. The Appraisal Foundation: *Uniform Standards of Professional Appraisal Practice (USPAP)*
2. American Society of Appraisers (ASA): Business Valuation Standards
3. Institute of Business Appraisers (IBA): Business Appraisal Standards
4. National Association of Certified Valuation Analysts (NACVA): Valuation Standards

A brief overview of these four important sets of professional standards was presented in this chapter. Obviously, CPAs must comply with all AICPA professional standards when performing any management advisory service, including the valuation of accounting practices.

3

PURPOSE AND OBJECTIVE OF THE ACCOUNTING PRACTICE APPRAISAL

This chapter presents the following basic elements of accounting practice valuation:

1. Defining the objective and purpose of the accounting practice appraisal
2. Selecting the appropriate standard of value
3. Selecting the appropriate premise of value
4. Describing the business interest subject to appraisal
5. Describing the bundle of legal rights subject to appraisal
6. Stating the appropriate valuation date
7. Selecting the appropriate form of the valuation report

OBJECTIVE AND PURPOSE OF THE APPRAISAL

The objective of the appraisal states the who, what, where, when, and why of the appraisal assignment. The analyst should prepare a clear and concise statement of the purpose and objective of the appraisal before starting the accounting practice valuation.

The objective of the appraisal should clearly articulate, at least:

1. What specific accounting practice business interest is being appraised
2. What ownership interest (or what bundle of legal rights) related to that business interest is being appraised
3. What standard, or definition, of value is being estimated
4. What constitutes the "as of" date of the appraisal

The purpose of the appraisal describes the audience (i.e., the expected reader) of the appraisal and states what decisions (if any) will be influenced by the appraisal. The purpose of the appraisal should clearly indicate, at least:

1. Why the appraisal is being performed
2. What is the intended use of the appraisal
3. Who is expected to rely upon the appraisal

It is highly recommended that the analyst and client agree, in writing, on both the objective and purpose of the accounting practice appraisal before it is begun.

ALTERNATIVE STANDARDS OF VALUE

The terms *standard of value* and *definition of value* may be considered to be synonyms. The standard, or definition, of value identifies the type of value being estimated. Alternative standards of value generally answer the question, Value to whom? This question is important because different parties may not value the same accounting practice ownership alike. For example, an accounting practice may have one value to its current partners, another value to an acquiring regional or national accounting firm, and yet another value to one of the firm's managers who wants to buy into the partnership.

The more common alternative standards, or definitions, of value include the following:

1. *Fair market value:* the most probable price paid by a typical (hypothetical) willing buyer to a typical (hypothetical) willing seller when neither is under undue influence to transact, both are fully cognizant of all relevant facts and circumstances, and both seek their maximum economic self-interest
2. *Fair value:* equitable recompense for a business interest when its owner has been involuntarily deprived of its benefit and where there is neither a willing buyer nor a willing seller (this is primarily a legal concept, possibly the appropriate standard of value when, say, a partner is involuntarily squeezed out of an accounting practice)
3. *Market value:* the most probable price that a business interest should bring in a competitive and open market under all conditions requisite to a fair sale, the buyer and seller each acting prudently and knowledgeably and the price unaffected by undue stimulus
4. *Acquisition value:* the price that a particular identified buyer would be expected to pay for a business interest given any unique benefits of the business interest to that identified buyer
5. *Use value:* the value of a business interest in a particular specified use (which may be different from either the current use or the highest and best use of the business interest)

6. *Investment (or investor) value:* the value of a business interest given a well-defined set of individual investment criteria (e.g., investment criteria for internal rate of return or payback period)—this standard of value does not necessarily contemplate a sale transaction

7. *Owner value:* the value of a business interest to its current owner given the owner's current use of the business interest, current resources, and capabilities for economically exploiting the business interest—this standard of value does not necessarily contemplate a sale transaction

8. *Insurable value:* the amount of insurance proceeds necessary to replace the subject business interest with an amount of compensation of comparable income-producing capacity (e.g., this standard of value may be appropriate with regard to business interruption insurance)

9. *Collateral value:* the amount that a creditor would be willing to loan when a subject business interest serves as security for the loan

10. *Ad valorem value:* the value of a business interest for ad valorem property taxation purposes given the statutory and judicial standards of the particular taxing jurisdiction

The purpose (or intended use) of an appraisal will greatly influence the selection of a standard of value. The selection of an appropriate standard of value will, in turn, directly impact the value estimate.

For most transactional analyses, appraisers will be estimating the fair market value of the accounting practice—that is, the most likely selling price of the practice (or an ownership interest in the practice). However, for purposes of financing, litigation, taxation, or various other activities, analysts should be familiar with other common standards of value.

At this point it is important to emphasize that while an appraiser may *estimate* value, only the market *determines* value. In some regards, professional practice appraisers are like reporters: They report—and, to an extent, interpret—available market data. They do not make a market, and they do not create a value. Rather, as all of the professional literature will agree, appraisers *estimate* how the appropriate market will quantitatively react to the subject practice. Actual buyers and sellers *make,* or *determine,* the market value. Appraisers may only interpret market value indicators and estimate how the appropriate market will react to the subject practice.

ALTERNATIVE PREMISES OF VALUE

The *valuation premise* is the hypothetical set of assumptions regarding accounting practice sale transactions under which the subject practice ownership interest will be analyzed. The selection of the appropriate valuation premise is typically dictated by the highest and best use of the subject accounting practice business interest.

The *highest and best use* of the accounting practice business interest is the reasonably probable and legal use of the interest that is physically possible, appropriately supported, financially feasible, and that results in the highest value.

The highest and best use must meet the following four criteria:

1. Legal permissibility
2. Physical possibility
3. Financial feasibility
4. Maximum profitability

Among all reasonable alternatives, the use of the practice business interest that yields the highest present value—after payments are made for labor, capital, and coordination—typically represents the highest and best use of the subject interest. The assessment of the highest and best use of the subject business interest will determine, in good measure, which of the four following fundamental premises of value should be applied in the appraisal of the subject accounting practice.

1. *Value in continued use,* as part of a mass assemblage of assets and as part of a going-concern business enterprise; this premise incorporates the contributory value of the subject practice's intangible assets to the other assets of the practice.
2. *Value in place,* as part of a mass assemblage of assets not currently used to produce income or as part of a going-concern business enterprise; this premise encompasses the economic value of many intangible assets of the practice, but it would probably not include the value of the practice goodwill.
3. *Value in exchange as part of an orderly disposition,* on a piecemeal basis (not part of a mass assemblage of assets); this premise recognizes that the various tangible and intangible assets of the practice will be sold individually and will enjoy normal exposure to their appropriate secondary market.
4. *Value in exchange as part of a forced liquidation,* on a piecemeal basis (not part of a mass assemblage of assets); this premise recognizes that the various tangible and intangible assets of the practice will be sold individually but that these assets will experience less than normal exposure to their appropriate secondary market.

These four alternative premises can produce dramatically different value conclusions for the same accounting practice. To select the appropriate premise of value, the analyst will consider:

- The purpose and objective of the accounting practice appraisal
- The actual functional and economic status of the subject accounting practice

Appraisers involved in transactional analyses will typically analyze the accounting practice under premise 1, value in continued use. However, for practice dissolution, financing and refinancing, litigation and various other purposes, the alternative premises of value may be more appropriate for the subject appraisal.

DESCRIBING THE BUSINESS INTEREST SUBJECT TO APPRAISAL

The description of the particular accounting practice business interest subject to appraisal should be complete enough to clearly identify the particular business interest to the reader of the appraisal.

For an accounting practice valuation to be meaningful at all, the analyst must have a clear understanding of exactly what business interest is being valued. And, the analyst's clear understanding must be effectively communicated in the valuation report.

Appraisers commonly err by concluding valuations with statements such as "the fair market value of the subject accounting practice, as of a certain date, is $XXX,XXX." Though perhaps economically correct, that valuation conclusion does not tell the typical reader of the valuation report what they want to know—namely, just *what* interest in the subject accounting practice is worth $XXX,XXX.

Exhibit 3.1 illustrates the various business interests that may be subject to appraisal of the typical accounting firm of Tick and Tie, CPAs.

The analyst could estimate the value of the total assets (both tangible and intangible) of Tick and Tie, CPAs, as in column A of Exhibit 3.1. The analyst could estimate the value of the capital structure of this accounting practice. The capital structure represents the total equityholders' interests plus all of the long-term interest-bearing debt of the practice. This is sometimes referred to as the *total invested capital* of the practice and is represented by column B in Exhibit 3.1.

The analyst could estimate the value of the equity structure of the practice. This represents the total amount of the equityholders' equity interests (or capital) in the practice. However, it excludes consideration of any outstanding long-term debt of the practice. This is represented by column C in Exhibit 3.1.

Finally, the analyst could estimate the value of a fractional ownership interest in the equity structure of the firm. In this case, the appraisal subject is less than 100 percent of the total equityholders' capital. For example, the appraisal subject may be a 20 percent equity interest in Tick and Tie, CPAs. This appraisal subject would be relevant, for example, if Tick and Tie were a five-partner firm (with equal equity ownership) and the appraisal assignment involved one partner's ownership interest only.

As will be described below, the valuation of a fractional ownership interest in a professional practice often involves the identification and quantification of appropriate practice valuation discounts. For example, the illustrative 20 percent equity interest in Tick and Tie, CPAs, is a nonmarketable, minority equity interest that may be

Assets	Liabilities and Owners' Equity	Business Interest Subject to Appraisal			
TICK AND TIE, CPAS					
STATEMENT OF FINANCIAL POSITION					
Current assets	Current liabilities				
Real estate	Long-term liabilities				
Tangible personal property	Owners' equity				
Intangible assets					
Total assets	Total liabilities and owners' equity	A	B	C	D

A = Asset structure = total assets = total liabilities and owners' equity
B = Capital structure = long-term debt and owners' equity
C = Equity structure = total owners' equity
D = Fractional interest = a fractional (or partial) ownership interest in the
      total owners' equity

Exhibit 3.1. Typical Accounting Practice Alternative Business Interests
            Subject to Appraisal.

subject to a buy-sell agreement, a partnership agreement, or other transferability restrictions. Each of these factors should be carefully considered in the analysis of the
20 percent equity interest appraisal subject.

THE BUNDLE OF LEGAL RIGHTS SUBJECT TO APPRAISAL

An important step in the accounting practice valuation process is the identification of the
specific bundle of legal rights subject to appraisal. According to the bundle-of-rights
theory of valuation, complete property ownership, or title in fee, comprises a group of
distinct rights, each of which can be separated from the bundle and conveyed by the fee
owner to other parties in perpetuity or for a limited time. Separating and transferring a
right from the bundle creates a partial, or fractional, property ownership interest.

Practice ownership interests may be examined from many perspectives because
the legal, economic, and financial aspects of accounting practice ownership rights
overlap. The ownership of accounting practice business interests can be divided in
various ways.

Separate economic and legal interests derived from the bundle of rights are involved in the ownership or a partial ownership in an accounting practice, and each of

these interests is distinct in its form and content. Fractional business interests are created when less than a total, 100 percent–equity, ownership interest in the accounting practice is conveyed in accordance with established legal procedures.

Among the more common bundles of legal rights related to accounting practice fractional ownership interests are the following:

1. Fee simple interest
2. Life or term estates
3. Licenser/franchiser interests
4. Licensee/franchisee interests
5. Reversionary interests
6. Other fractional ownership interests

Obviously, the selection of the appropriate bundle of legal rights to be appraised—as well as the fractional business interest to be appraised—will directly impact the accounting practice value estimate.

STATING THE APPROPRIATE VALUATION DATE

The accounting practice value estimate must be "as of" a specified valuation date. The value of an accounting practice changes over time, due to both endogenous and exogenous factors. The valuation dates may be:

- Historical—as of a previous date
- Contemporaneous—as of a current date
- Prospective—as of a future date

Hypothetical, or prospective, valuation dates always result in what are called *hypothetical appraisals*. According to the professional standards of the American Society of Appraisers, all hypothetical appraisals should be clearly identified as such.

The selection of the appropriate valuation date will be a function of the purpose of the appraisal assignment. Obviously, the analyst and client should agree in advance on an appropriate valuation date.

THE FORM OF THE VALUATION REPORT

The form of the accounting practice valuation report will be greatly influenced by the purpose of the valuation assignment. To avoid misunderstandings, the appraiser and client should agree in advance on the form of the valuation report.

The Uniform Standards of Professional Appraisal Practice (USPAP) defines a *report* as "any communication, written or oral, of an appraisal, review, or consulting service that is transmitted to the client upon completion of an assignment." USPAP allows for two types of appraisal:

1. A *complete appraisal,* which is performed without invoking the Departure Provision
2. A *limited appraisal,* which *does* invoke the Departure Provision

USPAP also allows for three forms of an appraisal report:

1. A *self-contained* appraisal report (see USPAP Standards, Rule 2-2(a))
2. A *summary* appraisal report (see USPAP Standards, Rule 2-2(b))
3. A *restricted* appraisal report (see USPAP Standards, Rule 2-2(c))

The American Society of Appraisers (ASA) Business Valuation Standard VIII describes the requirements for a "full written business valuation report." However, other, more limited forms of valuation reports are allowed under ASA standards. All of the promulgated ASA Business Valuation Standards are presented in Appendix F of this book.

A further discussion on the form, format, and content of accounting practice valuation reports is presented in Chapters 12 and 13.

DIFFERENCES BETWEEN OVERALL PRACTICE VALUATION AND FRACTIONAL BUSINESS INTEREST APPRAISAL

As mentioned above, the statement of the business interest subject to appraisal should clearly indicate whether the subject of the appraisal is the overall accounting practice or some fractional business interest in it. This distinction is important because it introduces the concepts of control (or lack of control) and of marketability (or of lack of marketability). When appropriate to the business interest subject to appraisal, valuation discounts for lack of control (typically called the *minority interest discount*) and for lack of marketability (sometimes called the *illiquidity discount*) can materially affect the pro rata value of the business interest subject to appraisal.

Degree of Control

The relationship between a control and a minority position in an accounting firm typically varies from firm to firm. Relevant state statutes, the practice's articles of incorporation or partnership bylaws, and the way the overall ownership of the practice is distributed all have a bearing on the relative rights of minority and controlling equityholders.

Statutes affecting the relative rights of controlling versus minority equityholders vary from state to state. As with state statutes, the subject accounting practice's articles of incorporation or partnership bylaws may require supermajorities for certain actions and/or may confer special rights to minority equityholders under certain conditions. The variety of possibilities is almost without limit. The appraiser should be sure to read the articles of incorporation or partnership bylaws (and all amendments thereto) to clearly understand any factors affecting the minority equityholders' degree of control.

If one accountant owns 49 percent of the equity and another owns 51 percent, then the 49 percent owner typically has little or no control of any kind. However, if two equityholders own 49 percent each and a third owns 2 percent, then the 49 percent equityholders may be on a par with each other, depending on who owns the other 2 percent. The 2 percent equityholder may be able to command a considerable price premium over the pro rata value for that particular equity interest because of its power to swing voting control.

Accordingly, the distinction between controlling and minority interests in an accounting practice may well be a matter of degree of influence. Control is only as valuable as the actual power it confers to exercise any or all of a variety of rights typically associated with control of the practice. Consequently, if the degree of control of the practice ownership interest is an issue in the valuation, then the appraiser should assess the extent to which the various elements of control do or do not exist in the particular situation and consider the impact of each element on the value of control.

Some of the more common prerogatives of control in a typical accounting practice include:

1. The ability to appoint management of the firm and of the various departments or practice areas of the firm
2. The ability to determine management, partner, and staff compensation and perquisites
3. The ability to set office and firm policy and to change the course of practice operations (from an operational or a strategic perspective)
4. The ability to acquire or liquidate practice assets
5. The ability to hire and fire (and promote and demote) staff
6. The ability to influence partnership admission and/or termination (i.e., the ability to make partners and to fire partners)
7. The ability to accept or reject individual client engagements and/or types of client engagements (i.e., types of professional services offered by the firm)

8. The ability to make acquisitions of other practices (or portions of other practices)

9. The ability to control the liquidation, dissolution, sale, or recapitalization of the practice

10. The ability to grant additional shares of stock (or partnership units) to individual equityholders (or partners)

11. The ability to declare and pay bonuses, profit distributions, or other partner distributions (or dividends)

12. The ability to change the practice articles of incorporation or partnership bylaws

13. The ability to contractually bind the practice, related to leases, loan agreements, or other contracts

14. The ability to change engagement staffing, office staffing levels, fee schedules, billing rates, utilization targets, partner and/or staff compensation plans, and similar operational issues

From the above list, it is apparent that the owner of a controlling interest in an accounting practice enjoys some very valuable rights that an owner of a minority position does not. However, many factors can limit a majority-equity-owner's right or ability to exercise many of the prerogatives normally associated with the control of the accounting practice. The analyst should carefully consider each of these factors when assessing the appropriate control premium, if any, to assign to a particular practice ownership interest.

Distinction between Discount for Minority Interest and Discount for Lack of Marketability

The minority interest discount (also called the *discount for lack of control*) and the discount for lack of marketability are two separate concepts, although there is some interrelationship between them. *Minority interest* refers to the relationship between the ownership interest being valued and the total accounting practice, based on the factors summarized above. The value of the minority interest in relation to the value of the total practice depends primarily on how much control the minority interest has.

Marketability refers to the liquidity of the practice ownership interest—how quickly and certainly it can be converted to cash at the equityholder's discretion. Even controlling practice ownership interests typically suffer to some degree from lack of marketability. It usually takes at least a few months to sell an entire accounting practice. However, minority interests in a professional practice are harder still to sell, even after being discounted for lack of control. In this market reality, the relationship between the discount for lack of marketability and the discount for minority interest is clearly manifested.

APPROACHES TO THE VALUATION OF MINORITY INTERESTS

Minority ownership interests in an accounting practice can be valued in three basic ways:

1. As a proportionate share of the total overall accounting practice value less a discount from this value (sometimes called a *top-down* approach)
2. By direct comparison with values of other minority ownership interests
3. By estimating the economic benefits the minority interest holder will realize over the life of the investment (sometimes called a *bottom-up* approach)

Proportion of the Overall Practice Value Less a Discount

One approach to the valuation of a minority ownership interest in an accounting practice is the following three-step process:

1. Estimate the overall value of the total accounting practice.
2. Compute the minority equityholder's pro rata interest in the total practice.
3. Estimate the amount of the discount, if any, applicable to the pro rata value of the total practice—in order to properly reflect the value of the subject minority ownership interest.

Valuation by Comparison with Other Minority Interests

Empirical data on actual sales of comparable or guideline minority ownership interests in accounting practices (either in the subject practice itself or in guideline or comparable accounting practices) can, if available, help the analyst reach a conclusion of value through direct comparison with the subject practice. Through such direct comparison, the analyst may reach this valuation conclusion without ever estimating a total value for the overall accounting practice.

The analyst can value the subject minority ownership interest using parameters similar to those used for valuing the total accounting practice. Such parameters would include, for example: capitalization of earnings, capitalization of cash flow, capitalization of dividends or partnership withdrawals, a ratio of price to book value or to adjusted net asset value, and so on. Guidance for the quantification of the market value parameters would be taken from the guideline or comparative minority ownership interest transfer transaction data.

Bottom-up Approach

In the two previous approaches, we started with something—some estimation of all of or part of a practice value—and applied a discount (or two) to estimate the value of a minority ownership interest. In the bottom-up approach, we start with nothing and try to estimate what the minority ownership interest owner might sometime realize.

In most cases, the economic benefits that the minority ownership interest holder may realize fall into two simple categories:

1. Continued receipt of dividends or other partnership withdrawals or profit distributions
2. The ultimate receipt of any proceeds realized on the sale of the subject equity ownership interest

What this really amounts to is an application of some version of a discounted economic-income analysis. The steps in this bottom-up approach are as follows:

1. Project the expected profit distributions to the subject equity interest (e.g., dividends or partnership withdrawals).
2. Project a point in time and a dollar amount at which the subject ownership interest can be expected to be sold.
3. Estimate an appropriate present value discount rate.
4. Discount the projected profit distributions and the projected sale price to a present value.

The concepts of controlling versus minority ownership interest, of lack of marketability, and of the effect of transferability and other restrictions on the value of an equity interest in an accounting practice will be discussed in greater detail in Chapters 10, 11, and 12.

SUMMARY

The analyst should clearly delineate the purpose and objective of an appraisal before starting any quantitative and qualitative valuation analyses. This statement of the purpose and objective of the appraisal will clarify the assignment in the analyst's mind, and later it will effectively communicate the scope of the analysis to the reader of the valuation report. It will also help the analyst identify valuation analyses that need to be performed. For example, if the subject of the appraisal is less than a 100 percent equity interest in the overall accounting practice, the analyst will want to consider carefully and to quantify various influences affecting value, including minority ownership interest, marketability, and transferability restrictions.

4

BASIC ACCOUNTING PRACTICE VALUATION APPROACHES

Professional accounting practices are frequently subject to valuation. Knowing the value of an accounting practice is important to the practice partners, to their spouses and heirs, to potential partners (including both partners to be admitted to the subject practice and possible merger partners), and to other interested parties.

Three basic approaches to accounting practice valuation are introduced in this chapter:

1. The market approach
2. The income approach
3. The asset-based approach

This chapter then takes up the important steps of preparing the valuation synthesis and conclusion and reporting the conclusion of the value estimate. Next, several of the most common approaches for the valuation of accounting practices are introduced; each will be discussed in greater detail in the following chapters. Finally, several caveats regarding accounting practice valuation approaches are explained.

Each valuation approach draws from a group of similar valuation methods. Accordingly, within the treatment of each general valuation approach, several valuation methods are introduced.

ACCOUNTING PRACTICE VALUATION APPROACHES

Many methods and procedures are commonly used to estimate the value of a professional accounting practice. All, however, can be subsumed within three general approaches to practice valuation:

1. The market approach
2. The income approach
3. The asset-based approach

Market Approach

The market approach is, arguably, the approach most commonly used to value professional accounting practices. This valuation approach involves (1) the analysis of actual arm's-length market transactions (i.e., sales of accounting practices) and (2) the selection of relevant market-derived valuation pricing multiples.

The market approach has several practical limitations. To be most effective, it requires access to a substantial database of confidential information regarding actual sale transactions of accounting practices. Moreover, for the valuation approach to be valid, the database must be reasonably comprehensive and the data must be reasonably current. Even then, the analyst must use considerable professional judgment (1) in selecting the sample of *comparable,* or *guideline,* transactions and (2) in adjusting the valuation multiples derived from the guideline practices. (The adjustments are based on a comparison of the operating results/attributes of the subject practice with those of the guideline practices.)

When applying this valuation approach, comparable transactions will involve substantially similar practices that are easily and directly comparable to the subject practice. In contrast, guideline transactions will involve practices less similar to the subject practice but enough alike to provide useful valuation guidance to the analyst. As guideline practices may not be directly comparable to the subject practice, numerous adjustments to the guideline practice data—or to the valuation pricing multiples derived from the guideline transactions—may be needed for them to provide useful guidance to the analyst.

In using this approach, the appraiser first analyzes the subject accounting practice by professional service line. Undertaking this analysis involves performing a relative revenue and profit analysis by audit, accounting, taxation, and management advisory service. But this analysis may also include very specific areas of practice specialization such as estate planning, litigation services, and so on.

Next, the analyst selects comparability criteria to be used (1) in the selection of comparable or guideline practice sale transactions and (2) in the valuation multiple selection procedures. These comparability criteria may include service mix, revenues per partner, profits per partner, partner/staff ratios, billing rate levels, partner/staff utilization levels, industry or service line specializations, and so forth.

Having selected comparability criteria, the analyst accesses the comprehensive database and selects a sample of comparable or guideline accounting firms that were sold recently.

The analyst first searches for comparable accounting practices, those very similar to the subject practice. If the selected practices are truly comparable to the subject practice, then a very few (and sometimes only one) transactions are required to perform this valuation approach.

If no comparable practice transactions are available, then the analyst will search for guideline accounting practices, those that share investment characteristics of risk and expected return with the subject practice. Typically, a larger sample of guideline transactions is required to perform this valuation approach.

When selecting and analyzing guideline accounting practice sale transactions in the market valuation approach, 10 basic elements of comparison are often considered:

1. The legal rights of ownership conveyed in the guideline transaction(s)

2. Any special financing terms or arrangements (e.g., between the buyer and the seller) such as earn-outs, low- or no-interest seller financing, employment agreements with the seller, and so on

3. Any elements of arm's-length sale conditions (whether, for example, the seller was forced to sell due to age, pending litigation, competitive conditions, etc.)

4. The economic conditions in the appropriate secondary market at the time of the sale transaction(s)

5. The market (i.e., geographic, industry, and firm specialization) in which the guideline practice(s) operated

6. The physical characteristics of guideline practice assets compared with those of the subject practice assets (e.g., age of office equipment, number and size of practice offices, etc.)

7. The functional characteristics of the guideline practice(s) compared with those of the subject practice (e.g., the number and scope of the firms' specialty practices)

8. The technological characteristics of the guideline practice(s)—compared to the subject practice (e.g., the degree of practice automation, the degree of sophistication of office equipment, etc.)

9. The economic characteristics of the guideline practice(s) compared with those of the subject practice (including consideration of local economic conditions and economic conditions in the industry/practice areas in which the firm(s) specializes)

10. Other factors in the guideline sale transactions such as seller covenants not to compete, earn-out provisions, seller consulting agreements or other transition period employment agreements, or other assets and/or agreements not directly (or, at least, not historically) associated with the guideline accounting practice

Finally, after reviewing and adjusting the sample data, the analyst selects valuation pricing multiples. The most common valuation pricing multiple for an accounting practice, of course, is a multiple of gross or net revenues. Also relevant for this type of analysis, however, are valuation pricing multiples related to other measures of economic income (e.g., net operating income, net income, net cash flow, etc.) or to other measures of operating statistics (e.g., number of professional staff, total billed/billable hours, etc.).

After selecting the sample of comparable and/or guideline transactional data, the analyst must carefully adjust the valuation multiples to reflect the differences between the subject practice and the comparable or guideline accounting firms. Comparability, or lack thereof, is a function of the similarity of the historical economic returns of the subject practice and the nonsystematic risk features of the subject practice as compared to the same elements for the sample firms.

Income Approach

Under the income approach, the value of the accounting practice is estimated as the present value of the prospective economic income that will be generated by the practice and distributed to the equityholders of the firm. For purposes of an accounting practice valuation, economic income may be defined in many different ways. However, the most common measure of economic income for accounting practice valuations is net cash flow. Net cash flow is typically defined as net revenues less total operating expenses (excluding depreciation) less incremental investments for capital expenditures.

There are two common general valuation methods within the income approach to accounting practice valuation:

1. The direct capitalization method
2. The yield capitalization method

In a direct capitalization method, the analyst first estimates the appropriate measure of economic income for one period after the valuation date, typically this measure represents a normalized or stabilized level of income for the practice. Next, the analyst divides that measure by an appropriate investment rate of return, called the *capitalization rate*. The capitalization rate may be appropriate for either an indefinite time or for a specified period, depending on how long the subject practice will, in the analyst's judgment, continue to generate an economic income stream.

In a yield capitalization method, the analyst projects the appropriate measure of economic income for several discrete future periods. This projection is then converted into a present value using a present value discount rate. The present value discount rate is the investor's required rate of return, or yield rate, over the expected term of the projection. In this valuation method, it is the duration of the discrete projection period (and whether or not a residual or terminal value should be considered at its conclusion) that depends on how long the subject practice will, in the analyst's judgment, continue to generate an economic income stream.

In any event, the result of the direct capitalization—or of the yield capitalization—indicates the value of the subject accounting practice according to the income approach. Because the measure of economic income typically analyzed in the yield capitalization method is net cash flow (as defined above), this method is often called a *discounted net cash flow analysis*.

There are several features of an accounting practice that affect the traditional income valuation approach. This is true both when the direct capitalization method is used and when the yield capitalization method is used.

First, economic income is projected to estimate a return on the equityholders' ownership interest only. Therefore, the valuation model typically should postulate a salary expense for the equityholders equal to what nonpartner staff members with comparable experience and tenure would earn. Also, cash flow normally should be estimated before any partner profit distributions.

Second, the income approach analysis is typically performed on a before-tax basis because most accounting firms are (nontaxpayer) partnerships, and therefore the present value discount rate should be determined on a before-tax basis.

Third, because most accounting firms enjoy very little leverage in their capital structure, the weighted average cost of capital used to calculate the present value discount rate will typically approximate the cost of equity capital for the subject accounting practice.

Using the income approach, the value of the capital structure of a practice is (a) the present value of the prospective economic income generated over a finite projection period (typically between 5 and 10 years) plus (b) the present value of the residual value of the practice at the conclusion of the discrete projection period. The residual value is typically estimated by capitalizing the discrete economic income projection in the terminal year, using an appropriate terminal value capitalization rate. This rate is usually (a) the appropriate present value discount rate less (b) an expected long-term growth rate in the practice.

Using the income approach, the value of the equity of the accounting practice is (a) the value of the capital structure less (b) the current value of any long-term debt outstanding.

As with the market approach, the analyst must exercise considerable professional judgment when using the income approach. Certainly, professional judgment is required to prepare the projections of revenues, expenses, and so forth used in the economic income model, to estimate the appropriate employee-equivalent compensation to be substituted for the partner's draw (i.e., base compensation) in the model, and to estimate the appropriate residual value of the subject accounting practice at the end of the discrete projection period.

Nonetheless, the income approach is widely used and has many advantages. Clearly, this valuation approach does require a rigorous economic analysis of the accounting practice operations in order to prepare the required financial projections. However, such an analysis should be performed in any event before the purchase or sale of an accounting practice.

Asset-Based Approach

Under the asset-based approach, the value of an accounting practice is estimated as the fair market value of all the accounting firm's assets less the current value of all its liabilities.

Obviously, this appraisal approach closely follows the basic accounting premise that a firm's total assets must equal its total equities. However, when using this appraisal approach, the analyst prepares a valuation-based, fair market value balance sheet instead of a GAAP-based, historical cost balance sheet. Nonetheless, the basic accounting equation—total assets less total liabilities equals owners' equity—still applies in this valuation-based balance sheet.

The total assets of an accounting practice typically can be grouped into several categories: financial assets, tangible personal property, tangible real estate, and intangible assets. Financial assets include cash, client receivables, and prepaid expenses. Tangible personal property includes office furniture and fixtures, data processing equipment, and so on. Real estate includes owned and leased land, buildings, and building improvements. Intangible assets typically include client work paper files (sometimes called the *accounting plant*), client relationships, a trained and assembled workforce, going-concern value, and the value of goodwill.

Accounting firm liabilities typically can be grouped into two categories: current and noncurrent. Current liabilities include accounts payable, salaries payable, and accrued expenses. Noncurrent liabilities include notes payable and other long-term obligations. In addition, the "value" of the accounting firm's contingent liabilities—if any—should be considered in an asset-based valuation.

Using the asset-based valuation approach, the value of an accounting practice is the fair market value of its assets less the current value of its liabilities.

SELECTING A VALUATION APPROACH

Before selecting the appropriate approach to use in the valuation of an accounting practice, the analyst should carefully define the appraisal problem by identifying the following:

1. The purpose and objective of the appraisal
2. The standard, or definition, of value
3. The premise of value
4. The business interest to be appraised
5. The quantity and quality of available data

When each of the first four items, discussed previously in Chapter 3, has been identified, the analyst should consider both the quantity and quality of available data regarding the subject firm. These data may be both financial and operational as well as both historical and prospective. After synthesizing these data, the analyst must ultimately rely upon experience and professional judgment to select the appropriate valuation approach or approaches for the particular appraisal.

PRACTICE FRACTIONAL INTEREST VALUATION DISCOUNTS AND PREMIUMS

In an independent analysis or in the course of an overall accounting practice valuation, analysts are often called upon to identify and quantify the various discounts and premiums associated with the appraisal of a partial ownership interest in the accounting practice. The following list, while not exhaustive, presents some typical nonsystematic risk factors that affect accounting practice valuation discounts:

- Illiquidity (of the overall accounting practice)
- Lack of marketability (of the subject fractional ownership interest)
- Blockage (associated with the size of the subject ownership interest)
- Key employee dependence (on the practice founder, the managing partner, or a key "rainmaker")
- Key client dependence
- Lack of industry diversification
- Lack of any defined firm specializations
- Lack of service line diversification
- Lack of service line innovation
- Productive capacity obsolescence
- Lack of geographic diversification
- Inappropriate capital structure (e.g., unfavorable debt-to-equity mix)
- Unfavorable contractual agreements (e.g., onerous lease agreements)
- Excess nonproductive assets (e.g., computer equipment not used in practice operations)
- Restrictions on ownership disposition (e.g., holding-period restrictions, buy-sell agreement restrictions)
- Minority (noncontrolling) ownership interest

Some of the typical nonsystematic return factors that affect accounting practice valuation premiums include:

- Majority (controlling) ownership interest
- Superior service line diversification

- Superior geographic diversification
- Excess income-producing assets
- Favorable capital structure
- Favorable cost-of-capital components
- Favorable contractual agreements
- Service line technological innovation
- Ready marketability of security interest
- Favorable industry specialization
- Favorable service line specialization

Instead of relying simply on professional judgment, professional appraisers often use advanced quantitative analysis to identify and quantify these practice valuation discounts and premiums. Professional appraisers perform a practice-specific analysis of each discount and premium. Moreover, they often customize these economic analyses to the specific accounting practice valuation approach employed.

Professional appraisers also consider, in addition to an economic analysis, judicial precedent and all published literature (i.e., empirical data analyses) when quantifying practice valuation discounts and premiums.

INTRODUCTION TO THE PRACTICE VALUATION SYNTHESIS AND CONCLUSION

The analyst must synthesize the various indications of value obtained by the various valuation approach methods to produce final valuation estimate for the subject accounting practice. A synthesis is required because different value indications result from the use of multiple valuation approaches—and from the application of various methods—within a single valuation approach.

To perform the valuation synthesis, the analyst reviews the entire appraisal to ascertain that its data, procedures, and logic are sound and consistent. Inconsistencies among the valuation approaches should be reconciled. Approaches and methods used should be pertinent to the bundle of ownership legal rights being appraised to the standard of value under consideration, and to the purpose and objective of the appraisal. A final, independent check of all mathematical calculations is recommended.

The conclusion of the final value estimate is not derived simply by applying technical and quantitative procedures. Rather, it is reached through the application of the analyst's professional judgment and experience to the practice valuation process.

INTRODUCTION TO REPORTING
VALUATION CONCLUSIONS

Regardless of the form or format of the basic accounting practice valuation report, it should:

1. Conform to the Uniform Standards of Professional Appraisal Practice (USPAP) adopted by the Appraisal Standards Board of The Appraisal Foundation
2. Be sufficiently descriptive to enable the reader to ascertain the estimated defined value and the rationale for that estimate, providing detail and depth of analysis that reflect the complexity of the accounting practice appraised
3. Analyze and report on current market conditions and trends that will affect the projected income or the marketability of the accounting practice
4. Contain sufficient supporting documentation to adequately describe the appraiser's logic, reasoning judgment, and analysis in arriving at the defined value reported
5. Follow a valuation methodology that includes the market approach, the income approach, and the asset-based approach; reconcile the three approaches; and explain the elimination of any valuation approach not used

UNACCEPTABLE REPORTING PRACTICES

The following practices should be considered unacceptable in an accounting practice valuation report:

1. Including inaccurate or incomplete data about the subject accounting practice
2. Failing to report and consider any apparent factor that has an adverse effect on the value and marketability of the subject accounting practice
3. Relying in the valuation analysis on comparable market transactions that were not confirmed by the appraiser
4. Relying, without adequate explanation, on valuation analyses of inappropriate "comparable" sales or failing to use comparable sales that are more similar, without adequate explanation
5. Developing value and marketability conclusions that are not supported by available market data
6. Failing to provide in the appraisal report a signed appraisal certification, statement of appraisal contingent and limiting conditions, and the professional qualifications of the responsible appraiser

The following accounting practice valuation reporting standards, have already been introduced:

1. USPAP Standards 9 and 10
2. ASA Business Valuation Standards (included in Appendix F)
3. IBA Business Appraisal Standards (included in Appendix G)
4. NACVA Business Appraisal Standards (included in Appendix H)

SUMMARY

While numerous methods and procedures may be used to estimate the value of an accounting practice, all of them may be grouped into three categories of practice valuation approaches:

1. The market approach
2. The income approach
3. The asset-based approach

Each of these valuation approaches will be described in greater detail in the Chapters 6, 7, and 8.

Based upon the results of these three valuation approaches, the analyst synthesizes various indications of value for the subject accounting practice and concludes a final estimate of its value. This valuation synthesis and conclusion will depend in part on (1) the purpose and objective of the appraisal, (2) the quantity and quality of available data, and (3) in good measure the experience and judgment of the professional appraiser. The process leading to the accounting practice valuation synthesis and conclusion will be discussed in greater detail in Chapter 11.

The present chapter also introduced the topic of reporting the results of the accounting practice valuation. Several valuation reporting dos and don'ts were presented. The topic of reporting the results of the accounting practice valuation will be presented in greater detail in Chapter 12.

5

DATA GATHERING AND DUE DILIGENCE FOR AN ACCOUNTING PRACTICE APPRAISAL

The data needed for valuing an accounting practice can be generally categorized into the following five groups:

1. Data from the subject accounting practice
2. Relevant economic and investment data, including data on interest rates and required rates of return relative to risk
3. Guideline transaction data
4. Other relevant information, such as data for use in quantifying appropriate valuation discounts and/or premiums
5. Relevant accounting industry data, for comparative analysis

The information needed for an accounting practice valuation need not be gathered in the order shown above. In fact, the data usually are gathered more or less simultaneously, either by one analyst or by a team of analysts. It is important to get an overview of the subject practice at an early meeting with the practice management (either by telephone or in person) so that the analyst will get a sense of what information will be relevant and can begin collecting it right away.

If time allows, the analyst should request financial statements and other readily available information before visiting the subject practice. The analyst can use this information to prepare questions and topics for discussion and thus maximize the productivity of interviews with the practice management.

GENERALIZED ACCOUNTING PRACTICE INFORMATION CHECKLIST

Exhibit 5.1 presents a generalized checklist of documents and information commonly used in accounting practice appraisals. Not every item on the list will necessarily be

FINANCIAL STATEMENTS

Balance sheets, income statements, statements of changes in financial position or statements of cash flow, and statements of stockholders' equity or partners' capital accounts for the last five fiscal years, if available

Income tax returns for the same years

Latest interim statements, if valuation date is three months or more beyond end of last fiscal year, and interim statement for the comparable period the year before

Service line income statements (if applicable) by department or service line, including:

- Audit
- Accounting and write-up
- Personal tax
- Corporate tax
- Management advisory services
- Specialized consulting services

OTHER FINANCIAL AND OPERATING STATISTIC DATA

Detailed equipment list and depreciation schedule

Aged accounts receivable list

Aged accounts payable list

List of all prepaid expenses

List of all unbilled work in progress

Number of days of billed receivables outstanding (in relation to standard fees)

Number of days of unbilled receivables outstanding (in relation to standard fees)

Copies of office or other real estate lease or leases (if lease does not exist or is not transferable, determine what new lease or rental terms will be)

(continued)

Exhibit 5.1.   Generalized Documents and Information Checklist for the Valuation of a Typical Accounting Practice. All information is current as of the valuation date.

Copies of any other existing contracts (employment agreements with partners and/or key accountants, covenants not to compete with former owners and/or with others, supplier agreements, maintenance agreements, software agreements, equipment leases or rental contracts, loan agreements, employee benefit plans, and so on)

List of all stockholders or partners, with:

- Number of shares owned by each or percentage of each partner's interest (or points) in earnings and capital
- Date each equityholder first became an equityholder
- Dollar amount of investment of each equityholder in the practice's equity (i.e., the amounts on which any return on capital calculations are made)

Compensation schedule for all owners for the last five years, including all benefits and personal expenses, with detailed descriptions of:

- Base salary levels (and method used to set)
- Any return on capital investment payments (and method used to set)
- Any profit distribution (and method used to set)
- Any performance or other bonus (and method used to set)

Copies or descriptions of all employee benefit plans:

- For all equityholders
- For all staff

Schedule of insurance in force, including key-person life, property and casualty, professional liability

Copies of all budgets or financial projections, prepared during the last five years—including current budget or financial plan

List of all clients served during past year, indicating fees collected from each client, by the following categories:

- Audit
- Accounting and write-up
- Personal tax
- Corporate tax
- Management advisory services
- Specialized consulting services

(continued)

Exhibit 5.1.   *(continued)*

Revenue analysis for the last three years, by service line (including audit, accounting and write-up, personal tax, corporate tax, management advisory services, specialized consulting services, any other departments/functions of the firm, and total), indicating:

- Number of clients served
- Number of engagements performed
- Gross fee revenue generated (at standard billing rates)
- Gross fee revenue unbilled (and written off)
- Gross fee revenue billed but uncollected (and written off)
- Net fee revenue collected
- Number of hours billed
- Utilization percentage of staff associated to service line

List of all employees (disaggregated by partner, nonpartner professional, and support staffing), including:

- Name
- Tenure (years) with firm
- Base compensation
- Total compensation
- Standard billing rate (for professionals)
- Number of hours billed (for professionals)
- Standard annual fees (for professionals)
- Actual annual fees generated (for professionals)
- Utilization percentage by standard hours (for professionals)
- Utilization percentage by standard fees (for professionals)

PRACTICE AND OTHER DOCUMENTS RELATING TO RIGHTS OF OWNERS

If a corporation, articles of incorporation, by-laws, any amendments to either, and corporate minutes

If a partnership, articles of partnership, with any amendments

Any existing equityholder or partner buy-sell agreements, options to purchase stock or partnership units, points, or other interests, rights of first refusal, trust agreements, or other documents affecting the ownership rights—and the transferability—of the ownership interest being valued

(continued)

Exhibit 5.1.   *(continued)*

OTHER INFORMATION

Brief history of the subject practice, including how long in business and details of any changes in ownership and/or bona fide offers to purchase the practice (or any interest in the practice) received during the last five years

Brief description of the subject practice, including:

- Any industry specialization
- Any geographic specialization
- Any service line specialization
- Competitive assessment of the subject practice compared to five most direct principal competitors (and names of these five competitors) in terms of:
  —Number of partners
  —Number of professionals
  —Annual professional fee revenue
  —Perceived reputation in the market

Description of any awards or other professional or service recognitions received by practice during last five years

Organization charts, by department

Information on related-party transactions (between partners, or otherwise)

Copies of all marketing literature (brochures, advertisements, newsletters, and so on)

List of all locations where the practice operates, with:

- Physical size of the office
- Indication of whether owned or leased space
- Total number of employees
- Total number of partners
- Total number of non-partner professionals

If the client base is concentrated, list of top 20 major accounts, with annual dollar professional fee revenue for each, principal service provided to each, principal industry of each and principal firm partner contact of each

List of all direct CPA firm competitors:

- By geography specialization
- By industry specialization
- By service line specialization

(continued)

Exhibit 5.1. *(continued)*

Resumes of all partners and all senior nonpartner professional personnel, with age, position, compensation, length of service, education, accounting industry special service, continuing education status, and prior experience

Any existing indicators of asset values, including latest property tax assessments and any appraisals (of real estate, equipment, or of practice value) that have been performed during last five years

Any contingent or off-balance-sheet assets or liabilities (pending lawsuits, compliance requirements, and so on)

Any filings or regulatory correspondence with professional agencies or associations including state CPA societies and AICPA

Information on all prior equity interest transactions that have occurred during the past five years, including:

- Partner retirements or other departures
- New partner admissions
- Sales between partners

Copy of all professional peer review reports received during the past five years

Exhibit 5.1.   *(continued)*

required for every practice appraisal, and in many instances special circumstances will require the analyst to review documents not listed.

Having requested whatever documents seem likely to be available, the analyst should be flexible enough to work within the limits of the documentation that the practice is able to provide. It would be unusual to find every item on the checklist readily available. Therefore, the analyst usually will need to obtain some of the information through interviews with practice management. As the valuation progresses, the analyst can review the written information and supplement it, when necessary, by requesting more documents through interviews with practice management and by reference to written information obtained from outside of the subject practice.

PRACTICE MANAGEMENT INTERVIEWS AND FIELDWORK

The need for the valuation analyst to visit the practice offices and to have personal contact with practice management and other related people varies greatly from one valuation situation to another. The extent of the necessary fieldwork depends on many things, including the purpose of the valuation, the nature of the practice, and the size and complexity of the case. Another factor is how extensively the written materials discussed above cover the many subjects that the appraiser needs to investigate.

The objectives of the valuation fieldwork range from gaining a broad, general perspective on the subject practice and its operations to filling in necessary minutiae. Generally, a visit to the practice offices to observe daily operations provides substantial insight beyond what can be gleaned from financial statements and other written materials. Seeing the practice operate firsthand and participating in face-to-face interviews with practice management typically make the practice come alive for an analyst. Also, the analyst can ascertain many details more easily and productively through direct conversation than via written material.

The analyst can get the most out of the field trip and interview process by thinking and planning in terms of accomplishing three objectives:

1. To gain a better overall understanding of the subject accounting practice
2. To understand better the implications of the practice's financial statements, operating statistics, and other written information used for the accounting practice valuation
3. To identify current or potential changes that might cause the accounting practice's future to differ from that indicated by a mere extrapolation of historical financial and operational data

SCHEDULING THE SEQUENCE OF DUE DILIGENCE STEPS

During due diligence the valuation expert reads and analyzes various aspects of the written material, visits the practice offices, and conducts interviews. The schedule established for the various due diligence steps must be worked out to suit the unique conditions of each valuation assignment. Scheduling should be a priority at the beginning of a valuation, along with defining the valuation assignment. Once established, a schedule should be reviewed and modified as necessary throughout the valuation process.

Generally, it is advisable to prepare in advance a thorough list of questions to ask during valuation fieldwork. While the specific issues pertinent to a practice valuation will vary from case to case, a standard laundry list of questions can be useful in preparing for field interviews. Review of such a list may ensure that an important question is not overlooked.

Valuation fieldwork also helps identify other analytical and research steps to take. A field trip can likewise clarify the utility of the myriad written materials discussed above. Some items may be dismissed as irrelevant. Some items may be examined at the practice offices but not copied for the analyst's files. In other cases, the valuation fieldwork may turn up circumstances suggesting the need for certain additional documentation.

For these reasons, it usually is best to visit the practice offices and interview the practice management fairly early in the valuation process—after obtaining and reviewing enough preliminary information to get a general overview of the practice. The analyst can then conduct follow-up interviews, if needed, either in person or by telephone.

FINANCIAL DATA GATHERING AND DUE DILIGENCE

When valuing an accounting practice—as when valuing most professional practices and small businesses—it is generally important to analyze and make appropriate adjustments to the practice's tangible and intangible assets and liabilities. The valuation of an accounting practice differs from that of a typical small business, however, because the types of assets used by an accounting practice differ significantly from those used by a typical small business. Perhaps the most important difference is that intangible value in the nature of goodwill plays a much more important part in an accounting practice than in a typical small business.

The whole process of valuing tangible and intangible assets is further complicated by the cash-basis accounting used by most accounting practices. The balance sheets of a cash-basis entity may reveal a good deal of value in unrecorded assets such as accounts receivable, work-in-process inventory, and prepaid expenses. Furthermore, fully depreciated equipment still being used by—and having substantial economic value to—the subject practice may have a negligible value on the historical-cost-based balance sheet. Also, leasehold improvements of questionable value to other businesses may be integral to the subject accounting practice operations. By the same token, such liabilities as accounts payable, accrued vacation time for employees, and accrued taxes may not be recorded on a cash-basis balance sheet. The analyst must determine whether these assets and liabilities are necessary to the operations of the accounting practice and how they affect its value.

ASSETS

The following discussion presents some of the more common types of assets that the analyst can find in a typical accounting practice. The list is not all-inclusive. When developing a list of potential assets, the analyst should consider carefully the type of accounting practice being appraised.

Cash

If there is reason to believe that the recorded cash balance may be incorrect, the analyst should request copies of bank statements and statement reconciliations and should review the deposit activity for a period of time just following the valuation date.

Accounts Receivable

Having first estimated the gross value of the accounts receivable, the analyst should adjust for uncollectible and slow-pay accounts. The two most common methods for estimating uncollectible accounts are:

1. Accounts receivable aging—discounting the accounts on the basis of how long past due they are
2. Actual payment history—analyzing the payment trends of the specific practice and assessing whether the trend is for more or fewer write-offs

Both methods have positive and negative characteristics. The analyst should determine which is more appropriate for the subject accounting practice.

Work-in-Process Inventory

Some accounting practices have unrecorded assets for work they have performed but not yet billed. Typically, work in process is an asset found in professional practices such as CPA firms that charge an hourly rate for professional or staff time. This asset might be called *unbilled accounts receivable.*

Since work in process is based on time spent by the practice's professional staff, there are usually time records available from which to estimate the amount of unbilled services. To make a reasonable estimate of the work-in-process inventory at a prior date, the analyst should understand the billing procedures of the practice—how often and on which day(s) of the month the work in process is billed, what procedures are used to compile and bill work in process, what criteria are used to determine accounts billable, and what records show work in process that has been written off.

Exhibit 5.2 presents a typical method of calculating the value of work-in-process inventory for an accounting firm using cash-basis or modified-accrual-basis accounting. Exhibit 5.2 presents the work-in-process inventory of the illustrative firm of Foot & Crossfoot, CPAs. From lines 4 and 7 in this table it is apparent that $32,000 worth of unbilled accounting services is not equal to $32,000 of expected cash collection. Hours are often written down or written up for a variety of reasons, and the analyst should calculate a historical percentage to estimate how much of the firm's billable time actually is billed. Time actually billed is then discounted for uncollectible receivables, as discussed above, to estimate how much is likely to be finally collected. If fixed-fee contracts are in force, the analyst should calculate their value on the basis of the estimated percentage of completion at the valuation date.

One final adjustment may be necessary. The analyst who finds a significant number of old unbilled hours still in "inventory" should determine how diligently the

FOOT & CROSSFOOT, CPAS CALCULATION OF VALUE OF WORK-IN-PROCESS INVENTORY AS OF SEPTEMBER 31, 1996.

	Foot	Crossfoot	Total
Hours in Unbilled Inventory	130	210	
Hourly Billing Rate	×$125	×$75	
Gross Value of Unbilled Inventory	$16,250	$15,750	
Total Gross Value of Unbilled Inventory			$32,000
Less: 3-Year Historical Adjustment to Work in Process (Amount Not Billed Is Equal to 7% of Total)			(2,240)
Estimated Work-in-Process Inventory that Will Be Billed			29,760
Less: 3-Year Historical Write-Off on Accounts Receivable (Amount of Charges Not Collected Is Equal to 9% of Total Charges)			(2,678)
Estimated Cash Value of Work in Process before Calculation of Discount for Time to Collect			$27,082
Indicated Market Value of Work-in-Process Inventory (Rounded)			$27,000

Exhibit 5.2.   Calculation of Value of Work-in-Process Inventory for a Typical Accounting Practice.

firm has house-cleaned its work-in-process inventory. If housecleaning has been haphazard or nonexistent, then the appraiser probably needs to age the work-in-process inventory and to significantly discount (or even eliminate) the old unbilled (and, likely, unbillable) hours.

Inventory of Supplies

The value of the supplies inventory depends on the type of practice. The office supplies of an accounting firm will typically have a small value. Without a detailed catalog of all inventory items, the analyst can usually estimate the amount of inventory on hand for practices that do not have substantial value in inventory. Nevertheless, the analyst should tour the subject practice offices and at least check the level of supplies normally maintained there.

Prepaid Expenses

Rent and insurance (including insurance policies for errors and omissions and for professional liability) are almost always prepaid. From an accounting perspective, because these expenses are continuing, their amounts are not necessarily allocated to the periods when they are used. The analyst, on the other hand, generally is concerned with a specific valuation date. Therefore, from a valuation perspective, prepaid expenses should be classified properly on the balance sheet in order to recognize the fact that future expenses have already been paid.

Equipment

As was true of supplies, the amount and value of equipment necessary to operate any given practice depends on the type and specialty (if any) of the subject accounting practice. For purposes of data collection during valuation, *equipment* includes all office furniture and fixtures, all office automation equipment, and all computer equipment.

The analyst may examine the list of all equipment included on the practice's depreciation schedule. To the extent possible, and practical, any such list should be physically verified: Sometimes fixed assets on a listing have been removed from the practice office; other times assets in place and fully functional within the practice office remain unlisted on the fixed asset schedule.

Leasehold Improvements

Often, leasehold improvements constitute another important asset of the subject practice. During the tour of the accounting practice office, the analyst should pay attention to the condition of the leasehold improvements—in other words, note how well the office is "packaged." If the leasehold improvements are in good condition and have been fully depreciated on the balance sheet, then the analyst may want to adjust their value upward, considering both their life expectancy and the term of the current office lease.

Intangible Assets

Many intangible assets may exist in, and add substantial value to, a professional accounting practice. Intangible assets that, should they exist, warrant investigation during the appraiser's analysis are presented in Exhibit 5.3.

Computer software	Management contracts
Computerized data bases	Marketing and promotional
Client files and records contracts	materials
Client lists	Noncompete covenants
Client relationships	Permits
Employment contracts	Procedural manuals
Favorable leases	Supplier contracts
Going-concern value	Technical and specialty libraries
Goodwill	Trained and assembled workforce
Historical documents	

Exhibit 5.3. Intangible Assets Typically Found in Professional Accounting Practices.

LIABILITIES

Several categories of liabilities may not be reflected on the books of an accounting practice. On the other hand, from a valuation standpoint, some liabilities such as deferred rent may appear there (and even be required by GAAP) even though they are not real economic (cash expenditure) liabilities of the practice.

Accounts Payable

Cash basis financial statements typically do not show accounts payable. Since accounting practices sell services, their accounts payable usually relate to continuing operating expenses such as supplies, telephone, utilities, taxes, and so forth rather than materials for manufacturing or for sale. If accounts payable need to be recorded, the analyst should review all unpaid invoices at the valuation date. If the valuation fieldwork is performed substantially after the appraisal date, the analyst should ask to see all canceled checks written during a reasonable period of time after the valuation date, along with the corresponding invoices. With this information the analyst can estimate how much money the practice owed (from an operating-expense perspective) as of the appraisal date.

Accrued Liabilities

Accrued liabilities are expenses such as payroll, payroll taxes, or interest that are allocated to a prior period but are not yet due. For example, if a note payable calls for interest payments at the end of the year and the appraisal date is at midyear, then the analyst should adjust for accrued interest (unless it is already shown on the financial statements), even though it is not payable for another six months.

Deferred Liabilities

Deferred liabilities typically fall into three categories:

1. Deferred revenues
2. Deferred expenses
3. Deferred income taxes

Deferred Revenues

Deferred revenues are amounts that have been received for services not yet performed. Deferred revenues may need to be considered in accounting firms that receive a retainer before beginning work on a case.

Deferred Expenses

Deferred expenses are relatively unusual. One example might be deferred rent. A landlord may offer several months of free occupancy in return for a tenant's signing a long-term lease. This situation would warrant a liability account for deferred rent because the tenant could theoretically have negotiated a lease for the same period of time at a lower monthly rent had he or she opted not to accept the free rent, even though the total payments under each option would be equal.

Deferred Income Taxes

Deferred income taxes appear on financial statements to match income tax expense with the related financial accounting income for the appropriate accounting period.

Long-Term Debt

Long-term debt in accounting practices is usually associated with equipment purchases. If the analyst has reason to believe that the amounts listed in long-term debt are incorrect, copies of the debt instrument(s) and payment records should be obtained. Also, the debt instrument should disclose if the subject accounting practice has an accrued interest liability that is not shown on the balance sheet.

Lease Obligations

The analyst should always obtain copies of all leases of the subject accounting practice, whether the practice is a lessor or a lessee. The financial statements usually show capital lease obligations, under which the practice will ultimately be obliged to purchase the leased equipment.

Contingent Liabilities

Contingent obligations are liabilities about which too little of the outcome is known to account for them on the financial statements. For example, the accountant may be a defendant or plaintiff in a malpractice suit or there may be disputed billings, and these facts may be disclosed on the financial statement. The analyst should investigate these types of liabilities.

DUE DILIGENCE SUMMARY

In accounting practice appraisals, the practice financial statements generally need to be adjusted from a cash basis to an accrual basis, as discussed in considerable detail in this chapter. This chapter has also discussed other balance sheet adjustments particular to accounting practices.

Gathering and analyzing the foregoing information will give the analyst the groundwork on which to perform the accounting practice valuation analyses. The specific material needed will vary with the particular practice valuation; its selection requires the analyst's judgment. Following the guidelines in this chapter will help the analyst to avoid the all-too-common pitfall of overlooking certain practice data that may have a significant bearing on the value of the accounting practice or accounting practice ownership interest subject to appraisal.

An experienced analyst can gain a great deal of insight into an accounting practice through an office visit and management interview process. The due diligence process should provide the analyst with a perspective on the subject accounting practice and yield a multitude of details relevant to the valuation assignment. What the analyst gets from the process will depend partly on the thoroughness of preparation and partly on the degree of cooperation provided by the subject practice and by the practice management being interviewed.

PUBLIC ACCOUNTING INDUSTRY COMPARATIVE INFORMATION

It is important for the analyst to obtain information regarding the financial performance and operating statistics of firms in the public accounting industry, to analyze and synthesize that data, and to compare the results of that analysis to the financial performance and operating statistics of the subject accounting practice. Collecting and comparing such data and analyses will be useful in all three standard accounting practice valuation approaches: the income approach, the market approach, and the asset-based approach.

When these valuation approaches are discussed in the next several chapters, the uses of this comparative information from the accounting industry will become more obvious. By way of introduction, the following list presents some of the reasons for (or uses of) the collection and analysis of accounting industry financial performance and operating statistics (and the comparison of these data to the subject accounting practice):

1. Income approach
    a. Test of reasonableness of practice management's financial and operating projections (when compared to industry average data)
    b. Adjustment (if necessary) of practice management's financial and operating projections (to bring them more in line with industry average data)
    c. Identification of financial and operational strengths and weaknesses of the subject practice (compared to industry average data)
    d. Selection of the appropriate practice-specific present value discount rate (and/or capitalization rate), based upon strengths and weaknesses of the subject practice compared to industry average benchmarks

2. Market approach
    a. Assessment of the subject practice compared to the "average" accounting practice
    b. Selection and analysis of guideline practices (based upon financial results and operating statistics)
    c. Adjustment (if necessary) of data obtained from guideline practices (based upon industry average financial results and operating statistics)
    d. Comparison of the financial and operating performance of the subject accounting practice to the selected guideline practices (based upon key financial and operating statistics identified in industry data)

3. Asset-based approach
    a. Analysis and adjustment (if necessary) of on-balance-sheet financial asset and liability accounts to bring them in line with industry benchmarks (based upon industry average data)
    b. Identification of valuable off-balance-sheet intangible assets of the subject accounting practice (by comparing subject practice financial and operating data to industry average data)
    c. Development of valuation models (and, if necessary, assessment of management's projections) to account for specific intangible assets (such as a trained and assembled workforce, client relationships, goodwill, etc.)

d. Selection of a present value discount rate (and/or capitalization rate) appropriate for the valuation analysis of the practice's identified intangible assets (based on industry average rates of return and profit margins as well as on the risk of the subject practice relative to the industry average)

In summary, the collection and analysis of accounting industry financial and operating data is a useful procedure in any accounting practice valuation approach.

Sources of Accounting Practice Industry Financial Data

Numerous published sources (most of which are updated annually) report financial ratio and other financial information by industry. Many of these published sources track and report data for accounting firms. Of these, most present their financial ratio and other information by size of firm, determined by size of assets, of revenues, or of both.

It is noteworthy that the financial statistics presented for a given industry (e.g., accounting firms) may vary a great deal in these published sources. This occurs when different publications extract their data from different sources. For example, some publications obtain their data from income tax returns, other publications obtain their data from financial statements filed with banks, and so forth.

Exhibit 5.4 presents some of the representative sources for statistics on accounting firm (among other industries) financial ratios. While not absolutely comprehensive, this list does include all of the more common published industry financial data sources relied upon by professional practice appraisers. Exhibit 5.4 also includes the addresses and many of the telephone numbers for the publishers of these periodic published data sources.

As an example of one source for financial ratio data, Exhibit 5.5 presents relevant pages from the 1995 edition of *Tax and Financial Statement Benchmarks,* by Neil Sheflin, Ph.D., published by John Wiley & Sons, Inc. While formats of presentation underlying data sources may differ among publications, this one is typical of published sources on accounting services industry financial data.

Sources of Accounting Practice Industry Operating Data

Several published sources (some updated annually) report operating statistics specifically related to public accounting firms. These statistics usually generalize such information as sizes of firms, numbers of partners, partner-to-staff ratios, partner compensations, firm profitability, firm staff and partner billing rates, and firm staff and partner utilization rates.

Probably the most widely referenced of such resources is the *Practice Manage-*

Almanac of Business and Industrial Financial Ratios, by Leo Troy. Prentice Hall, Englewood Cliffs, NJ 07632. Phone: (800) 922-0579. Fax: (201) 592-0696. Annual. Contains financial ratios derived from federal tax returns. Ratios for about 200 industries are arranged by size of company assets.

Cost of Doing Business—Partnerships and Proprietorships. Dun & Bradstreet, 99 Church St., New York, NY 10007. Phone: (800) 234-3867 or (212) 593-6800. Fax: (212) 593-6622. Annual. Covers operating expenses for over 200 lines of business.

Financial Statement Studies of the Small Business. Financial Research Associates, 510 Avenue J, S.E., Winter Haven, FL 33880. Phone: (813) 299-3969. Annual.

Income and Fees of Accountants in Public Practice. National Society of Public Accountants, 1010 N. Fairfax St., Suite 700, Alexandria, VA 22314. Phone: (703) 549-6400. Fax: (703) 684-0540. Triennial.

Corporation Income Tax Returns: Statistics of Income. Internal Revenue Service, Superintendent of Documents, U.S. Government Printing Office, Washington, DC 20402. Annual.

Industry Norms and Key Business Ratios. Dun & Bradstreet, 99 Church St., New York, NY 10007. Phone: (800) 234-3867 or (212) 593-6800. Fax: (212) 593-6622. Annual.

IRS Corporate Financial Ratios. Schonfeld & Associates, 1 Sherwood Drive, Lincolnshire, IL 60069. Phone: (847) 948-8080. Annual.

RMA Annual Statement Studies. Robert Morris Associates, One Liberty Place, 1650 Market Street, Suite 2300, Philadelphia, PA 19103. Phone: (800) 677-7621. Fax: (215) 851-9206. Annual.

Statistics of Income Source Book. Internal Revenue Service, Superintendent of Documents, U.S. Government Printing Office, Washington, DC. Annual.

Tax and Financial Statement Benchmarks, by Neil Sheflin. John Wiley & Sons, One Wiley Drive, Somerset, NJ 08875. Phone: (800) 225-5945. Annual.

Exhibit 5.4. Published Sources of Financial Ratio and Other Financial Data for the Accounting Services Industry.

ment Survey: National Results, published annually by the Texas Society of Certified Public Accountants in Dallas. This survey is generally considered the most comprehensive resource with regard to accounting firm operating statistics.

Several other state CPA societies periodically survey accounting firm operating statistics (typically in a given region). For example, the California Society of Certified

SERVICES: Other services
Accounting, auditing, and bookkeeping services

SIC: 872	PBA: 8930									ASSET SIZE			
WITH & WITHOUT NI	All	0	1 to 99 K	100 to 249 K	250 to 499 K	500 to 999 K	1 to 4 M	5 to 9 M	10 to 24 M	25 to 49 M	50 to 99 M	100 to 249 M	250 M & Over
1. Number of Corporations	23,431	1,014	18,557	2,986	638	103	111	15	3	•	3	•	•
INCOME STATEMENT % of Net Sales													
2. Net Sales Per Firm $000	237	253	102	364	984	1,628	8,164	2,191	13,301	•	180,814	•	•
3. Cost of Sales and Ops %	19.7	5.1	7.7	23.1	4.9	23.2	60.5	10.4	7.0	•	10.8	•	•
4. Gross Margin %	80.3	94.9	92.3	76.9	95.1	76.8	39.5	89.6	93.0	•	89.2	•	•
5. Other Operating Expenses%	33.9	45.1	43.7	36.5	35.0	31.0	14.8	22.0	18.8	•	23.0	•	•
6. Compensation of Officers %	16.2	23.7	24.4	17.7	20.1	14.3	2.0	7.5	8.7	•	1.9	•	•
7. Repairs %	1.0	0.7	0.8	0.7	0.7	1.0	1.9	0.0	•	•	0.9	•	•
8. Bad Debts %	0.1	•	0.0	0.0	•	3.3	•	0.8	0.0	•	0.2	•	•
9. Rent on Business Property %	5.5	8.3	7.7	4.5	4.2	4.1	1.3	2.5	2.8	•	7.1	•	•
10. Depr., Depl., Amort. %	2.2	1.7	2.9	1.2	2.5	1.2	0.6	2.7	6.7	•	3.9	•	•
11. Advertising %	0.5	0.0	0.8	0.6	0.2	1.0	0.3	•	•	•	0.4	•	•
12. Pension and Ann Plans %	0.6	0.0	0.3	0.4	1.7	2.2	0.1	2.1	•	•	1.6	•	•
13. Employee Benefit Pgms %	3.0	6.2	2.2	7.5	1.1	•	0.6	2.7	•	•	2.6	•	•
14. State & Local Taxes Paid %	4.9	4.5	4.5	3.9	4.5	3.9	8.1	3.8	0.5	•	4.3	•	•

(continued)

Exhibit 5.5. Typical Industry Financial Data Source. *Source:* Specimen data table from Neil Sheflin's, *Tax and Financial Statement Benchmarks,* 1995 ed. (New York: John Wiley & Sons, 1995). Reprinted by permission of John Wiley & Sons, Inc.

SIC: 872	PBA: 8930						ASSET SIZE						
WITH & WITHOUT NI	All	0	1 to 99 K	100 to 249 K	250 to 499 K	500 to 999 K	1 to 4 M	5 to 9 M	10 to 24 M	25 to 49 M	50 to 99 M	100 to 249 M	250 M & Over
15. Net Operating Inc. %	46.4	49.8	48.6	40.4	60.1	45.8	24.6	67.6	74.2	•	66.2	•	•
16. Interest Expense %	1.4	0.8	1.5	1.7	2.6	0.0	0.6	0.7	2.1	•	1.5	•	•
17. Other Income %	2.4	0.6	1.8	4.0	1.0	15.3	0.4	1.6	19.0	•	2.2	•	•
18. Interest Income %	0.5	0.0	0.3	0.5	0.3	0.2	0.1	0.9	1.4	•	2.0	•	•
19. Net Capital Gains %	0.1	0.0	0.4	0.0	•	•	•	•	•	•	0.1	•	•
20. Other Expenses %	41.4	45.2	38.9	37.9	56.3	58.6	24.3	61.3	85.8	•	56.6	•	•
21. Contributions and Gifts %	0.0	•	0.0	0.1	•	•	0.0	•	•	•	0.0	•	•
22. Earnings Before Taxes %	6.0	4.4	10.0	4.8	2.2	2.5	0.1	7.1	5.3	•	10.4	•	•
23. Federal Income Tax %	0.4	0.1	0.1	0.4	0.0	0.9	0.1	0.8	1.7	•	2.8	•	•
24. Net Income %	5.5	4.3	9.9	4.4	2.2	1.6	0.0	6.3	3.6	•	7.6	•	•
BALANCE SHEET % of Assets/Liabilities & Net Worth													
25. Total Assets Per Firm $000	75	•	22	149	297	721	2,204	7,351	13,115	•	76,570	•	•
26. Cash %	15.9	•	15.0	20.0	22.3	19.6	16.9	1.4	24.9	•	7.6	•	•
27. Receivables %	20.5	•	13.3	17.9	9.6	0.6	48.4	5.2	20.0	•	31.3	•	•
28. Inventory %	0.8	•	0.6	2.7	•	•	•	•	•	•	0.1	•	•
29. Other Current Assets %	7.5	•	2.7	12.0	5.8	38.8	2.9	1.2	2.4	•	7.8	•	•
30. Net Fixed Assets %	26.4	•	33.1	17.5	28.7	41.0	9.6	28.0	52.7	•	37.5	•	•
31. Other Long-Term Assets %	28.8	•	35.2	29.8	33.6	0.1	22.1	64.2	0.0	•	15.7	•	•

(continued)

Exhibit 5.5. *(continued)*

SIC: 872	PBA: 8930						ASSET SIZE						
WITH & WITHOUT NI	All	0	1 to 99 K	100 to 249 K	250 to 499 K	500 to 999 K	1 to 4 M	5 to 9 M	10 to 24 M	25 to 49 M	50 to 99 M	100 to 249 M	250 M & Over
32. Liabs & Net Worth PF $000	75	•	22	149	297	721	2,204	73,51	13,115	•	76,570	•	•
33. Accounts Payable %	7.5	•	2.0	10.2	0.8	22.1	16.1	0.3	24.5	•	4.2	•	•
34. Notes & Loans Payable %	19.7	•	18.3	2.5	50.9	•	16.1	47.0	2.3	•	30.0	•	•
35. Other Current Liabilities %	11.0	•	9.8	4.2	4.0	•	47.1	1.8	0.8	•	3.7	•	•
36. Long-Term Debt %	32.5	•	48.4	42.5	42.8	8.2	25.7	13.5	26.9	•	1.6	•	•
37. Other Long-Term Liabs %	3.3	•	5.2	0.7	•	•	0.2	26.8	0.2	•	1.5	•	•
38. Net Worth %	25.9	•	16.3	40.0	1.5	69.8	-5.2	10.7	45.3	•	59.0	•	•
RATIOS													
39. Current Ratio	1.2	•	1.1	3.1	0.7	2.7	0.9	0.2	1.7	•	1.2	•	•
40. Quick Ratio	1.0	•	0.9	2.4	0.6	2.6	0.8	0.1	1.6	•	1.2	•	•
41. Working Cap/Sales %	2.1	•	0.4	14.7	-5.4	16.3	-3.0	•	19.5	•	3.8	•	•
42. Inventory Turnover (EOY)	•	•	•	91.0	•	•	•	•	•	•	•	•	•
43. Inventory Days (EOY)	1.0	•	0.5	4.0	•	•	•	•	•	•	0.2	•	•
44. Avg Collection Pd (EOY)	23.6	•	10.7	27.0	10.6	1.0	47.7	63.2	78.7	•	48.6	•	•
45. Net Fixed Asset Turnover	12.0	•	13.9	13.9	11.6	5.5	38.6	1.1	1.9	•	6.3	•	•
46. Total Asset Turnover	3.2	•	4.6	2.4	3.3	2.3	3.7	0.3	1.0	•	2.4	•	•
47. Debt to Total Assets %	74.1	•	83.7	60.0	98.5	30.2	•	89.3	54.7	•	41.0	•	•

(continued)

Exhibit 5.5. *(continued)*

SIC: 872	PBA: 8930					ASSET SIZE							
WITH & WITHOUT NI	All	0	1 to 99 K	100 to 249 K	250 to 499 K	500 to 999 K	1 to 4 M	5 to 9 M	10 to 24 M	25 to 49 M	50 to 99 M	100 to 249 M	250 M & Over
48. Times Interest Earned	5.2	6.3	7.7	3.9	1.8	•	1.1	10.5	3.6	•	8.1	•	•
49. Return on Assets %	17.6	•	45.5	10.7	7.1	3.5	0.1	1.9	3.7	•	17.9	•	•
50. Return on Equity %	68.0	•	•	26.8	•	5.1	•	17.5	8.1	•	30.3	•	•
51. EBIT/Total Assets %	23.6	•	52.7	15.8	15.8	5.7	2.6	2.3	7.5	•	27.9	•	•
52. Cash Flow/Sales %	7.7	6.0	12.9	5.6	4.7	2.8	0.6	9.0	10.3	•	11.5	•	•

For accounting periods ending 7/91–6/92. $000 = $thousands   EOY = End of Year.

(continued)

Exhibit 5.5.   *(continued)*

SERVICES: Other services
Accounting, auditing, and bookkeeping services

SIC: 872   PBA: 8930

							ASSET SIZE						
WITH NI	All	0	1 to 99 K	100 to 249 K	250 to 499 K	500 to 999 K	1 to 4 M	5 to 9 M	10 to 24 M	25 to 49 M	50 to 99 M	100 to 249 M	250 M & Over
1. Number of Corporations	15,899	690	12,304	2,261	503	52	70	•	•	•	•	•	•
INCOME STATEMENT % of Net Sales													
2. Net Sales Per Firm $000	256	372	116	354	1,192	3,200	2,944	•	•	•	•	•	•
3. Costs of Sales and Ops %	12.4	5.1	7.6	26.3	5.1	23.2	19.1	•	•	•	•	•	•
4. Gross Margin %	87.6	94.9	92.4	73.7	94.9	76.7	80.9	•	•	•	•	•	•
5. Other Operating Expenses %	34.1	45.1	42.0	30.2	33.2	30.5	20.1	•	•	•	•	•	•
6. Compensation of Officers %	15.8	23.7	23.1	10.7	19.0	14.4	52	•	•	•	•	•	•
7. Repairs %	1.1	0.7	0.8	0.5	0.7	1.0	8.3	•	•	•	•	•	•
8. Bad Debts %	0.2	•	0.0	0.0	•	3.4	•	•	•	•	•	•	•
9. Rent on Business Property %	5.8	8.3	7.6	4.2	4.3	3.7	0.9	•	•	•	•	•	•
10. Depr., Depl., Amort. %	2.4	1.7	2.7	1.1	2.6	0.9	1.4	•	•	•	•	•	•
11. Advertising %	0.5	0.0	0.7	0.4	0.3	1.0	0.3	•	•	•	•	•	•
12. Pension and Ann Plans %	0.5	0.0	0.2	0.2	0.8	2.2	•	•	•	•	•	•	•
13. Employee Benefit Pgms %	3.7	6.2	2.6	9.3	1.0	•	0.2	•	•	•	•	•	•
14. State & Local Taxes Paid %	4.1	4.5	4.3	3.8	4.5	3.9	3.8	•	•	•	•	•	•

(continued)

Exhibit 5.5. (continued)

SIC: 872	PBA: 8930						ASSET SIZE						
WITH NI	All	0	1 to 99 K	100 to 249 K	250 to 499 K	500 to 999 K	1 to 4 M	5 to 9 M	10 to 24 M	25 to 49 M	50 to 99 M	100 to 249 M	250 M & Over
15. Net Operating Inc. %	53.5	49.8	50.4	43.5	61.7	46.2	60.8	•	•	•	•	•	•
16. Interest Expense %	1.5	0.8	1.7	1.5	2.7	0.0	1.2	•	•	•	•	•	•
17. Other Income %	2.8	0.6	1.9	5.0	0.5	15.4	1.2	•	•	•	•	•	•
18. Interest Income %	0.4	0.0	0.2	0.5	0.3	0.2	0.5	•	•	•	•	•	•
19. Net Capital Gains %	0.2	0.0	0.5	0.0	•	•	•	•	•	•	•	•	•
20. Other Expenses %	45.2	45.2	33.7	40.3	57.2	57.8	59.3	•	•	•	•	•	•
21. Contributions and Gifts %	0.0	•	0.0	0.1	•	•	0.1	•	•	•	•	•	•
22. Earnings Before Taxes %	9.6	4.4	16.9	6.6	2.3	3.8	1.4	•	•	•	•	•	•
23. Federal Income Tax %	0.6	0.1	0.1	0.6	0.0	0.9	0.2	•	•	•	•	•	•
24. Net Income %	9.0	4.4	16.8	6.1	2.3	2.8	1.2	•	•	•	•	•	•
BALANCE SHEET % of Assets/Liabilities & Net Worth													
25. Total Assets Per Firm $000	83	•	26	142	274	795	2,528	•	•	•	•	•	•
26. Cash %	16.9	•	11.7	26.6	14.4	27.9	23.4	•	•	•	•	•	•
27. Receivables %	18.4	•	16.7	15.8	13.2	•	48.4	•	•	•	•	•	•
28. Inventory %	0.2	•	0.8	•	•	•	•	•	•	•	•	•	•
29. Other Current Assets %	6.5	•	1.8	14.9	5.5	3.1	2.4	•	•	•	•	•	•
30. Net Fixed Assets %	28.2	•	27.9	15.0	39.3	69.0	10.0	•	•	•	•	•	•
31. Other Long Term Assets %	29.7	•	41.1	27.8	27.5	•	15.8	•	•	•	•	•	•

(continued)

Exhibit 5.5. *(continued)*

SIC: 872	PBA: 8930						ASSET SIZE						
WITH NI	All	0	1 to 99 K	100 to 249 K	250 to 499 K	500 to 999 K	1 to 4 M	5 to 9 M	10 to 24 M	25 to 49 M	50 to 99 M	100 to 249 M	250 M & Over
32. Liabs & Net Worth PF $000	83	•	26	142	274	795	2,528	•	•	•	•	•	•
33. Accounts Payable %	9.3	•	1.4	14.1	1.1	39.6	20.8	•	•	•	•	•	•
34. Notes & Loans Payable %	20.6	•	18.9	2.5	70.1	•	21.2	•	•	•	•	•	•
35. Other Current Liabilities %	9.0	•	9.7	5.7	5.4	•	28.8	•	•	•	•	•	•
36. Long-Term Debt %	29.4	•	37.6	38.5	52.1	14.7	22.5	•	•	•	•	•	•
37. Other Long-Term Liabs %	4.2	•	6.2	0.9	•	•	•	•	•	•	•	•	•
38. Net Worth %	27.4	•	26.2	38.2	−28.7	45.8	6.5	•	•	•	•	•	•
RATIOS													
39. Current Ratio	1.1	•	1.0	2.6	0.4	0.8	1.0	•	•	•	•	•	•
40. Quick Ratio	1.0	•	0.9	2.1	0.4	0.7	1.0	•	•	•	•	•	•
41. Working Cap/Sales %	1.0	•	0.2	14.0	−10.0	−2.1	2.8	•	•	•	•	•	•
42. Inventory Turnover (EOY)	•	•	•	•	•	•	•	•	•	•	•	•	•
43. Inventory Days (EOY)	0.2	•	0.6	•	•	•	•	•	•	•	•	•	•
44. Avg Collection Pd (EOY)	22.1	•	14.0	23.4	11.1	•	151.7	•	•	•	•	•	•
45. Net Fixed Asset Turnover	10.9	•	15.7	16.7	11.1	5.8	11.7	•	•	•	•	•	•
46. Total Asset Turnover	3.1	•	4.4	2.5	4.4	4.0	1.2	•	•	•	•	•	•
47. Debt to Total Assets %	72.6	•	73.8	61.8	•	54.2	93.5	•	•	•	•	•	•

(continued)

Exhibit 5.5. *(continued)*

SIC: 872	PBA: 8930						ASSET SIZE							
WITH NI	All	0	1 to 99 K	100 to 249 K	250 to 499 K	500 to 999 K	1 to 4 M	5 to 9 M	10 to 24 M	25 to 49 M	50 to 99 M	100 to 249 M	250 M & Over
48. Times Interest Earned	7.3	6.3	10.9	5.5	1.9	•	2.2	•	•	•	•	•	•
49. Return on Assets %	27.6	•	74.0	15.2	10.0	11.3	1.4	•	•	•	•	•	•
50. Return on Equity %	•	•	•	39.7	•	24.7	21.6	•	•	•	•	•	•
51. EBIT/Total Assets %	34.1	•	81.9	20.3	21.9	15.1	3.1	•	•	•	•	•	•
52. Cash Flow/Sales %	11.3	6.0	19.5	7.1	4.9	3.7	2.6	•	•	•	•	•	•

For accounting periods ending 7/91–6/92. $000 = $thousands   EOY = End of Year.

Exhibit 5.5. *(continued)*

Public Accountants has published *Management of an Accounting Practice Surveys* for several states. These surveys give accounting firm operating statistics in each particular state.

To illustrate the type of firm operating statistics available, Exhibit 5.6 presents the table of contents page from the 1994 Results of Illinois CPA Firms *Management of an Accounting Practice Survey.*

Other state accounting societies also conduct surveys of accounting practice operating statistics from time to time. These occasional survey results may or may not be published as stand-alone studies. However, the state CPA societies typically keep the survey results on file (and available) for research and other purposes.

Accounting practice analysts are strongly recommended to contact the CPA society in the state (or nearby states) where the subject practice is located to ascertain whether any current surveys of accounting firm operating statistics are available. For this reason, Exhibit 5.7 presents the addresses and telephone numbers of the 53 state, territory, and capital district CPA societies.

Lastly, the *Management of an Accounting Practice Handbook* represents an excellent data source with regard to accounting firm operating statistics. These operating statistics are gathered at the annual American Institute of Certified Public Accountants practice management and small firm conferences. The *Management of an Accounting Practice Handbook* is updated annually and is published by the AICPA and Practitioners Publishing Company in Fort Worth, Texas.

Exhibit 5.6. Example of Available Operating Statistics on Accounting Practices. *Source:* Table of Contents for the *1994 Results of Illinois CPA Firms Management of an Accounting Practice Survey* (Redwood City, CA: California Society of Certified Public Accountants, 1994). Reprinted with permission.

STATE CPA SOCIETIES

State Society Executives

ALABAMA SOCIETY OF CPAS
Bryan M. Hassler, Exec. Dir.
P.O. Box 5000
Montgomery, AL 36103-5000
Street Address
1103 South Perry Street
Montgomery, AL 36104
(334) 834-7650
Fax: (334) 834-7310

ALASKA SOCIETY OF CPAS
Linda Plimpton, Exec. Dir.
341 W. Tudor, Suite 105
Anchorage, AK 99503
(907) 562-4334
Fax: (907) 562-4025

ARIZONA SOCIETY OF CPAS
Gary L. Julian, Exec. Dir.
432 N. 44th Street, Suite 300
Phoenix, AZ 85008-7602
(602) 273-0100
Fax: (602) 275-2752

ARKANSAS SOCIETY OF CPAS
Barbara S. Angel, Exec. Dir.
415 North McKinley, Suite 970
Little Rock, AR 72205-3022
(501) 664-8739
Fax: (501) 664-8320

CALIFORNIA SOCIETY OF CPAS
James R. Kurtz, Exec. Dir.
275 Shoreline Drive
Redwood City, CA 94065-1412

(415) 802-2600
Fax: (415) 802-2661

COLORADO SOCIETY OF CPAS
Mary E. Medley, Exec. Dir.
7979 E. Tufts Avenue, Suite 500
Denver, CO 80237-2843
(303) 773-2877
Fax: (303) 773-6344

CONNECTICUT SOCIETY OF CPAS
Jack Brooks, Exec. Dir.
179 Allyn Street, Suite 201
Hartford, CT 06103-1491
(203) 525-1153
Fax: (203) 549-3596
Voice Mail: (203) 527-0783,
   ext. 14

DELAWARE SOCIETY OF CPAS
Margaret W. Mahood, Exec. Dir.
28 The Commons
3520 Silverside Road
Wilmington, DE 19810
(302) 478-7442
Fax: (302) 478-7412

DISTRICT OF COLUMBIA INSTITUTE
   OF CPAS
John J. McNally, Exec. Dir.
1023 15th Street, NW, 8th Floor
Washington, DC 20005-2602
(202) 789-1844
Fax: (202) 789-1847

(continued)

Exhibit 5.7.   Accounting Practice Operating Statistics Reference Sources.

FLORIDA INSTITUTE OF CPAS
Lloyd "Buddy" Turman, Exec. Dir.
P.O. Box 5437
Tallahassee, FL 32314-5437
Street Address
325 West College Avenue
Tallahassee, FL 32301
(904) 224-2727
Fax: (904) 222-8190

GEORGIA SOCIETY OF CPAS
James P. Martin, Jr., Exec. Dir.
3340 Peachtree Road, NE
Suite 2700
Atlanta, GA 30326
(404) 231-8676 (Voice Mail: x808)
Fax: (404) 237-1291

HAWAII SOCIETY OF CPAS
Clarence T. Kuwahara, Exec. Dir.
P.O. Box 1754
Honolulu, HI 96806
Street Address
900 Fort Street, Suite 850
Honolulu, HI 96813
(808) 537-9475
Fax: (808) 537-3520

IDAHO SOCIETY OF CPAS
Melissa Nelson, Exec. Dir.
P.O. Box 2896
Boise, ID 83701
Street Address
250 Bobwhite Court, Suite 240
Boise, ID 83706

(208) 344-6261
Fax: (208) 344-8984

ILLINOIS CPA SOCIETY
Martin Rosenberg, Exec. Dir.
222 South Riverside Plaza, 16th Floor
Chicago, IL 60606
(312) 993-0407, x204
Fax: (312) 993-9432

Jo Ann Benzer, Asst. Exec. Dir.
(312) 993-0407, x206
Fax: (312) 993-9954

INDIANA CPA SOCIETY
Gary M. Bolinger, Exec. Dir.
P.O. Box 40069
Indianapolis, IN 46240-0069
Street Address
8250 Woodfield Crossing Blvd.
Suite 305
Indianapolis, IN 46240-0069
(317) 726-5000
Fax: (317) 726-5005

IOWA CPA SOCIETY
Stanton Bonta, Exec. Dir.
950 Office Park Road, Suite 300
West Des Moines, IA 50265-2548
(515) 223-8161
Fax: (515) 223-7347

KANSAS SOCIETY OF CPAS
T.C. Anderson, Exec. Dir.
P.O. Box 5654
Topeka, KS 66605-0654

(continued)

Exhibit 5.7. *(continued)*

Street Address
400 Croix
Topeka, KS 66611
(913) 267-6460
Fax: (913) 267-9278

KENTUCKY SOCIETY OF CPAS
Bernard W. Gratzer, Exec. Dir.
P.O. Box 436869
Louisville, KY 40253
Street Address
1735 Alliant Avenue
Louisville, KY 40253
(502) 226-5272
Fax: (502) 261-9512

SOCIETY OF LOUISIANA CPAS
Grady Hazel, Exec. Dir.
2400 Veterans Blvd., Suite 500
Kenner, LA 70062
(504) 464-1040
Fax: (504) 469-7930

MAINE SOCIETY OF CPAS
Wendy A. Whiting, Exec. Dir.
P.O. Box 7406
Portland, ME 04112-7406
Street Address
120 Exchange Street, #307
Portland, ME 04101
(207) 772-9639
Fax: (207) 772-4986

MARYLAND ASSOCIATION OF CPAS
Barbara A. Zorn, Exec. Dir.
P.O. Box 4417
Lutherville, MD 21094-4417

Street Address
1300 York Road, Suite 10
Lutherville, MD 21093
(410) 296-6250
Fax: (410) 296-8713

MASSACHUSETTS SOCIETY OF CPAS
Theodore J. Flynn, Exec. Dir.
105 Chauncy Street, 10th Floor
Boston, MA 02111
(617) 556-4000
Fax: (617) 556-4126

MICHIGAN ASSOCIATION OF CPAS
Robert A. Bogan, Jr., Exec. Dir.
P.O. Box 9054
Farmington Hills, MI
  48333-9054
Street Address
28116 Orchard Lake Road
Farmington Hills, MI
  48333-3737
(810) 855-2288
Fax: (810) 855-9122

MINNESOTA SOCIETY OF CPAS
Clair G. Budke, Exec. Dir.
N.W. Financial Center, #1230
7900 Xerxes Avenue South
Bloomington, MN 55431
(612) 831-2707
Fax: (612) 831-7875

MISSISSIPPI SOCIETY OF CPAS
Jack Coppenbarger, Exec. Dir.
P.O. Box 16630
Jackson, MS 39236

(continued)

Exhibit 5.7. *(continued)*

Street Address
Highland Village, Suite 246
Jackson, MS 39211
(601) 366-3473
Fax: (601) 981-6079

MISSOURI SOCIETY OF CPAS
Cynthia S. Lund, Exec. Dir.
P.O. Box 66934
St. Louis, MO 63166-6934
Street Address
275 N. Lindbergh Blvd., #10
St. Louis, MO 63146
(314) 997-7966
Fax: (314) 997-2592

MONTANA SOCIETY OF CPAS
Jane Campbell, Exec. Dir.
P.O. Box 138
Helena, MT 59624-0138
Street Address
44 West Sixth Avenue, 3d Floor East
Helena, MT 59601
(406) 442-7301
Fax: (406) 443-7278

NEBRASKA SOCIETY OF CPAS
Dan Vodvarka, President
635 South 14th Street
Suite 330
Lincoln, NE 68508
(402) 476-8482
Fax: (402) 476-8731

NEVADA SOCIETY OF CPAS
Darlene Reed, Exec. Dir.
5250 Neil Road, Suite 205
Reno, NV 89502

(702) 826-6800
Fax: (702) 826-7942

NEW HAMPSHIRE SOCIETY OF CPAS
Marlene Gazda, Exec. Dir.
3 Executive Park Drive
Bedford, NH 03110
(603) 622-1999
Fax: (603) 626-0204

NEW JERSEY SOCIETY OF CPAS
Merryl Bauer, Exec. Dir.
425 Eagle Rock Avenue
Roseland, NJ 07068-1723
(201) 226-4494
Fax: (201) 226-7425

NEW MEXICO SOCIETY OF CPAS
Gari Fails, Exec. Dir.
1650 University NE, Suite 450
Albuquerque, NM 87102
(505) 246-1699
Fax: (505) 246-1686

NEW YORK STATE SOCIETY OF CPAS
Robert L. Gray, Exec. Dir.
530 Fifth Avenue, 5th Floor
New York, NY 10036-5101
(212) 719-8300
Fax: (212) 719-3364

NORTH CAROLINA ASSN. OF CPAS
James T. Ahler, Exec. Dir.
P.O. Box 80188
Raleigh, NC 27623-0188

(continued)

Exhibit 5.7. *(continued)*

Street Address
3100 Gateway Center Blvd.
Morrisville, NC 27560
(919) 469-1040
Fax: (919) 469-3959

NORTH DAKOTA SOCIETY OF CPAS
James Abbott, Exec. Dir.
2701 South Columbia Road
Grand Forks, ND 58201
(701) 775-7100
Fax: (701) 775-7430

OHIO SOCIETY OF CPAS
J. Clarke Price, Exec. Dir.
P.O. Box 1810
Dublin, OH 43017-7810
Street Address
535 Metro Place South
Dublin, OH 43017
(614) 764-2727 (Voice Mail: x305)
Fax: (614) 764-5880

OKLAHOMA SOCIETY OF CPAS
Daryl J. Hill, Exec. Dir.
50 Penn Place, Suite 910
Oklahoma City, OK 73118
(405) 841-3800
Fax: (405) 841-3801

OREGON SOCIETY OF CPAS
Cheryl L. Langley, Exec. V.P.
10206 S.W. Laurel Street
Beaverton, OR 97005-3209
(503) 641-7200
Fax: (503) 626-2942

PENNSYLVANIA INSTITUTE OF CPAS
Albert E. Trexler, Exec. Dir.
1608 Walnut Street, 3d Floor
Philadelphia, PA 19103
(215) 735-2635
Fax: (215) 735-3694

COLEGIO DE CONTADORES PUBLICOS
AUTORIZADOS DE PUERTO RICO
Edna I. Jimenez, Exec. Dir.
Call Box 71352
San Juan, PR 00936-1352
Street Address
Edif. Capital Center
Ave. Arterial Hostos #3
Buzon 1401
Hato Rey, PR 00918
(809) 754-1950
Fax: (809) 753-0212

RHODE ISLAND SOCIETY OF CPAS
Raymond C. Church, Exec. Dir.
One Franklin Square
Providence, RI 02903
(401) 331-5720
Fax: (401) 454-5780

SOUTH CAROLINA ASSN. OF CPAS
Lollie B. Coward, Exec. Dir.
570 Chris Drive
West Columbia, SC 29169
(803) 791-4181
Fax: (803) 791-4196

SOUTH DAKOTA CPA SOCIETY
Laura Coome, Exec. Dir.
P.O. Box 1798
Sioux Falls, SD 57101-1798

(continued)

Exhibit 5.7. *(continued)*

Street Address
250 Blake Greeley Building
231 S. Phillips Avenue
Sioux Falls, SD 57102
(605) 334-3848
Fax: (605) 334-3848

TENNESSEE SOCIETY OF CPAS
Brad Floyd, Exec. Dir.
Box 187
Brentwood, TN 37024-0596
Street Address
201 Powell Place, Suite 120
Brentwood, TN 37024
(615) 377-3825
Fax: (615) 377-3904

TEXAS SOCIETY OF CPAS
Don Weldon, Exec. Dir.
14860 Montford Drive, Suite 150
Dallas, TX 75240
(214) 687-8500

UTAH ASSOCIATION OF CPAS
Jeannie Patton, Exec. Dir.
455 East 400 South, Suite 202
Salt Lake City, UT 84111
(801) 359-3533
Fax: (801) 359-3534

VERMONT SOCIETY OF CPAS
Deborah Riley, Exec. Dir.
100 State Street
Montpelier, VT 05602
(802) 229-4939
Fax: (802) 223-0360

VIRGIN ISLANDS SOCIETY OF CPAS
John DeLuca, President
P.O. Box Y
Christiansted
St. Croix, VI 00822-3016
(809) 773-4305
Fax: (809) 773-9850

VIRGINIA SOCIETY OF CPAS
Thomas M. Berry, Exec. V.P.
P.O. Box 4620
Richmond, VA 23058-4620
Street Address
4309 Cox Road
Glen Allen, VA 23060
(804) 270-5344
Fax: (804) 273-1741

WASHINGTON SOCIETY OF CPAS
John R. Plymyer, Exec. Dir.
902 140th Avenue, N.E.
Bellevue, WA 98005-3480
(206) 644-4800
Fax: (206) 562-8853

WEST VIRGINIA SOCIETY OF CPAS
Patricia M. Moyers, Exec. Dir.
P.O. Box 1142
Charleston, WV 25324
Street Address
One Huntington Square
Suite 1201
Charleston, WV 25301
(304) 342-5461
Fax: (304) 344-4636

(continued)

Exhibit 5.7. *(continued)*

WISCONSIN INSTITUTE OF CPAS
LeRoy Schmidt, Exec. Dir.
P.O. Box 1010
Brookfield, WI 53008-1010
Street Address
235 North Executive Drive
Brookfield, WI 53005
(414) 785-0445
Fax: (414) 785-0838

WYOMING SOCIETY OF CPAS
Lora C. Lissman, Exec. Dir.
1721 Warren Avenue
Cheyenne, WY 82001
(307) 634-7039
Fax: (307) 634-5110

Exhibit 5.7.   *(continued)*

6

INCOME APPROACH

The income approach theoretically yields the most correct estimate of the value of a going-concern accounting practice, since the value of an ownership interest in an accounting practice is equal to the present worth of its expected future economic income. As mentioned previously, net cash flow is the measure of economic income typically used in an income approach analysis. However, other measures of economic income are also suitable for this valuation approach.

Estimating the value of an accounting practice with the income approach appears deceptively easy. However, in practice this valuation approach requires considerable professional judgment to estimate the various valuation model inputs. These include: (1) appropriate projections of cash flow (or other measure of economic income) and (2) the appropriate present value discount rate (or direct capitalization rate).

The income approach may be used in appraisals completed for a variety of purposes, including taxation, financing, and litigation. However, this valuation approach is best suited to the context of the transaction pricing and structuring of an actual purchase or sale of either a controlling interest or of a minority ownership interest in an accounting practice.

THEORETICAL CONCEPTS AND PRACTICAL APPLICATIONS

Using the income approach, the value of the accounting practice is estimated as the present value of the economic income expected to be generated by the subject practice. Two methods are commonly used in the income approach for the appraisal of accounting practices: the direct capitalization method, based on a single-period estimate of expected economic income, and the yield capitalization method, based on a multi-period estimate of expected economic income.

Direct Capitalization Method

Under the direct capitalization method, the value of the accounting practice is estimated by dividing expected economic income by a capitalization rate. For a given accounting practice, this entails:

1. Estimating the expected (stabilized or normalized) economic income to be generated in the year following the appraisal date
2. Estimating the appropriate capitalization rate to apply to the expected economic income

The present value formula for the single-period direct capitalization model is

$$PV = \frac{E_1}{c}$$

where

$$
\begin{aligned}
PV &= \text{present value of the practice} \\
E_1 &= \text{next year's projected economic income} \\
c &= \text{capitalization rate}
\end{aligned}
$$

The direct capitalization method proves most useful for appraising ownership interests in accounting practices when the earnings of a practice are predictable and when the practice has matured to a point where growth is relatively constant. Practices that serve a diverse, solid base of clients frequently generate earnings streams that are relatively predictable. An analysis of the earnings history of the practice and a review of clients and client fees over the previous three to five years will provide insights regarding

1. The predictability of the earnings
2. A reasonable projected long-term growth rate

Yield Capitalization Method

The yield capitalization method requires: (1) the projection of a stream of prospective economic income and (2) the estimation of an appropriate yield capitalization rate—or present value discount rate—in order to convert the projected economic income to a present value. For a given accounting practice, this entails

1. Making a discrete estimation of the prospective economic income to be generated over a finite period—typically, five to ten years—after the appraisal date
2. Estimating the appropriate present value discount rate to apply to the prospective economic income

3. Estimating the terminal value—or residual value—of the accounting practice at the end of the discrete projection period

The present value formula for the multi-period yield capitalization model is

$$PV = \sum_{i=1}^{i=n} \frac{E_1}{(1 + k)^i} + \frac{Terminal\ Value_n}{(1 + k)^n}$$

where

$$
\begin{aligned}
PV &= \text{present value of the practice} \\
E &= \text{economic income for each period} \\
k &= \text{present value discount rate} \\
i &= \text{time period 1 through } n \\
Terminal\ Value_n &= \text{value of the practice at the end of year } n
\end{aligned}
$$

In general, the yield capitalization method is more appropriate than the direct capitalization method

1. When the subject accounting practice has not yet reached a level of maturity (in terms of client development, service line mix, or expected revenues)
2. When a single growth estimate is not reasonable to assume into perpetuity
3. When the recent earnings reported by the subject practice are not a good indication of the expected future earnings of the practice

The yield capitalization method would be an appropriate method for the appraisal of accounting practices that have

1. A short earnings history
2. Been growing at a high rate
3. Recently expanded the scope of services they offer clients (e.g., a recent addition of consulting expertise)

The yield capitalization method is most appropriate in these circumstances because it allows for the estimation of economic earnings through a discrete time period until the practice is expected to generate a constant rate of growth.

DEFINITIONS OF ECONOMIC INCOME

The first step in the income approach valuation process is the estimation of the expected economic income of the accounting practice. The direct capitalization method requires the estimation of next year's economic income, and the yield capitalization method requires the projection of several years of economic income (typically from five to ten years).

Measures of Economic Income

Several measures of economic income are acceptable in the direct capitalization and yield capitalization methods. Often, for the appraisal of an accounting practice, economic income is defined as follows:

	Projected pretax adjusted income (or net revenues less total operating expenses)
+	Depreciation and amortization expense
−	Necessary capital expenditures
−	Necessary working capital increases
−	Debt principal repayments
+	Debt additions
=	Economic income subject to capitalization

As mentioned previously, in an accounting practice valuation, the firm's partners are typically treated as employees for purposes of compensation. That is, the partners' draw is usually not considered as an operating expense. Rather, a hypothetical "salary" such as would be paid to nonpartner accountants of comparable experience and expertise is subtracted as an operating expense. In this way, the economic income subject to capitalization represents, as much as possible, a profit distribution on the equity ownership instead of compensation for professional services rendered.

However, alternative measures of economic income can be used in developing an estimate of a practice's value. It is important that the estimated rate of return (i.e., capitalization rate) be consistent with the selected measurement of economic income. Thus, an equity discount rate should be used with a measurement of an equity stream of income, a weighted average cost-of-capital discount rate should be used with a measurement of income available to pay both equityholders and debtholders, and so forth. For the definition of economic income as presented above, the analyst would typically rely on a pretax equity required rate of return, since the economic income is based on the pretax income available to the practice equityholders.

If the subject practice has interest-bearing debt in its capital structure, then the practice can be appraised by relying on projections of debt-free economic income. Debt-free economic income is the economic income available to both the practice debtholders and the practice equityholders. In this instance, the analyst would typically use a weighted average cost of capital as the expected rate of return on investment. The weighted average cost of capital is a blend of the cost of debt capital and the cost of equity capital of the subject accounting practice.

Several other measures of economic income may be used in an income approach analysis. They include net fee income, operating income, income before distribution to equityholders, pretax income, and after-tax income (in the case of professional corporations).

Methodology for Projecting Economic Income

To properly estimate the economic income for an accounting practice, the appraiser should make a thorough analysis of all relevant factors affecting the practice. These include the following:

1. The historical earnings reported by the practice
2. The types and mix of professional services offered by the practice
3. The mix of clients and types of clients served
4. The degree of seasonality of the practice revenues
5. The degree of maturity or seasoning of the practice
6. The average duration of the client relationships
7. The degree of industry specialization of the practice
8. The degree of service line specialization of the practice
9. The location of the practice (particularly with regard to the state of the local economy)
10. The average age of the partners
11. The average utilization of the partners
12. The average tenure and turnover of the staff
13. The average utilization of the staff
14. The average billing rates of the partners and staff
15. The relationship of billing rates and typical engagement fees to competing practices
16. The size of the subject practice relative to competing practices
17. The operating expenses (and operational efficiency) of the practice
18. The current utilization and the expansion capacity of the physical facilities

Typically, an estimate of expected income requires an analysis of economic income generated by the accounting practice over a historical time period, such as five years. It is important to adjust the level of historical income to eliminate any nonrecurring or extraordinary items. In addition, reported income should be adjusted when the accounting firm's past financial practice—for instance, its compensation of equity-holders—has been inconsistent with industry and regional norms.

In the direct capitalization method, an analysis of the historical trends in the economic income reported by the practice can result in an estimate of expected income growth rate for the practice. This expected growth rate can be applied to historical results in order to estimate expected future income.

The type of services offered by the practice also affects the estimation of prospective economic income. For example, the recent addition of staff with consulting expertise—to complement a practice with established tax and audit expertise—would affect the estimation. Likewise, a recent emphasis on (or expected addition of) specialty service lines—business valuations, litigation support, personal financial planning, and so on—would result in a significantly different economic income projection than a continuing focus on more traditional audit, write-up, or tax preparation services.

The mix of clients served by the practice can also affect projected economic income. Projections for a practice with a broad mix of audit and tax services for clients in a variety of industries may differ substantially from projections for a practice with a heavy reliance on audit, tax, and consulting clients in a single specialized industry, especially if this single industry is cyclical. However, accounting practices that specialize in a single successful, growing industry may deserve very optimistic economic income projections (and such practices may actually sell at substantially higher values than otherwise comparable firms with a more generalized, nonspecialized client base).

Specific Factors Affecting the Estimation of Economic Income for Accounting Practices

Several unique features of accounting practices affect the appropriate estimation of economic income. They include the following:

1. The model for estimating economic income should incorporate a hypothetical salary expense for the partners equal to what nonpartner staff members with comparable experience, expertise, and tenure would earn.
2. Cash flow projections should be estimated before any partner profit distributions (i.e., any distributions or withdrawals based solely on equity ownership—as opposed to professional services).
3. The economic income should be measured on a pretax basis for accounting firms, which are typically nontaxpayer partnerships (or other nontaxpayer legal entities).

SELECTION OF A CAPITALIZATION RATE
OR A DISCOUNT RATE

The second step in the income approach is the estimation of the expected rate of return for investing in the subject accounting practice. In the single-period direct capitalization model, this expected rate of return is referred to as the *direct capitalization rate*. (In this text it will be referred to simply as the *capitalization rate*.) In the multi-period yield capitalization model, the expected rate of return is referred to as the *yield capitalization rate*—or *present value discount rate*. (In this text it will be referred to simply as the *discount rate*.)

A capitalization rate is a divisor used to convert economic income to present value. A discount rate is the rate of return that an investor would demand on the purchase of an investment given the level of risk associated with the investment. The difference between the two rates is that, basically, the capitalization rate equals the discount rate less the expected growth rate.

BASIS FOR THE ESTIMATION
OF A CAPITALIZATION RATE OR A DISCOUNT RATE

The expected rate of return for an investment in an accounting practice is based on

1. The risk associated with the investment
2. The rates of return available on alternative investments

Exhibit 6.1 presents various yields available on alternative investments. As can be seen in the exhibit, the expected yields increase as the risk of investment increases. For example, the risk associated with an investment in a long-term Treasury bond is less than the risk associated with an investment in a B-rated industrial bond. Therefore, the 11.0 percent yield for the industrial bond is greater than the 7.1 percent yield for the Treasury bond. This incremental yield (or rate of return) is required to compensate investors for the additional risk inherent in an investment in industrial bonds.

Historical and expected returns on equity investments are presented in Exhibit 6.2. Investors in common stocks and in small capitalization common stocks expect an even greater rate of return than investors in fixed-income securities. The higher return compensates them for the additional risk of owning part of the business instead of being either a secured or an unsecured creditor.

As can be seen in Exhibit 6.2, investors in common stocks have received total returns averaging 12.5 percent over the past 69 years, and investors in small-company (i.e., small-capitalization) common stocks have earned an average of 17.7 percent in

	Yield (%)
Short-term government bonds	6.0
Long-term government bonds	7.1
Industrial bonds	
AAA	7.4
AA	7.6
A	8.1
BBB	8.5
BB	9.2
B	11.0
Source: The Outlook, 8 May 1996 (New York: Standard & Poor's) Data as of 1 May 1996.	

Exhibit 6.1.   Yields for Alternative Fixed-Income Investments.

	Arithmetic Mean of the Historical Annual Total Returns for the Period of 1926–1995 (%)		
All common stocks	12.5		
All small-company common stocks	17.7		

	Historical Risk Premium (%)	+	Long-term Government Bond Returns (%)	=	Implied Expected Total Returns (%)
All common stocks	7.4		7.1		14.5
All small-company common stocks	12.6		7.1		19.7

Source: Stocks, Bonds, Bills, and Inflation, 1996 Yearbook (Chicago: Ibbotson Associates, 1996) and The Outlook, 8 May 1996 (New York: Standard & Poor's).

Exhibit 6.2.   Total Returns for Equity Investments.

income and capital gains over the same period. Exhibit 6.2 also shows that the additional risk associated with an investment in common and small-company stocks has been (and is) offset by a premium added to the rate of return for long-term government bonds, bringing the implied expected total return on common stocks and small-company stocks to 14.5 percent and 19.7 percent, respectively.

An investment in an accounting practice may require an even higher rate of return than the yields presented in Exhibit 6.1 and the total rates of return for equity investments presented in Exhibit 6.2. This additional rate of return may be needed to compensate for the additional risk associated with ownership of the accounting practice. Obviously, if an investor had to choose between a common stock index fund (i.e., a portfolio of liquid securities in large, publicly traded companies) and an accounting practice, and if each offered the same expected return, then the investor would buy shares in the common stock index fund.

In practice, estimating the appropriate risk premium to add to the historical equity rates of return is a complex process. Such an estimation requires an analysis of the specific public accounting industry characteristics and specific accounting practice characteristics that influence the degree of risk and expected return of the particular investment in the subject practice.

The many factors important to consider when estimating the appropriate risk premium include:

1. The degree of diversification of the practice's client base
2. The degree of diversification of the practice's service lines
3. The reliance of the practice on any one partner (or any other rainmaker) for a large percentage of business
4. The geographic territory served by the practice (and the state of the local economy)
5. The profitability of the practice (and the historical variability of the practice's profitability)
6. The practice's competitive strengths and weaknesses (in terms of perceived quality of service, perceived quality of partners/staff, etc.) as compared with competing firms
7. The seasonality of client work and of revenues generated
8. The historical (and anticipated) turnover of the partners and staff
9. The actual ages (and levels of experience) of the partners and staff
10. The tenure—and rate of annual turnover—of clients (by type of client and by type of service)

The magnitude of the appropriate risk premium for a specific accounting practice is fairly subjective and is based, to a large degree, on the experience and judgment of the analyst.

In summary, the expected equity rate of return for an investment in a particular accounting practice is composed of the following three factors:

1. A risk-free rate
2. A general risk premium reflecting the additional risk associated with an equity investment
3. A subject-practice-specific risk premium reflecting the risk of an investment in the public accounting industry and in the specific accounting firm

If the subject accounting practice has outstanding debt in its capital structure, and if debt-free economic income is projected, then the appropriate present value discount rate is the subject practice's weighted average cost of capital. The weighted average cost of capital is estimated by

1. Multiplying the percentage of outstanding debt capital relative to the total practice capital by the appropriate cost of debt
2. Multiplying the percentage of outstanding equity capital relative to the total practice capital by the appropriate cost of equity
3. Adding the results of steps 1 and 2

ESTIMATION OF THE TERMINAL VALUE

Formula for Estimating Terminal Value

For the yield capitalization method, a third step is necessary in order to complete the income approach valuation analysis. Once the discrete projection period cash flows and the present value discount rate have been estimated, then the terminal value must be estimated. The terminal value is the estimated value of the subject accounting practice at the end of year n in the present value equation presented below

$$PV = \sum_{i=1}^{i=n} \frac{E_i}{(1 + k)^i} + \frac{Terminal\ Value_n}{(1 + k)^n}$$

where

$$
\begin{aligned}
PV &= \text{present value of the practice} \\
E &= \text{economic income for each period} \\
k &= \text{present value discount rate} \\
i &= \text{time period 1 through } n
\end{aligned}
$$

The appropriate estimation of the terminal value is crucial since the terminal value can often represent a large percentage of the total value of the subject accounting practice. To estimate the value of an accounting practice as of the terminal date, the analyst must (1) determine an appropriate terminal value date and (2) select a valuation model to use for the estimation.

Methods for Estimating the Terminal Value

Several of the most common methods used to estimate a terminal value are described below. The most appropriate method depends upon (1) the specific characteristics related to the subject accounting practice and (2) the most likely ownership event that will occur to the subject practice at or before the terminal date.

For example, by the end of the discrete projection period, is it more likely that the practice will be sold, merged, liquidated, or owned by its current partners? The answer to this question will determine, in part, the most appropriate terminal value estimation method.

Constant Growth Method

Terminal values of accounting practices are usually calculated using the constant growth model, often called the *Gordon model* (or the *Gordon dividend capitalization model*). The Gordon model assumes that the economic income of the practice will increase at a constant rate into perpetuity.

To estimate the terminal value of the accounting practice using the Gordon model, the analyst capitalizes the prospective economic income for the year following the last discrete projection period, using the following formula:

$$FV = \frac{E_1}{k - g}$$

where

FV	=	terminal value of the practice
E_1	=	estimated next period economic income
k	=	present value discount rate
g	=	projected long-term growth rate

The Gordon model is extremely sensitive to changes in the expected growth rate of the economic income of the accounting practice. Since the growth rate is projected to continue indefinitely, it is important that the growth rate estimate is reasonable. Unusually high rates of growth reported by an accounting practice in the short run typically cannot be sustained into perpetuity. The use of an unreasonably high terminal growth rate will result in an unrealistically high value for the accounting practice. In order for the Gordon model to be appropriate, projections of economic income are required until the point in time when real growth in economic income stabilizes.

In the Gordon model, it is also critical that the estimate of the economic income in the terminal year is normalized, or adjusted, to exclude nonrecurring or extraordinary economic income. If the economic income stream for the terminal year is not normalized, then the resulting value for the accounting practice likely will be incorrect.

Guideline Transaction Method

Another method that can be used in order to estimate the terminal value of the accounting practice is the guideline transaction method. This method assumes that the value of the subject accounting practice in the terminal year will equal the indicated value that investors currently pay for guideline or comparable accounting practices.

In this method, the terminal value is estimated by

1. Selecting and analyzing recent sale transactions of guideline accounting practices
2. Calculating various valuation pricing multiples from these completed sale transactions
3. Applying these valuation pricing multiples to the projected values of the corresponding financial fundamental measures (e.g., net revenues, pretax income, etc.) of the subject accounting practice at the terminal date

For this terminal value estimation method to be appropriate, it is essential that the guideline accounting practices be reasonably similar to the subject accounting practice, especially in their expected growth rates and in the variability of their prospective cash flows. The analyst may need to make subjective adjustments to the indicated guideline valuation multiples to account for differences between the guideline and the subject accounting practices.

In addition, changing economic conditions may make it inappropriate to apply valuation multiples from guideline transactions to the financial fundamentals of the subject accounting practice at a future date. For example, the valuation multiples paid for accounting practices at the peak of an economic cycle may apply to the earnings measures of the accounting practice projected for the terminal date.

Estimation of Appropriate Terminal Value Date

In the yield capitalization method, projections are made for economic income for a discrete, finite period of time—typically, a period of 5 to 10 years. Economic income projections are normally made until the subject accounting practice matures to a point where expected growth is relatively stable.

ILLUSTRATIVE EXAMPLE

Exhibits 6.3 through 6.6 illustrate the valuation of an accounting practice using the income approach—specifically, the yield capitalization method. The objective of this appraisal is to estimate the fair market value of 100 percent of the partners' equity capital for a hypothetical accounting practice, Addit, Upp & Billem, CPAs, as of December 31, 1996.

Based upon the purpose and objective of the appraisal, and also on the analyst's conclusion of the highest and best use of the subject practice, this analysis will be performed under the valuation premise of value in continued use as a going-concern business enterprise.

Estimate of Projected Economic Income

Exhibit 6.3 presents the projected economic income for Addit, Upp & Billem for calendar years ended 1997 through 2001. This projection presents the pretax net cash flow measure of economic income.

The projected net client revenues are based upon a detailed projection of the number of partners and staff for each year, the expected billing rate for each accountant, the expected utilization for each accountant, the expected billability of the work performed, and the expected collectibility of the fees billed.

The projected operating expenses are based upon a detailed analysis of the historical levels of operating expenses of the relationship between operating expenses and client revenues (or to other factors, such as number of accountants, amount of floor space, etc.) and of the nature of fixed costs versus variable costs of the firm's operating expense structure.

For purposes of simplicity, we will assume that Addit, Upp & Billem does not have any long-term, interest-bearing debt outstanding. That is, all of the capital in the Addit, Upp & Billem capital structure is equity capital.

In addition, Exhibit 6.3 also presents the calculation of projected "normalized" economic income for the subject accounting practice. Several adjustments have been required to estimate normalized economic income in this example.

1. An adjustment has been made to add back the partner compensation in excess of the amount that nonpartner staff members with similar experience and expertise would earn.
2. Depreciation expense has been added back to net income since depreciation is a noncash expense item.
3. Planned capital expenditures have been deducted since these capital expenditures were deemed necessary to sustain the indicated level of growth in the economic income projections.
4. Additional working capital investments necessary to fund the subject practice's growth have been deducted; these investments represent decrements in the cash flow available for distribution to the equityholders.

ADDIT, UPP & BILLEM, CPAS
STATEMENT OF PROSPECTIVE RESULTS OF OPERATIONS
AS OF DECEMBER 31, 1996
(in $000s)

	Projected for the Calendar Years Ended December 31				
	1997	**1998**	**1999**	**2000**	**2001**
Net client revenues	1,200	1,260	1,323	1,389	1,459
Operating expenses					
Total partner compensation	350	366	382	399	417
Staff salaries	330	345	360	377	394
Employment taxes and benefits	70	73	76	80	83
Rent expense	96	96	96	96	96
Telephone and utilities	54	56	58	61	63
Postage and stationery	50	53	55	58	61
Professional liability and other insurance	50	53	55	58	61
Data processing expenses	50	53	55	58	61
Depreciation expense	40	42	44	46	49
Other expenses	20	20	20	20	20
Total operating expenses	1,110	1,155	1,203	1,253	1,305
Net income	90	105	120	137	154

Derivation of the Normalized Economic Income to Partners

		1997	**1998**	**1999**	**2000**	**2001**
	Net income	90	105	120	137	154
+	Partner incentive compensation	150	157	164	171	179
+	Depreciation expense	40	42	44	46	49
−	Capital expenditures	(35)	(35)	(45)	(45)	(45)
−	Increase in working capital	(3)	(3)	(3)	(3)	(3)
=	Normalized economic income	242	265	280	306	333

Note: Mathematical differences are due to rounding.

Exhibit 6.3. Projected Economic Income for Addit, Upp & Billem, CPAs, Calendar Years 1997 through 2001.

Based upon these projections, Exhibit 6.3 presents the projected "normalized" economic income available for distribution to the partners in the subject practice for the next five years.

Estimation of the Present Value Discount Rate

Since the economic income estimated in this example is the amount available to the equityholders of the practice, the appropriate present value discount rate to apply to this measure of earnings stream is the equity cost of capital. Exhibit 6.4 presents the estimation of the appropriate present value discount rate for Addit, Upp & Billem.

In this example, the equity discount rate has been derived through the rate build-up procedure, beginning with (1) the risk-free rate of return, adding (2) the equity risk premium and (3) the small company stock risk premium, and then adding (4) a practice-specific risk premium. This practice-specific risk premium has been derived through a detailed analysis of the various factors affecting the level of risk associated with an investment in Addit, Upp & Billem. This rate build-up procedure results in an appropriate present value discount rate of 25 percent.

ADDIT, UPP & BILLEM, CPAS
ESTIMATION OF THE APPROPRIATE PRESENT VALUE DISCOUNT RATE
AS OF DECEMBER 31, 1996

Capital Market and Money Market Data As of December 31, 1996	Indicated Rate
Risk-free rate of return	7.1%
+ All common stocks equity risk premium	7.4%
+ Incremental small company common stock equity risk premium	5.2%
+ Practice-specific nonsystematic equity risk premium	5.0%
= Indicated present value discount rate for the subject practice equity	24.7%
Present value discount rate (rounded)	25.0%

Exhibit 6.4.   Calculation of the Equity Discount Rate for Addit, Upp & Billem, CPAs, Using the Rate Build-up Procedure.

Estimation of the Terminal Value

Exhibit 6.5 presents the estimation of the terminal value of the subject practice using the Gordon model as the terminal value estimation method. The terminal value was estimated through a two-step process:

Step 1. As presented in Exhibit 6.3, the year 2001 normalized economic income of the subject accounting practice has been projected at $333,000. To estimate the projected economic income for the year 2002, the year 2001 economic income of $333,000 has been multiplied by one plus the long-term growth rate of 4 percent. This 4 percent long-term growth rate represents the appropriate nominal long-term growth rate for the subject accounting practice. This long-term growth rate has been based upon an analysis of the competitive position of this accounting practice (and of its industry specialization and its service line specialization). This analysis results in projected economic income in year 2002 of $346,000.

Step 2. Next, year 2002 economic income must be divided, or "capitalized," by the present value discount rate less the expected long-term growth rate. As presented in Exhibit 6.5, subtracting the expected long-term growth rate of 4 percent from the present value discount rate of 25 percent results in a terminal value capitalization rate of 21 percent. Dividing the projected year 2002 economic income of $346,000 by the 21 percent terminal value capitalization rate results in an indicated terminal value of $1,648,000.

ADDIT, UPP & BILLEM, CPAS ESTIMATION OF THE APPROPRIATE TERMINAL VALUE AS OF DECEMBER 31, 2001 (in $000s)	
	Projected economic income for year 2001	333
×	The expected long-term income growth rate	1.04
=	Projected economic income in year 2002	346
÷	The appropriate long-term capitalization rate	
	Present value discount rate	25.0%
	Less the expected long-term growth rate	4.0%
	Equals long-term capitalization rate	21.0%
=	Indicated terminal value of the subject practice	1,648

Exhibit 6.5.   Calculation of the Estimated Terminal Value of Addit, Upp & Billem, CPAs, Using the Gordon Model.

ADDIT, UPP & BILLEM, CPAS
VALUATION INDICATION
AS OF DECEMBER 31, 1996
(in $000s)

	Calendar Years Ended					Terminal Value
	1997	1998	1999	2000	2001	
Normalized economic income	242	265	280	306	333	1,648
Present value discount factor	0.8065	0.6504	0.5245	0.4230	0.3411	0.3411
Present value of economic income	195	172	147	129	114	562
Practice valuation indication	1,319					
Indicated practice value (rounded)	1,320					

Note: Mathematical differences are due to rounding.

Exhibit 6.6. Calculation of the Valuation Indication of Addit, Upp & Billem, CPAs, Using the Income Approach and Yield Capitalization Method Analysis.

Valuation Indication

Exhibit 6.6 presents the valuation indication of the Addit, Upp & Billem practice based on the income approach and yield capitalization method analysis. Based on the present value discount rate of 25 percent, the present value of the discrete period cash flow projection and of the terminal value is as presented in Exhibit 6.6.

The sum of the present values of all of the prospective cash flow (i.e., both the discrete projection and the terminal value) is $1,320,000. Therefore, the indicated value of the total partners' capital of Addit, Upp & Billem, CPAs, based on this income approach analysis, as of December 31, 1996, is $1,320,000.

7

MARKET APPROACH

The market approach to valuation assumes that pricing relationships based on past sales of comparable (or guideline) accounting firms can provide relevant indications of value for a subject practice. When an adequate quantity of verifiable information regarding arm's-length, guideline transactions is available for collection and analysis, transactional data for merged and acquired practices provide the most relevant valuation indicators for controlling-interest professional practice valuations.

When sufficient verifiable data regarding actual sales of minority ownership interests are available, they can also be used to value minority ownership interests. But this is typically not the case. Rather, minority interest discounts (also called lack-of-control discounts) are often required to reflect the true market values for the fractional minority ownership interests in a practice because available data relates to consummated sales of entire practices or of controlling ownership interests in practices.

THEORETICAL CONCEPTS AND PRACTICAL APPLICATIONS

In practice, the market approach is applied by thoroughly analyzing negotiated, arm's-length transfers of accounting practices in the market. Based upon the analysis of these transfers, pricing indicators—or valuation pricing multiples—are established. Careful consideration is advised in the selection of valuation pricing multiples derived from guideline transactional data. This is because the subject practice may be less rather than more comparable to the guideline practices. Differences in the financial and operational fundamentals between the subject practice and the guideline practices should be considered in the selection of the valuation pricing multiples.

Applying these valuation pricing multiples to comparative financial and/or operational fundamentals ascertained for the subject practice, the appraiser arrives at indications of value for it. The appraiser should give careful consideration to the amount and the validity of the information supporting each indication of value before using it in estimating an overall valuation for the accounting practice. Obviously, the availability of adequate and verifiable guideline or comparable market information with regard to the transfer of accounting practices is of primary importance regarding the application of the market approach.

As described previously, the analyst first attempts to collect and analyze transactional data regarding comparable practices. If transactional data regarding sufficiently comparable practices are not available, then the analyst attempts to collect and analyze transactional data regarding guideline practices.

If transactional data regarding specific guideline practices are not available, sometimes a portfolio, or group, of individually dissimilar practices can be assembled that collectively have investment risk/expected return characteristics similar to the subject practice. In that case, the collective portfolio of practices could be used as a guideline—that is, could give valuation guidance to the analyst, even though no individual practice sale transaction may provide an individual valuation guideline.

As an important point of distinction, guideline transactional data involve the sale of practices similar enough to the subject practice (in terms of risk/expected return investment characteristics) to be useful for analytical purposes. Sometimes the guideline transactions are only similar enough to the subject practice to be used for benchmark comparison purposes.

Comparable transactional data involve the sale of practices very similar to—or, at least, directly comparable to—the subject practice in terms of risk and expected return. The transactional pricing multiples regarding these comparable practice sales may be applied more directly to the subject practice financial and/or operational fundamentals.

The successful application of the market approach depends on the analyst's ability to complete each phase of the market transaction analysis. Only then will a value indication provided by the market approach offer relevant information for making decisions about the potential transfer of an accounting practice.

Typically, analysts attempt to apply the market approach (sometimes called the *sales comparison approach*) methods first in the valuation process. This is because the market—that is, the economic environment where arm's-length transactions between unrelated parties occur—is typically the best indicator of the value of an accounting practice. Analysts will analyze the market for sale transactions and/or merger transactions that may be useful in the analysis of the subject accounting practice.

There is a general systematic process—or framework—to the application of market approach methods to the valuation of accounting practices. The basic steps of this systematic process are summarized as follows:

1. Research the appropriate exchange market to obtain as much information as possible on recent sale or merger transactions involving accounting practices that may be—in any way—comparative to the subject practice.

2. From the information gathered in step 1, select a sample of guideline (i.e., similar from a risk/expected return investment prospective) or comparable (i.e., similar from an operational perspective) accounting practices that are enough like the subject practice—in terms of characteristics such as industry specialization, service line specialization, geographic markets served, historical and prospective practice growth, and so forth—to provide meaningful valuation guidance.

3. Verify that the data obtained are factually accurate and that the sale or merger transactions reflect arm's-length market considerations. (If the guideline transactions were not at arm's-length market conditions, then adjustments to the transactional data may be necessary.) This verification procedure may also elicit additional information about current market conditions for the possible sale or merger of the subject accounting practice.

4. Select relevant units of pricing comparison or valuation pricing multiples (e.g., price to professional fees billed, price to professional fees earned, price to practice net income before partner compensation, price to practice net income after partner draw/normal compensation, etc.).

5. Compare the guideline accounting practice sale or merger transactions with the subject practice, using the basic elements of comparison. Then, either adjust the sale or merger price of each guideline transaction appropriately to the subject practice or eliminate that transaction as a guideline for future consideration.

6. Reconcile the various value indications produced from the analysis of the guideline transactions into a single value indication or into a range of values. In an imprecise market subject to varying economics, a range of values may sometimes prove a more useful conclusion for the subject accounting practice than a single value estimate.

In the market approach valuation of an accounting practice, 10 basic elements of comparison should be considered when selecting and analyzing each guideline sale or merger transaction:

1. The legal rights of practice equity ownership (whether stock ownership or partnership units) that were conveyed in the guideline transaction

2. The existence of any special financing terms or arrangements between the buyer and the seller, such as short-term or interim employment agreements with the selling accountant and (quite frequently) earn-out provisions with regard to the payment of the practice purchase price

3. Whether the elements of arm's-length sale conditions existed; whether the practice transaction was, in any way, a distress sale; or whether there were

any transferability restrictions related to the practice ownership interest that would indicate anything other than an arm's-length, independent sale

4. The economic conditions that existed in the appropriate secondary market at the time of the sale or merger transaction—especially conditions in the local area and in the industry principally served by the practice

5. The degree of industry specialization of the guideline practice and the state of the industry in which the practice specializes (is that industry growing or declining?)

6. The physical characteristics of the guideline practices—number of office locations, offices, favorable versus unfavorable leases, short-term versus long-term leases, new/modern offices versus old/antiquated offices, and so on

7. The functional characteristics of the guideline practices—practice service lines (e.g., audit versus accounting versus corporate tax versus individual tax) and practice specializations (e.g., personal financial planning, estate planning, litigation support, business valuations, etc.)

8. The human capital characteristics of the guideline practices—number of partners, age and credentials of partners, utilization of partners, business development effectiveness of partners, partner to staff ratios, age and qualifications of managers, age and qualifications of staff accountants, annual turnover at the manager and/or staff levels, and so forth

9. The economic characteristics of the guideline practices—average billing rates for each level of professional, average utilization rates for each level of professional, average collection rates for each level of professional, amount of recurring annual client work, current backlog of client work, and so forth

10. The inclusion of other assets in the guideline practice sale transaction, possibly including the sale of a bundle—or portfolio—of assets, which could include owned real estate (and/or below market leases on real estate owned by the partners), noncompete agreements from the selling partners, and so on

The reconciliation step is the last phase of any market approach valuation analysis in which two or more value indications have been derived from guideline market data. In the reconciliation step, the analyst summarizes and reviews the data and analyses that resulted in each of the value indications. These value indications are then resolved into a range of value, a single value indication, or a point estimate. It is important that the analyst consider the strengths and weaknesses of each guideline value indication derived, examining the reliability and appropriateness of the market data compiled and the analytical procedures applied.

Each of the above listed six phases or basic steps in the market approach is discussed during the remainder of this chapter.

SEARCH FOR GUIDELINE MARKET TRANSACTIONS

The search for guideline market transactions seeks only those market transactions that involve the transfer of entities similar to the subject accounting practice. Clearly, the key to appropriately identifying a group of either guideline or comparable market transactions is to have a clear understanding of the subject accounting practice.

To develop this understanding, the analyst should analyze both the historical and the prospective results of its operations. Such an exercise may involve interviewing the existing shareholders/partners of the subject practice as well as parties close to the consummated guideline transactions. Further, the analyst may perform a financial analysis of the subject practice, including a review of the practice's client mix, industry mix, service specialization, and so forth. In addition, the analyst may perform an operational analysis of the subject practice, including a review of average billing rates by staff level, utilization rates (i.e., number of billable hours) by staff level, partner-to-staff ratios, and so on.

These financial and operational analyses may be made to compare the subject accounting practice either to the portfolio of guideline practices or to public accounting industry benchmark financial and operational data. The sources of these public accounting industry benchmark data are presented in Chapter 5, "Data Gathering and Due Diligence for an Accounting Practice Appraisal."

Only after these requisite due diligence procedures and comparative analyses have been performed, and the true operating dynamics of the subject accounting practice have been understood, is the analyst in a position to identify and analyze potential guideline and/or comparable transactions. Now the obvious problem for the analyst becomes locating information on comparative market transactions. Although numerous transfers of accounting practices occur every year, the vast majority of these transfers occur among private parties. Consequently, it is difficult to obtain information about them, little, if any, information being available to the general public.

Although actual transactional information is often difficult to obtain, such information does exist. Probably the most reliable source of transactional information is the "practices for sale" advertisements in the various state CPA society journals, the *Journal of Accountancy,* and other accounting industry publications.

A typical course of action regarding the collection of transactional data is to respond (by phone, letter, or fax) to every practice for sale advertisement that appeared in a relevant publication for two or so years prior to the subject valuation date. Whether a publication is relevant depends on the size of the subject practice. If the subject practice is small, the data collection may be limited to the CPA society publications in its own and surrounding states. If the subject accounting practice is larger, then the data collection may be expanded to more states and to national accounting publications. In any event, the *Journal of Accountancy* often includes practice for sale advertisements that may be helpful in this data collection process.

A response to the practice for sale advertisement will allow the analyst to learn one of three things regarding the listed (and potentially guideline) practice:

1. It sold
2. It did not sell, and it is still for sale
3. It did not sell, and it is no longer for sale

If the practice sold, the analyst should obtain as much information as possible regarding the practice and the sale transaction. If the practice did not sell but is still for sale, then the analyst should obtain as much information as possible regarding the practice and the listing price. While listing prices may have to be reduced in order to estimate a cash equivalency value, guideline practice listing data may still be used in the market transaction analysis if no better data (regarding consummated transactions) are available.

If the practice did not sell and is no longer for sale, then the analyst should still obtain as much information as possible regarding the listed practice and the unsuccessful listing price. There is still useful information to be gleaned from such data. First, the data reveal specific valuation pricing multiples, implied by the listing price, that the market did not accept (presumably, lower valuation multiples would have attracted a market participant). Second, the implied valuation pricing multiples of the unsuccessful listing probably indicate a ceiling, or upper boundary, that may be relevant to the subject practice. And third, the analyst may obtain useful anecdotal data about the general market conditions for the sale of guideline accounting practices; these data are useful to the extent that the same market conditions face the subject accounting practice.

Data obtained during the research of these practice for sale advertisements as well as documentation of completed sale transactions (e.g., purchase agreements, the acquired practice's historical financial information for the three-year or five-year period preceding the transaction, and any covenants created as a result of the transactions) should provide the information needed to perform a market transaction analysis. When the usual sources for identifying potential market transactions are unavailable, the analyst can typically rely on local business brokers and professional practice brokers for leads and information regarding accounting transfers.

SELECTION OF GUIDELINE MARKET TRANSACTIONS

A thorough review of available sources and discussions with industry contacts will usually produce a list of several guideline transactions that may provide meaningful valuation guidance to the analyst. In some circumstances, a single sale transaction will be identified in which the acquired accounting practice is reasonably comparable to the practice subject to valuation. In that instance, one truly comparable practice sale transaction may provide sufficient valuation evidence to the analyst.

After several acquisitions of comparative accounting practices have been identified, it is extremely important to select for further analysis only those transactions involving practices whose operating dynamics come closest to those of the subject practice. Further, the practice sale transactions should have occurred within a reasonable period of time relative to the valuation date to be considered relevant market value indications. Stale (i.e., dated) market transaction data provides little or no meaningful valuation guidance.

Because CPAs are viewed by most professionals as having a broad base of business knowledge, many practices that operate as accounting firms are able to specialize entirely in service lines other than traditional audit or accounting services. These specialized practices provide such services as personal financial planning, business valuation, forensic accounting, and litigation support services. Transactional data regarding the sale of such practices generally should not be considered comparable for the purpose of valuing an accounting practice that emphasizes traditional accounting services (i.e., audit, review, compilation, write-up work, and taxation services). Similarly, sales of traditional service accounting practices may not provide meaningful valuation guidance for the appraisal of a specialized practice, all other things being equal. This is because specialized practices typically sell for different (and often greater) valuation pricing multiples than do traditional service accounting practices.

Even after limiting the base of transactional data to practices similar to the subject practice—in terms of the same services (i.e., traditional versus specialized) and the same client industry group (i.e., diversified industry base versus specialized industry base)—further consideration is required in order to concentrate on the practices that demonstrate economic income streams comparative to that of the subject practice.

For example, suppose that a financial analysis of a subject practice indicates that historically the economic income capacity of the practice has been driven by a revenue base comprising 25 percent audit services and 75 percent individual tax return services. Suppose also that the market transaction used to derive valuation pricing multiples involves an accounting practice that has generated its income from 75 percent audit work and 25 percent individual tax returns. Clearly, applying these valuation pricing multiples to the subject practice's fundamentals will probably produce an overstated indication of the subject practice's value because there is greater risk associated with the transfer of an economic income stream generated by 75 percent individual tax returns and 25 percent audit work as compared to an economic income stream reflecting the opposite service mix. This increased risk results from the fact that individual tax return work is dependent, to a large extent, on personal relationships between the service provider and the client. Although two tax providers may be equally qualified, personality differences may still result in a loss of clients.

On the other hand, audits generally result in repeat engagements and recurring clients, assuming that quality service is provided. Corporate clients, once comfortable with a particular accounting firm's service and fees, typically engage the same firm for the sake of efficiency (i.e., return engagements often involve the same audit team, which promotes efficiency on the job).

Applying valuation pricing multiples derived from a market transaction in which the service mix of the acquired practice is the inverse of that of the subject practice is tantamount to ascribing the same level of risk to the respective economic income of each practice. Based on the differences in the expected risk of these two economic income streams, this type of comparison would not be appropriate.

CONFIRMATION OF GUIDELINE MARKET TRANSACTIONS

The independent confirmation of market transaction data, when possible, is an important step in the market transaction analysis. Any word-of-mouth information provided by brokers or other contacts should be verified with the actual parties to the transaction, barring any confidentiality problems. To the extent possible, transaction-specific and practice-specific documentation such as the purchase agreement and related financial information should be obtained and thoroughly analyzed.

If actual transaction documentation is not available, then from discussions with the parties to the transactions the analyst may often glean specific practice sale terms and other circumstances that have otherwise not been made public. This information will enable the analyst to better understand the true economic circumstances of a particular practice sale transaction.

Additional information obtained through the interview process often proves to be useful during the actual process of developing valuation pricing multiples based on particular market transactions. Information obtained from the guideline transaction participants, may help the analyst recognize the need for adjustments to the economic income fundamentals reported by the transactional practices. In some cases, the need arises to adjust the reported transaction price to a cash equivalency price for reasons such as special financing terms, abnormal market conditions, and so on.

Only after the requisite adjustments have been made to the transaction fundamentals should the analyst comfortably rely on valuation pricing indicators derived from a particular transaction. Some of the more common adjustments required to actual transactional data are discussed in the following section.

ADJUSTMENTS TO GUIDELINE MARKET TRANSACTIONS

The objective of adjusting guideline market transaction information is to reflect both the actual practice sale price and the underlying practice financial fundamentals as realistically as possible. Without a doubt, the actual sale price agreed to by the buyer and the seller resulted from significant negotiation, with each party attempting to maximize his own economic self-interest.

Implicit within the ultimate transaction price are assumptions regarding time value of money considerations—as well as future owners' compensation and related ownership benefits. Further issues considered during the negotiation include owning versus leasing the existing premises, the duration of the existing office lease, the impact on future earnings of relocating the purchased practice, and nonrecurring revenue and expense items.

Time Value of Money Considerations

In the accounting field, it is not unusual for transactions to be structured such that the payout (often called the *earn-out*) for the transfer of the practice will occur over a period of time. For example, during the sale of a practice, it is common for the seller to agree to transfer his practice to the buyer if the buyer will remit to the seller 20 percent of estimated collected fees over a five-year period.

Normally, the buyer will not be required to compensate the seller for the opportunity costs relating to the seller's time value of money considerations. In other words, the buyer obtains interest-free financing.

When the analyst's assignment is to estimate fair market value for the subject accounting practice, time value of money issues must be considered when analyzing market transactions. Transactions requiring payment over time must be analyzed to reflect the way time value of money considerations impact the ultimate transaction price.

Obviously, discounting a stream of payments to be received over a five-year period to a present value, and assuming a reasonable required rate of return will result in a fair market value lower than the total gross payments estimated to be received. This scenario presents a clear example of why the terms of a particular transaction must be analyzed carefully before the actual price or the estimated fair market value of the practice transferred is clear. Once the "true" cash price—often called the *cash equivalency value*—for the transaction has been established, it can be used to estimate valuation pricing indicators that can be applied to the fundamentals of the subject accounting practice.

Owners' Compensation and Related Benefits

Typically, one of the first considerations for the prospective purchaser of a practice is the level of economic income that will be provided by the investment. To the extent that the buyer's financial analysis of historical operations reported by the target practice indicates a discretionary cash flow that exceeds his or her expectations, he or she will be willing to "give" more during the negotiation process. The opposite is true when the buyer anticipates that future discretionary cash flows will merely meet or fall slightly short of investment expectations.

Because an analyst is normally hired to estimate fair market value, he or she is usually required to assume a hypothetical willing buyer rather than a specific buyer. The analyst should therefore adjust the economic income for the purchased practice to a level that reasonably could be expected by a typical potential buyer. Comparing a reasonable expectation of economic income with the transaction sale price will result in a valuation pricing indicator more reflective of economic reality.

Facilities Ownership versus Facilities Lease

Many small- to medium-size accounting practices are operated from premises owned by the partners of the practice. Consequently, all of the costs associated with the ownership of real property (i.e., land and buildings) are included in the practice operating expenses. Related costs might include property taxes, interest expense on the outstanding mortgage balances, significant repairs and maintenance expenses, insurance costs, and other charges resulting from excess operating space.

From an economic perspective, it is normally more practical for an accounting practice to lease than to own office space. Therefore, the analyst should adjust the earnings fundamentals reported by an acquired practice operating from owned office space to reflect expenses (and consequently, earnings) at levels more commensurate with the level expected if the practice leased office space.

Along the same lines, "sweetheart" leasing arrangements that exist for the current practice may not be available to the new owners after a sale transaction. Accordingly, the analyst should examine all leasing terms reported by an acquired practice to estimate whether the practice buyer will experience similar lease-related expenses in future operating periods.

Like the adjustments for compensation and benefits discussed above, adjustments for facility operating expenses should be made to estimate the true economic benefits of ownership that a practice buyer should expect in future operating periods. Comparing these adjusted levels of economic benefits with the practice sale price (adjusted by time value of money and other appropriate considerations) should result in relevant valuation pricing indicators.

Nonrecurring Revenue or Expense Items

During any given accounting period, the results of operations for a particular practice may reflect the impact of significant nonrecurring revenue and/or expense items. The nonrecurring nature of these items generally renders the historical financial results reflecting these items inappropriate for comparative purposes.

In order to normalize the results of operations for a particular practice, all significant revenue and expense items determined to be nonrecurring should be removed from the historical results of operations. On the revenue side, one-time audit fees or compliance engagements, major litigation or insurance settlements, or significant revenues resulting from isolated transaction-related or similar services should be removed. On the expense side, significant charges relating to adverse litigation or similar claims, expenses relating to broken lease commitments, and other material nonrecurring expense items should be adjusted. Only after revenues and expenses have been adjusted to "normalized" amounts will the information provided through market transactional analyses result in meaningful valuation pricing indicators.

Comparative Analysis of Guideline Practices to the Subject Practice

If the data are available, the analyst will find it extremely useful to compute certain financial and operational ratios for both the guideline accounting practices and the subject accounting practice. This financial ratio analysis, which should encompass a period of several years, allows the analyst to assess the comparative strengths and weaknesses of the guideline practices as compared to the subject practice. It includes the following:

1. Liquidity ratios
   a. Current ratio
   b. Quick ratio
   c. Average working capital balance to annual fees
2. Operational activity ratios
   a. Annual fees to average receivables balance
   b. Average days fees outstanding in accounts receivable
   c. Annual fees per CPA
   d. Annual fees per professional
   e. Annual fees per employee
   f. Average billing rate per CPA
   g. Average billing rate per professional
   h. Average billing rate per employee
   i. Average annual billed hours per CPA
   j. Average annual billed hours per professional
   k. Average annual billed hours per employee

3. Coverage/leverage ratios
   a. Earnings before interest and taxes (EBIT) to interest expense coverage
   b. Net fixed assets to owners' equity
   c. Long-term debt to total capital (long-term debt + owners' equity)
   d. Interest-bearing debt to owners' equity
   e. Interest-bearing debt to total capital
4. Profitability ratios
   a. EBIT calculated before partners' profits distributions to average total assets
   b. Pretax income calculated before partners' profits distributions to average owners' equity
   c. Pretax income calculated before partners' profits distributions to average total assets
   d. EBIT calculated before partners' profits distributions to average total capital
   e. Debt-free net income (DFNI) calculated before partners' profits distributions to average total capital
   f. Pretax income per partner
   g. Pretax income per CPA
   h. Pretax income per professional

As mentioned earlier in this chapter, it is also appropriate for the analyst to compare the financial and operational ratios derived from the subject practice to accounting industry financial and operational data. Sources of financial and operational data for the accounting firm—both national and regional—were presented in Chapter 5, "Data Gathering and Due Diligence for an Accounting Practice Appraisal."

DEVELOPMENT OF VALUATION PRICING MULTIPLES

Examples of relevant valuation pricing indicators, or valuation pricing "multiples," that can be derived from the application of the market approach include the following:

- Price/Revenues (P/R) multiples
- Price/Earnings (P/E) multiples
- Price/Cash flow (P/CF) multiples

Although price/book value multiples are often applied in the valuation of manufacturing companies, holding companies, and other business concerns, they rarely apply when valuing accounting practices, other professional practices, or other service-oriented (i.e., non-asset-intensive) business concerns. Transfers of individual ownership interests between partners in accounting practices and other service businesses (e.g., law firms or consulting firms), however, are often based on an adjusted net asset value.

Analysts may disagree regarding the exact definition of revenues, earnings, and cash flow; however, all analysts would agree that consistency is the main issue. Revenues, earnings, and cash flow should be determined in a consistent manner for each market transaction analyzed, as well as for the subject practice. Further, revenues, earnings, and cash flow should represent normalized amounts, indicative of long-term operating expectations.

The indicated valuation multiples are derived by dividing the appropriate financial fundamentals (e.g., revenues, earnings, and cash flow) into the adjusted price for each market transaction. Applying the most appropriate valuation pricing multiples to the corresponding fundamentals demonstrated by the subject accounting practice will provide indications of the value for the subject practice.

CAPITALIZATION OF THE SUBJECT PRACTICE FUNDAMENTALS

If enough relevant market transactions have been identified, the market transaction analysis should result in a range of indicated valuation multiples. With an eye to how closely the guideline accounting practices in the market transaction analysis compare to the subject practice, the analyst selects relevant valuation pricing multiples and applies them to the corresponding fundamentals demonstrated by the subject practice's operating results.

Like the operating fundamentals reflected by the guideline transaction practices' financial performances, the operating fundamentals for the subject accounting practice should be adjusted to reflect normalized results. Only after the subject practice's financial fundamentals have been adjusted to normalized levels will the application of the indicated valuation pricing multiples produce meaningful indications of value.

ILLUSTRATIVE EXAMPLE

To illustrate the market approach, assume that Ican Foote, the sole owner of Tick & Tie, CPAs, has engaged you to perform a valuation of his accounting practice. Ican, who is 62 years old, has been offered $500,000 for his practice by Plentimore Taxes.

Plentimore, who is only 48 years old, believes that the purchase of Ican's predominantly audit-based practice will complement his tax practice nicely.

As part of your engagement, you will apply the market approach in order to conclude if the practice purchase offer to Ican for Tick & Tie is a good offer. Discussions with Ican and a comprehensive financial analysis of his practice indicate that his economic income stream is represented by approximately 70 percent audit work, 20 percent corporate tax work, and 10 percent write-up services.

As of March 31, 1996, the balance sheet for Tick & Tie, CPAs, reflected total assets of approximately $200,000, including intangible assets and accounts receivable. Tick & Tie, CPAs, reported total client revenues of $600,000 for calendar year 1995— that is, for the last full operating year prior to the March 31, 1996, valuation date.

Based on your financial analysis of Tick & Tie, CPAs, and on your discussions with Ican, you have performed a search for guideline market transactions. Three guideline transactions have been identified:

Transaction 1—a two-CPA practice with client revenues of approximately $700,000 for the last full year prior to the sale transaction. The practice has been operating for approximately 12 years at the same location and historically has generated revenues divided approximately evenly between audits of small company clients and related corporate income tax services.

At the sale transaction date, the guideline practice was operating with approximately $220,000 in total assets, including intangible assets and accounts receivable.

Transaction 2—a one-CPA practice with client revenues of approximately $375,000 for the last full year prior to the transaction. The guideline practice has been operating for approximately 22 years at the same location and historically has generated revenues divided evenly among individual tax services, write-up services, and financial review and compilation services.

At the sale transaction date, the guideline practice was operating with approximately $165,000 in total assets, including intangible assets and accounts receivable.

Transaction 3—primarily a two-CPA practice, although the owner's son-in-law, a CPA, assists during tax season. Client revenues for the practice totaled approximately $800,000 for the last full year prior to the sale transaction. The guideline practice has been operating approximately 6 years from the same location, after having operated approximately 18 years from a previous location one mile away. Historically, the practice revenues have been composed of 75 percent corporate audit services and 25 percent corporate tax services.

At the sale transaction date, the guideline practice was operating with approximately $270,000 in total assets, including intangible assets and accounts receivable.

Exhibits 7.1 through 7.3 present the market transaction analysis prepared for the valuation of Tick & Tie, CPAs, as of March 31, 1996. Exhibit 7.1 presents an analysis of the guideline purchased practices, focusing on client revenues as the primary financial fundamental. Exhibit 7.2 presents an analysis of the guideline acquired practices focusing on earnings. Exhibit 7.3 presents an analysis of the guideline purchased practices, focusing on cash flow as the primary financial fundamental.

Based on the transactional information analyzed and presented in Exhibits 7.1 through 7.3, Tick & Tie, CPAs, reflected operations over the three-year period preceding the valuation date that most closely parallel the operations of the practice represented by Transaction 3. Although analysts frequently use a five-year operating period in market transaction analysis, the three-year period was considered relevant in this instance because all three of the purchased practices and Tick & Tie, CPAs, are considered mature practices, each having operated more than 10 years. In addition, each guideline practice—and the subject practice—was determined to be operating in a low-growth phase.

As can be seen in Exhibit 7.1, the revenue growth rate of 4.9 percent experienced by Tick & Tie, CPAs, slightly exceeded the 4.6 percent rate experienced by the acquired practice of Transaction 3 during the three-year period preceding the valuation date.

Earnings and cash flow growth rates (Exhibits 7.2 and 7.3, respectively) experienced by Tick & Tie, CPAs, were 9.1 percent and 8.6 percent, respectively, slightly lower than the growth rates experienced by the guideline practice of Transaction 3.

From a profitability perspective, analyzed by comparing earnings (Exhibit 7.2) and cash flow (Exhibit 7.3) with client revenues, Tick & Tie, CPAs, reflects higher profitability than either guideline practice of Transactions 1 and 2, and is slightly less profitable than the guideline practice of Transaction 3.

Based on the market transaction analysis presented in Exhibits 7.1 through 7.3, the following valuation pricing multiples were selected to estimate the fair market value of Tick & Tie, CPAs:

Type of Valuation Pricing Multiple	Selected Valuation Multiple
Price/Revenues	0.9 times
Price/Earnings	7.2 times
Price/Cash Flow	6.3 times

VALUATION OF TICK & TIE, CPAS
MARKET APPROACH
GUIDELINE PRACTICE REVENUE ANALYSIS
AS OF MARCH 31, 1996

Guideline Transaction	Practice Purchase Price($)	Revenues[a] ($)					3-Year Average ($)	3-Year Growth Rate (%)
		1995	1994	1993	1992			
Transaction 1	550,000	700,000	668,000	658,000	638,000	675,333	3.1
Transaction 2	250,000	375,000	355,000	345,000	350,000	358,333	2.3
Transaction 3	820,000	800,000	770,000	750,000	700,000	773,333	4.6
Tick & Tie, CPAs	NA	600,000	570,000	545,000	520,000	571,667	4.9

Price/Revenues	1995
Transaction 1	0.79
Transaction 2	0.67
Transaction 3	1.03
Mean	0.83
Median	0.79

[a]Revenues have been adjusted to exclude all nonrecurring items.

Exhibit 7.1. Comparative Analysis of Growth and Growth Rates of Revenues for Guideline Purchased Practices and Tick & Tie, CPAs, 1992 through 1995.

VALUATION OF TICK & TIE, CPAS
MARKET APPROACH
GUIDELINE PRACTICE EARNINGS ANALYSIS
AS OF MARCH 31, 1996

Guideline Transaction	Practice Purchase Price ($)	Earnings[a] ($)					3-Year Average ($)	3-Year Growth Rate (%)
		1995	1994	1993	1992		
Transaction 1	550,000	77,000	80,160	72,380	63,800	76,513	6.5
Transaction 2	250,000	37,500	39,050	39,675	36,750	38,742	0.7
Transaction 3	820,000	112,000	103,950	97,500	84,000	104,483	10.1
Tick & Tie, CPAs	NA	81,000	74,100	65,400	62,400	73,500	9.1

Profitability (as a % of Revenues)

		1995	1994	1993	1992	3-Year Average (%)	
Transaction 1		11.0	12.0	11.0	10.0	11.3	
Transaction 2		10.0	11.0	11.5	10.5	10.8	
Transaction 3		14.0	13.5	13.0	12.0	13.5	
Tick & Tie, CPAs,	NA	13.5	13.0	12.0	12.0	12.9	

Price/Earnings	1995
Transaction 1	7.14
Transaction 2	6.67
Transaction 3	7.32
Mean	7.04
Median	7.14

[a]Earnings reflect normalized revenues less normal operating expenses (i.e., significant nonrecurring expenses have been eliminated).

Exhibit 7.2. Comparative Analysis of Growth and Growth Rates of Earnings for Guideline Purchased Practices and Tick & Tie, CPAs, 1992 through 1995.

VALUATION OF TICK & TIE, CPAS
MARKET APPROACH
GUIDELINE PRACTICE CASH FLOW ANALYSIS
AS OF MARCH 31, 1996

Guideline Transaction	Practice Purchase Price ($)	Cash Flow[a] ($)				3-Year Average ($)	3-Year Growth Rate (%)
		1995	1994	1993	1992		
Transaction 1	550,000	89,250	91,850	83,895	74,965	88,332	6.0
Transaction 2	250,000	43,125	44,375	44,850	42,000	44,117	0.9
Transaction 3	820,000	127,200	118,580	111,750	97,300	119,177	9.3
Tick & Tie, CPAs	NA	91,500	84,075	74,938	71,500	83,504	8.6

Profitability (as a % of Revenues)

	1995	1994	1993	1992	3-Year Average (%)
Transaction 1	12.8	13.8	12.8	11.8	13.1
Transaction 2	11.5	12.5	13.0	12.0	12.3
Transaction 3	15.9	15.4	14.9	13.9	15.4
Tick & Tie, CPAs	15.3	14.8	13.8	13.8	14.6

Price/Cash Flow	1995
Transaction 1	6.16
Transaction 2	5.80
Transaction 3	6.45
Mean	6.14
Median	6.16

[a]Cash flow reflects normalized earnings plus depreciation and amortization.

Exhibit 7.3. Comparative Analysis of Growth and Growth Rates of Cash Flow for Guideline Purchased Practices and Tick & Tie, CPAs, 1992 through 1995.

VALUATION INDICATION

Applying the selected valuation pricing multiples to the relevant operating fundamentals reflected in the Tick & Tie, CPAs, financial statements results in the following indications of value:

Financial Fundamental	1995 Operating Results	Selected Valuation Multiple	Indicated Fair Market Value
Revenues	$600,000	0.9 times	$540,000
Earnings	$81,000	7.2 times	$583,000
Cash Flow	$91,500	6.3 times	$576,000

The indicated values for Tick & Tie, CPAs, fall within a reasonable range. Because
each of the indicated values is based on actual market transactions, it is reasonable
for an analyst to conclude that each value is a reasonable estimation of the fair market value of Tick & Tie, CPAs.

Based on the analysis performed and the indicated range of values, a reasonable
estimation of the fair market value of Tick & Tie, CPAs, based on the market approach, as of March 31, 1996, is $566,000. As the analyses summarized above sug-
gest, the offer of $500,000 for Tick & Tie, CPAs, by Plentimore Taxes does not quite
measure up to the indicated value for the subject accounting practice, based on the
market approach.

SUMMARY

The following concepts regarding the market approach to the valuation of accounting practices were presented in this chapter:

1. The fundamental categories of alternative market approach valuation methods
2. The strengths of using the market approach to value accounting practices
3. The limitations of using the market approach to value accounting practices
4. Sources of guideline comparative data, both financial and operational
5. The selection and application of valuation methods and valuation pricing
   multiples
6. An example of the application of the market approach

When adequate verifiable transactional data regarding guideline practices are
available, the market approach is a powerful tool for accounting practice valuation.
Nonetheless, even when sufficient confirmed transactional data are available, this
valuation approach requires the application of considerable appraisal judgment.

8

ASSET-BASED APPROACH*

Because of the *accounting* principles related to the historical cost basis of accounting and because of the fundamental principle of the accounting identity, the book value of assets minus the book value of liabilities equals the book value of owner's equity. However, the basic principles of *economics* allow us to create a somewhat different valuation identity: the current value of assets minus the current value of liabilities equals the value of owner's equity. This latter principle is true for accounting practices, other types of professional practices, and businesses in general.

From the perspective of accounting practice valuation, the relevant standard (or definition) of value is the one appropriate for the purpose and objective of the appraisal. Chapter 3 presented several alternative standards of value, including fair market value, fair value, market value, intrinsic or fundamental value, and investment value. These and other, similar standards of value are the appropriate value definitions to use in the analysis and appraisal of an accounting practice using any of the asset-based valuation approach methods.

Accordingly, having determined the purpose and objective of the appraisal, the analyst will begin by selecting the appropriate standard of value to apply to the accounting practice ownership interest. In the asset-based valuation approach, the analyst will apply that appropriate standard of value to all of the assets and all of the liabilities of the subject practice. In other words, the analyst will restate the value of all assets and liabilities of the accounting firm from the historical cost basis to, say, fair market value. The analyst can then apply the axiomatic assets-minus-liabilities formula to estimate the fair market value of the firm's equity interests.

* This chapter is adapted and condensed, with permission, from Chapters 15 and 17 of Shannon P. Pratt with Robert F. Reilly and Robert P. Schweihs, *Valuing Small Businesses and Professional Practices,* 2d ed. (Burr Ridge, Ill.: Irwin Professional Publishing, 1993). For a broader discussion of these topics, please see *Valuing Small Businesses and Professional Practices,* 2d ed., or Shannon P. Pratt, Robert F. Reilly, and Robert P. Schweihs, *Valuing a Business: The Analysis and Appraisal of Closely Held Companies,* 3d ed. (Burr Ridge, Ill.: Irwin Professional Publishing, 1996).

At this point, the analyst has typically concluded the value of 100 percent owner-ship of the equity of the accounting practice on a marketable, controlling-interest basis. If the appraisal subject is some lesser ownership interest in the firm (e.g., the value of a nonmarketable, minority equity interest), then several security valuation discounts and/or premiums will also need to be considered.

FUNDAMENTALS OF THE ASSET-BASED VALUATION APPROACH

Properly applied, asset-based valuation approach methods are, from an analytical perspective, the most complex and challenging of accounting practice valuation pro-cedures. The costs and benefits of asset-based practice valuation methods will be de-scribed below. Before we consider these costs and benefits or the various asset-based valuation approach methods, several important fundamentals should be reiterated.

First, in properly applying asset-based valuation methods, historical-cost-based financial statements are only a starting point in the valuation analysis. They are never the ending point in such a valuation analysis. Analysts use the firm's statement of fi-nancial position (i.e., balance sheet) prepared in accordance with GAAP merely as a point of departure from which to begin the appraisal analysis. While the final format of the valuation-based balance sheet is cosmetically similar to that of the historical-cost-based balance sheet (e.g., the assets may be on the left-hand side and the liabili-ties may be on the right-hand side), the valuation-based balance sheet differs materi-ally from the historical-cost-based balance sheet both in content and intent. Specifically, for the valuation-based balance sheet:

1. The balances in the asset and the liability accounts have all been revalued to the appropriate standard of value for the subject appraisal, as of the valuation date
2. Several additional asset and liability accounts are likely to be added, and sev-eral original asset and liability accounts are likely to be deleted (or consoli-dated)

Second, in properly applying asset-based valuation methods, all assets and liabili-ties should be restated to a standard of value consistent with the standard of value se-lected for the overall practice valuation. As will be described below, if the asset and liability account balances are immaterial, or if the revaluation changes are imma-terial, then the analyst may elect to leave those account balances at their historical cost value. Otherwise, the analyst must separately consider and analyze each asset and liability account, either individually (item by item) or collectively (grouped by major account categories). The analyst will then conclude the defined value (e.g., fair market value) of each asset and each liability account, ultimately estimating the defined value (e.g., fair market value) of the subject accounting firm's equity structure.

Third, in properly applying asset-based valuation methods, all of the accounting practice's assets and liabilities should be considered for revaluation to the selected appropriate standard of value. Typically, many of an accounting practice's most valuable assets are not recorded on a historical-cost-based balance sheet. This omission may include the entire spectrum of the subject firm's intangible assets and intellectual properties.

ASSET-BASED VALUATION APPROACH METHODS

In the appraisal literature, several names are used for similar asset-based valuation methods. These valuation methods are sometimes referred to as the *net asset value* method, *adjusted net worth* method, *adjusted book value* method, *asset build-up* method, or *asset accumulation* method. In fact, these are all very similar valuation methods within the same broad asset-based valuation approach. Accordingly, these methods will be referred to collectively as *asset-based valuation methods* for the remainder of this chapter.

Asset-based valuation methods are balance-sheet-oriented valuation methods. Essentially, the accounting firm's balance sheet is restated to a current value (as defined). This typically involves the identification and valuation of otherwise unrecorded intangible assets as well as the revaluation of the asset and liability accounts already recorded on the GAAP-based balance sheet.

Two alternative methods are used in the application of the asset-based valuation approach:

1. The discrete (or individual) identification and revaluation of all of the firm's asset and liability accounts; this is typically called the *asset accumulation* method
2. The collective identification and revaluation of all (or major categories of) the firm's asset and liability accounts; as will be discussed shortly, the capitalized excess earnings method is the most common of these collective asset-based revaluation methods

Discrete (Separate) Revaluation of Assets and Liabilities

In the discrete revaluation, or asset accumulation method, the accounting practice's assets and liabilities are all analyzed and appraised individually. This involves a separate identification and revaluation of the accounting practice's:

1. Financial assets (e.g., cash, receivables, work in process, etc.)
2. Tangible personal property (e.g., computers, office equipment, furniture and fixtures, etc.)
3. Tangible real estate (e.g., land, land improvements, buildings, etc.)
4. Intangible real property (e.g., leasehold interests, easements, etc.)
5. Intangible personal property (e.g., computer software, client relationships, going-concern value, goodwill, etc.)
6. Current liabilities (e.g., salaries payable, accounts payable, etc.)
7. Long-term liabilities (e.g., notes and mortgages payable, etc.)
8. Contingent liabilities (e.g., pending tax dispute, pending litigation, etc.)

Under this valuation method, the value of the discretely appraised assets (both tangible and intangible) less the value of the discretely appraised liabilities (both recorded and contingent) represents the business value of the subject accounting practice.

Collective Revaluation of Assets and Liabilities

In the collective revaluation method, all of the accounting firm's assets and liabilities (and, hence, owners' equity) are revalued in one analysis and calculation. Typically, this collective revaluation is concluded in the identification and quantification of the accounting firm's incremental value over and above (or decremental value below) the book value of its recorded assets. Using this valuation method, the accounting firm's intangible goodwill is often defined globally as the total of all appreciation (or depreciation) in the value of the accounting firm, as compared to its book value.

Under the capitalized excess earnings method, the value of the accounting firm's equity is the value of the subject firm's net tangible assets plus the value of its collective intangible assets, much or all of which may be in the nature of goodwill. This collective intangible value is quantified using the capitalized excess earnings method.

So, when viewed from the perspective of the asset-based valuation approach, the capitalized excess earnings method is considered an asset-based valuation method, where the total amount of the accounting firm's asset revaluation is concluded on a collective basis. This single collective adjustment for the revaluation of all of the accounting firm's assets and liabilities is often labeled as *intangible value in the nature of goodwill.*

As will be noted below, in the strictest application of the excess earnings method, as discussed in Internal Revenue Service Revenue Ruling 68-609, all tangible assets are revalued to fair market value, and the excess earnings method is used only to quantify the total intangible value of the firm in excess of tangible asset value. Revenue Ruling 68–609 is presented in Appendix C.

Which Asset-Based Valuation Method to Use

Theoretically and practically, the accounting practice value concluded under the collective revaluation method should equal the accounting practice value concluded under this discrete revaluation method.

The determination of which revaluation method to use in a given accounting practice appraisal should be a function of

1. The experience and judgment of the professional analyst
2. The quantity and quality of available data
3. The purpose and objective of the appraisal
4. The scope and timing of the appraisal assignment

First, we will describe the steps in the application of the asset accumulation method—or the individual asset valuation method—in the asset-based practice valuation approach. Second, we will describe the steps in the application of the capitalized excess earnings method—or the collective asset valuation method—in the asset-based practice valuation approach.

THE ASSET ACCUMULATION METHOD

Steps in Applying the Asset Accumulation Method

This section lists and briefly discusses the asset accumulation method, as summarized in six steps.

1. Obtain or develop a GAAP-based—or historical-cost-based—balance sheet for the subject accounting practice.
2. Determine which categories of assets and of liabilities currently recorded on the GAAP-based balance sheet require a valuation adjustment, and then revalue these assets and liabilities to the appropriate standard of value.
3. Identify all off-balance-sheet assets—typically intangible assets—that should be recognized and valued.
4. Identify all off-balance-sheet—or typically contingent—liabilities that should be recognized and valued.
5. Value the previously unrecognized (under GAAP) assets and liabilities identified in steps 2 through 4 to the appropriate standard of value.
6. Construct a valuation-based balance sheet (based on the appropriate standard of value), building on the results of steps 1 through 5.

Obtain or Develop a GAAP-Basis Balance Sheet

As mentioned above, the analyst starts with a GAAP-based or historical-cost-based balance sheet for the subject accounting practice prepared as of the valuation date.

Identify Assets and Liabilities to Be Revalued

Second, the analyst carefully analyzes and understands each category of material recorded asset and recorded liability for the subject accounting practice. The objective of this analysis is to determine which categories of material recorded assets and liabilities will need to be revalued according to the selected standard of value appropriate for the subject practice valuation. As a convention throughout the remainder of this discussion, let's assume that fair market value is the appropriate standard of value for the subject accounting practice.

Identify Off-Balance-Sheet Assets That Should Be Recognized

Third, the analyst identifies which unrecorded (often called *off-balance-sheet*) assets need to be recognized on the valuation-based balance sheet of the accounting firm. For example, while intangible assets are not normally recorded on the firm's financial statements under GAAP, they often represent the largest component of economic value for an accounting practice.

Identify Off-Balance-Sheet and Contingent Liabilities That Should Be Recognized

Fourth, the analyst identifies which unrecorded material contingent liabilities, if any, need to be recognized on the valuation-based balance sheet of the subject accounting firm. Analysts do not often identify and value contingent liabilities in an asset accumulation method of practice valuation because most accounting firms do not have material contingent liabilities. Nonetheless, the analyst should consider this procedure in every such accounting practice valuation.

Value the Items Identified

Fifth, after the analysis of recorded assets and liabilities and after the identification of unrecorded assets and liabilities, the analyst begins the quantitative process of revaluing each of the subject firm's assets and, if necessary, liabilities. Typically, the analyst performs these valuation analyses by category of assets. The standard categorization of assets, for purposes of applying the asset accumulation method, is described above. These standard categories of assets are

1. Financial assets
2. Tangible personal property
3. Tangible real estate

4. Intangible real property

5. Intangible personal property

Construct a Valuation-Based Balance Sheet

Sixth, after concluding the defined value for all the accounting practice's financial, tangible, and intangible assets—and for all of the firm's recorded and contingent liabilities—the analyst constructs a valuation-based balance sheet for the accounting firm, as of the valuation date. From this valuation-based balance sheet, it is mathematically simple for the analyst to subtract the value of the firm's liabilities (recorded and contingent) from the value of the firm's assets (tangible and intangible). The remainder of this subtraction is the value of a 100 percent interest in the accounting firm's equity structure (on a marketable, controlling basis).

If the appraisal assignment relates to something less than the overall accounting practice value (e.g., to a nonmarketable, minority ownership interest in partnership units that are subject to a buy-sell agreement), then additional valuation discount and/or premium analyses and procedures are required.

Premises of Value for Individual Assets

Before considering the various methods for valuing the individual assets of the accounting firm, the analyst should first consider both the appropriate standard (or definition) of value and the appropriate premise of value for each asset category. Usually (but not always) the appropriate standard of value for each asset category should be the same standard selected for the overall accounting practice valuation.

When appraising individual assets, analysts may elect from among four alternative premises of value. Each of these four premises may apply under each of the alternative standards of value.

While the standard, or definition, of value answers the question, Value to whom? the premise of value answers the question, Value under what type of hypothetical market transaction? For example, under the fair market value standard of value, the same asset category may be appraised under any of the four premises of value. So, while fair market value answers the question, Value to whom? (i.e., value to a hypothetical willing buyer and hypothetical willing seller), the selected premise of value answers the question, In what type of market transaction—or under what set of transactional circumstances—will these parties interact?

The four alternative premises of value for individual asset appraisals are

1. Value in continued use, as part of a going concern

2. Value in place, as part of a mass assemblage of assets

3. Value in exchange, as part of an orderly disposition

4. Value in exchange, as part of a forced liquidation

Value in Continued Use, as Part of a Going Concern

Under this valuation premise, it is assumed that the subject accounting practice assets are sold as a mass assemblage of assets and as part of an income-producing, going-concern accounting practice. It is further assumed that the relationships between the firm's tangible and intangible assets are mutually synergistic.

Value in Place, as Part of a Mass Assemblage of Assets

Under this valuation premise, it is likewise assumed that the subject accounting practice assets are sold as a mass assemblage, but here it is also assumed that the mass assemblage is capable of but not currently operating as an income-producing accounting practice. So while this premise of value admits some degree of mutual synergy between tangible and intangible assets—in particular, it admits a value-in-place component to the subject assets—it specifically excludes the contributory value of such common intangible assets as a trained and assembled workforce, going-concern value, and goodwill, none of which apply to an inoperative practice.

Value in Exchange, as Part of an Orderly Disposition

Under this valuation premise, it is assumed that the subject accounting practice assets are sold piecemeal, not as part of a mass assemblage. It is also assumed that the assets are given an adequate exposure to their normal secondary market. However, since an orderly disposition market transaction is assumed, this premise does not contemplate any contributory value effect of the tangible on the intangible assets or vice versa.

Value in Exchange, as Part of a Forced Liquidation

Under this valuation premise, it is likewise assumed that the subject assets are sold piecemeal and not as part of a mass assemblage, but here it is also assumed that the assets are not allowed a normal exposure to their normal secondary market. Rather, the assets are permitted an abbreviated exposure to a market of the highest bidders present (who may or may not represent the collective-demand-side marketplace for that asset).

Selecting the Appropriate Premise of Value

Any of the four premises of value described above may be applied to the same asset (or category of assets) being appraised under a given standard of value. For example, an analyst may select the fair market value standard and assume that a willing buyer and a willing seller transact to exchange an asset.

Obviously, even under the same standard of value, the subject accounting practice will be subject to materially different overall practice valuation conclusions, given the alternative premise or premises of value selected for valuing the various practice assets.

Individual Asset Valuation Approaches and Methods

After the appropriate premise of value is selected, the next step in the asset accumulation valuation method is to apply one or more widely recognized appraisal approaches to each individual asset category. Since this text is not devoted to individual asset appraisal, the discussion here will be introductory in nature.

Financial Assets

The most common assets in this category include cash, accounts receivable, unbilled work in process, and prepaid expenses. No revaluation procedures are needed with cash, of course. With accounts receivable, the analyst estimates their net realizable value, which is, essentially, the present value of the expected realization (i.e., collection) of the receivables. With unbilled work in process, the analyst estimates its net realizable value after considering the amount of work in process that will ultimately be billed and collected. With prepaid expenses, the analyst estimates their net realizable value. Prepaid expenses typically include deposits and prepaid rent, insurance, utilities expenses, and so forth.

Tangible Real Estate

Tangible real estate includes such assets as owned land, land improvements, buildings, and building improvements. In the appraisal literature, real estate is technically considered to be tangible real property, distinguished from intangible real property, which represents a limited legal interest (i.e., less than a fee simple interest) in real estate.

A prodigious body of literature is devoted to the appraisal of real estate, and both the appraisal regulatory agencies and the various professional appraisal membership organizations have promulgated professional standards for the valuation of tangible real property. For example, the *Uniform Standards of Professional Appraisal Practice* (USPAP)—which principally concerns real estate—were discussed earlier.

All real estate is valued by reference to three traditional asset valuation approaches: (1) the cost approach, (2) the income approach, and (3) the market (or sales comparison) approach. However, each of these approaches subsumes several discrete appraisal methods. Since accounting practices typically do not own their own real estate treatment of these three valuation approaches will be saved for the discussion of the valuation of intangible assets, later in this chapter.

Tangible Personal Property

The asset category of tangible personal property typically includes office furniture, fixtures, and computers and office automation. A considerable body of literature exists on the appraisal of commercial tangible personal property. As with real estate, all of the various appraisal methods and procedures for appraising tangible personal property can be grouped into three traditional asset appraisal approaches: (1) the cost approach, (2) the income approach, and (3) the market (or sales comparison) approach.

Intangible Real Property

Intangible real property assets represent intangible legal claims on tangible real estate. These assets typically include leasehold interests and various other leasehold estates. As intangible claims on tangible real estate, the value of these assets is generally a subset of, or a derivative of, the value of the associated tangible real estate.

As with tangible real estate, individual methods and techniques have been published for appraising intangible real property. Once again, these methods can all be conveniently grouped into the three traditional appraisal approaches: (1) the cost approach, (2) the income approach, and (3) the market (or sales comparison) approach.

Intangible Personal Property

The intangible asset valuation concepts presented in this category will be developed within our overall framework of the valuation of an accounting practice. The identification and valuation of individual intangible assets is an integral and essential part of the asset accumulation method to the appraisal of accounting practices.

Identification of Intangible Assets

From valuation, accounting, and legal perspectives, an intangible asset must possess certain attributes to exist. Some of the requisite attributes that an intangible asset needs to be subject to valuation include the following:

- It should be subject to specific identification and recognizable description.
- It should be subject to legal existence and protection.
- It should be subject to the right of private ownership, and this private ownership should be legally transferable.
- There should be some tangible evidence or manifestation of the existence of the intangible asset (e.g., a contract or a license or a registration document).
- It should have been created or have come into existence at an identifiable time or as the result of an identifiable event.
- It should be subject to being destroyed or to a termination of existence at an identifiable time or as the result of an identifiable event.

In other words, there should be a specific bundle of legal rights (and other natural properties) associated with the existence of any intangible asset.

For an intangible asset to have a quantifiable value from an economic perspective, it should possess certain additional attributes, which include the following:

- It should generate some measurable amount of economic benefit to its owner. This economic benefit could be in the form of an income increment or of a cost decrement. This economic benefit may be measured in any of several ways, including the present value of net income, net operating income, net cash flow, and so on.
- It should enhance the value of other associated assets, which may include tangible personal property and tangible real estate.

Clearly, a substantial distinction may be made between the legal existence of an intangible asset and its economic value. An example of this distinction would be an accounting practice that created software for preparing tax returns and then immediately and permanently locked it in the firm's vault. If the newly created software was never used in the production or protection of income, then it would have no economic value, even though it had legal existence.

Categorization of Intangible Assets

Generally, professional appraisers will put individual intangible assets into one of several distinct categories. These categories aid appraisers in identifying and classifying assets, and therefore, they are relevant when appraising intangible assets for accounting practice valuation purposes.

Intangible assets in each category are generally similar in nature and function. Also, intangible assets are grouped in the same category when similar valuation methods apply to them. The most common categorization of intangible assets follows:

- Technology-related (e.g., technical databases)
- Customer-related (e.g., client lists)
- Contract-related (e.g., favorable supplier contracts)
- Data processing–related (e.g., computer software)
- Human capital–related (e.g., a trained and assembled workforce)
- Marketing-related (e.g., marketing brochures and materials)
- Location-related (e.g., leasehold interests)
- Goodwill-related (e.g., going-concern value)

There is a specialized classification of those intangible assets called *intellectual properties*. Intellectual properties manifest all of the legal existence and economic value attributes of other intangible assets. However, because of their special status, intellectual properties enjoy special legal recognition and protection.

Unlike other intangible assets that may be created in the normal course of business operations, intellectual properties are created by human intellectual and/or inspirational activity. Such creative activity (although not always planned) is specific and conscious, and as such it can be attributed to specific individuals. Because of this unique creation process, intellectual properties are generally registered under, and protected by, specific federal and state statutes.

Like other intangible assets, intellectual properties are typically grouped into categories. The intellectual properties within each category are generally similar in nature, feature, method of creation, and legal protection. Likewise, similar valuation, transfer pricing, and other methods of economic analysis apply to the intellectual properties in each category.

The most common categorization of intellectual properties follows:

- Creative (e.g., copyrights)
- Innovative (e.g., patents)

Obviously, not all categories of intangible assets and intellectual properties will apply to the typical accounting practice.

Valuation of Intangible Assets

Intangible assets are valued according to the three traditional approaches:

1. The market (or sales comparison) approach
2. The income approach
3. The cost approach

All individual appraisal techniques and methods used for intangible asset valuation are derived from these three traditional approaches to value. For every intangible asset appraisal, each of the three approaches may prove more or less relevant. Therefore, the prudent accounting practice appraiser will consider and (when possible) use all three generally accepted approaches during the appraisal of individual intangible assets.

Each valuation technique results in both a preliminary and (ultimately) a final indication of the value of the subject intangible asset. In the valuation synthesis step of the appraisal process, the analyst integrates the results derived from applying the various analytical procedures. The object of this integration is to reach a final conclusion that reflects consideration and synthesis of all appraisal approaches and methods used to estimate the value of the intangible asset.

Market (or Sales Comparison) Approach

The market (or sales comparison) approach provides a systematic framework for estimating the value of an intangible asset through analyzing actual sale or transfer transactions of intangible assets, these should be reasonable guideline comparatives to the subject intangible asset. This valuation approach is based on the economic principles of supply and demand and of market efficiency.

The market approach requires the appraiser to compare the intangible asset being studied with guideline intangible assets that have been listed for sale or sold in their appropriate primary or secondary markets. Correlations between actual sale transaction prices are also examined.

Factors that are considered include:

- The income-generating capacity of the guideline intangible asset
- The markets served by the guideline intangible asset
- The historical and expected prospective return on investment earned by the guideline intangible asset
- The historical age and the expected remaining useful life of the guideline asset
- The time of the sale
- The degree of—and the future risk of—obsolescence of the guideline intangible asset (including physical, functional, technological, and economic)
- Special terms and conditions of the sale (such as special seller financing, an earn-out agreement, a noncompete agreement, and so on)

These factors are analyzed discretely for each guideline or comparable intangible asset transaction, and the data are adjusted as appropriate.

From a practical standpoint, it is difficult for analysts to use the market approach to value many intangible assets. This is true for several reasons.

First, intangible assets often are not sold separately from other business assets. In other words, they are sold as part of a mass assemblage of income-producing (tangible and intangible) business assets. Therefore, the analyst faces the problem of allocating a lump sum transaction price among all of the assets transferred, including the specific guideline intangible asset.

Second, buyers and sellers of intangible assets tend to keep transactional data proprietary. Analysts thus face difficulty in obtaining, verifying, and confirming data on the actual terms of arm's-length sales of intangible assets.

Last, the analyst also faces the challenge of data purification and cash equivalency analysis. That is, even if the guideline intangible is sold without any accompanying fixed assets, the transfer is often accompanied by short-term servicing agreements and long-term noncompete agreements. And if there is an earn-out or other payment terms (as is often the case with the transfer of intangible assets), then the analyst has to perform a cash equivalency analysis to estimate the actual guideline transaction price to be used for further valuation analysis.

Nonetheless, most analysts would agree that—when it can be used—the market approach is the best method for estimating the value of an intangible asset. For intangible no less than for tangible assets, an actual and active secondary market provides the best indicator of value. Of course, this assumes that a secondary transfer market exists, that it is sufficiently active, and that the analyst can obtain verifiable empirical pricing data regarding the actual intangible asset transfers.

Income Approach

The income approach provides a systematic framework for estimating the value of an intangible asset based on income capitalization or on the present value of future economic income to be derived from the use, forbearance, license, or rental of that intangible asset. This valuation approach is based on the economic principle of anticipation.

Under the income approach to intangible asset appraisal, economic income can be defined several ways, including:

- Net income before tax
- Net income after tax
- Net operating income
- Gross or net rental income
- Gross or net royalty or license income
- Gross (or operating) cash flow
- Net (or net free) cash flow

The income capitalization procedure can also be accomplished in several ways, including:

- Capitalizing current year's income
- Capitalizing an average of several years' income
- Capitalizing a normalized or stabilized period's income
- Projecting future income over a discrete time period and estimating a present value

Quantifying the appropriate capitalization rate or present value discount rate is an essential step in the income approach to intangible asset valuation. The appropriate capitalization rate or present value discount rate should reflect a fair return on the owners' investment in the subject intangible asset. It should consider:

- The opportunity cost of capital
- The time value of money (including consideration of a real rate of return and expected inflation over the investment horizon)
- The term of the investment (including consideration of the expected remaining life of the subject intangible asset)
- The risk of the investment

When deriving the appropriate capitalization rate or discount rate, the most important factor to remember is that the rate selected must be consistent with the measurement of economic income used. In other words, a before-tax capitalization rate should be applied to a before-tax measurement of economic income; an after-tax capitalization rate should be applied to an after-tax measurement of economic income; an economic income stream representing a return to equityholders only should be capitalized by a rate based upon a cost of equity capital only; and so forth.

An economic income stream can be assigned to a particular intangible asset in several ways. When appraising intangible assets, economic income can be derived from two sources: (1) increments to revenue or (2) decrements to cost. In an appraisal, either source can contribute with equal validity to the value of the subject intangible asset.

With regard to incremental revenue, certain intangible assets may enable their owner to sell more services than otherwise, sell services at a higher average billing rate than otherwise, gain a larger market share, increase staff utilization, ensure a relatively sure source of recurring clients, and so on.

With regard to decremental costs, certain intangible assets may enable their owner to incur lower labor costs, enjoy lower rent expense, enjoy low utilities expense, enjoy lower advertising or promotional expenses, defer the costs of recruiting and training employees, avoid start-up costs, avoid or defer software development or ongoing data processing costs, and so forth.

Some intangible assets lend themselves well to the application of the income approach. Such contract-related or customer-related assets as favorable leases, favorable supply contracts, and recurring client lists are likely candidates. Obviously, when intangible assets generate a measurable and predictable stream of economic income—whether that be an increment to revenues or a decrement to costs—the analyst should seriously consider using the income approach as one method in the appraisal of the subject intangible asset.

When using an income approach valuation method, the analyst should be particularly mindful of the expected remaining life of the subject intangible asset. Clearly, the economic income projection associated with the subject intangible asset should not extend beyond the expected remaining useful life for that intangible asset.

Also, the analyst should be careful not to double-count the economic income associated with the subject intangible asset during the valuation process. That is, the analyst should ensure that the same stream of economic income (whether it be a revenue increment or a cost decrement) is not assigned to more than one asset. For example, the same stream of excess earnings for a particular accounting practice should not be assigned to both the firm's clients and its employees, as that specific stream is attributable to only one of these assets.

The analyst should also be careful to consider only that stream of economic income associated with the particular intangible asset in the valuation process. The analyst mindful of this caveat will be careful to assign a fair return on the tangible assets used to produce income related to the subject intangible asset. This fair return on associated fixed assets should be subtracted from the economic income stream assigned to the subject intangible asset so that intangible asset values are not double-counted during the valuation.

Cost Approach

The cost approach provides a systematic framework for estimating the value of an intangible asset based on the economic principle of substitution. In other words, a prudent investor will pay no more for an intangible asset than the cost of replacing it with a comparable substitute.

Replacement Cost New

It has been said that replacement cost new establishes the maximum amount that a prudent investor would pay for a fungible asset. Of course, the total cost of an intangible asset should include all the material, labor, developer's profit, and entrepreneurial incentive required to motivate someone to create it.

When an intangible asset is less useful than an ideal replacement asset, the value of the subject intangible asset must be adjusted accordingly. The subject intangible asset's replacement cost new is adjusted for losses in economic value due to

- Physical deterioration
- Functional obsolescence
- Technological obsolescence (a specific form of functional obsolescence)
- Economic obsolescence (often called external obsolescence)

Physical deterioration reduces the value of an intangible asset due to physical wear and tear resulting from continued use. It is unlikely that most intangible assets will ever experience physical deterioration. However, for conceptual completeness, the analyst should consider the existence of any physical deterioration during the valuation analysis.

Functional obsolescence reduces the value of an intangible asset when it is unable to perform the function (or yield the periodic utility) for which it was originally designed.

Technological obsolescence reduces the value of an intangible asset when improvements in technology make it less than the ideal replacement for itself. Technological obsolescence occurs when improvements in design or engineering technology produce a new replacement intangible asset with a greater standardized measure of utility.

Economic obsolescence reduces the value of the subject intangible asset when it is affected by events or conditions external to—and not controlled by—its current use or condition. The impact of economic obsolescence is typically beyond the control of the asset's owner, for which reason, economic obsolescence is typically considered incurable.

In estimating the amounts (if any) of physical deterioration, functional obsolescence, technological obsolescence, and economic obsolescence, consideration of the intangible asset's age and expected remaining useful life are essential to the proper application of the cost approach.

Under the cost approach, the typical formula for quantifying an intangible asset's cost is:

> Reproduction cost new
> − Curable functional and technological obsolescence
> = Replacement cost new

To estimate the value of the intangible asset, the following formula is used:

> Replacement cost new
> − Physical deterioration
> − Economic obsolescence
> − Incurable functional and technological obsolescence
> = Value

Curable versus Incurable Obsolescence

An intangible asset's deficiencies are considered curable when the prospective economic benefit of enhancing or modifying it exceeds the current cost (in terms of material, labor, and time) of changing it. An intangible asset's deficiencies are considered incurable when the current costs of enhancing or modifying it (in terms of material, labor, and time) exceed the expected future economic benefits of improving it.

Reproduction Cost   Reproduction cost is the cost of constructing at current price an exact duplicate or replica of the subject intangible asset. Therefore, an intangible asset's reproduction cost encompasses all the deficiencies, "superadequacies," and obsolescence that exist in the subject intangible asset. Many of these conditions or characteristics are inherent in the subject asset and are thus incurable.

Replacement Cost The replacement cost of an intangible asset is the cost of creating at current prices an asset having equal utility to the subject asset. However, the replacement asset would be created with the latest methods and constructed to current standards, state-of-the-art design and layout, and the highest available quality of workmanship.

The difference between an intangible asset's reproduction cost and its replacement cost is typically the cost of curing functional and technological obsolescence. That is, in an ideal replacement intangible asset, all elements of curable functional and technological obsolescence have been removed or reengineered from the subject intangible asset. An intangible asset's replacement cost is sometimes quantified using a green-field approach, which calculates the cost to redesign and reengineer an ideal replacement intangible asset on the drawing board from scratch—that is, on a virgin "green field."

Some intangible assets lend themselves well to the application of the cost approach. These intangible assets are typically used—or used up—in generating income for the firm. Examples of likely candidates include computer software and automated databases, proprietary staff training materials, technical libraries, client files and records, and so forth.

Obviously, when such intangible assets are used (or used up) by a firm—and when accurate replacement cost estimates are available—the analyst should seriously consider the application of the cost approach as one method in the appraisal.

Remaining Useful Life Analysis of Intangible Assets

One factor that has been mentioned in our discussion of all three valuation approaches is the estimation of the remaining useful life of the subject intangible asset. Estimating the remaining useful life (sometimes called *lifing* the intangible assets) is important in the market approach because the analyst will want to select guideline sale transactions where the intangible asset involved has about as much remaining useful life as the subject intangible asset.

Quantifying remaining useful life helps the analyst using the income approach estimate the time period or duration over which to project (and capitalize) the economic income associated with the subject intangible asset. This estimation is also important in the cost approach, where the analyst will need an assessment of the remaining functionality of the subject intangible asset to identify and quantify elements of physical depreciation (if any), functional obsolescence, technological obsolescence, and economic obsolescence.

Several methods are used for analyzing and estimating the remaining useful life of intangible assets. The most common of these are listed below:

1. Remaining legal (or legal protection) life
2. Remaining contractual term of period
3. Statutory or judicial life
4. Remaining physical life
5. Remaining functional life
6. Remaining technological life
7. Remaining economic life
8. Statistical (or analytical) mortality life

An analyst should usually consider all of these measures of remaining useful life in the analysis of an intangible asset. Also, generally, the shortest remaining useful life measured will be the one used in the appraisal of each intangible asset.

Illustrative Example

To illustrate the general application of the asset accumulation valuation method, consider a hypothetical accounting practice called Audits R. Us & Co.

To keep this example relatively simple, assume that the founder of Audits R. Us & Co. is contemplating the sale of the entire accounting practice and has engaged an analyst to perform a valuation of it. As the objective of this appraisal is to estimate the fair market value of the overall accounting practice, it will not be necessary to consider the identification and quantification of various valuation discounts and premiums.

Given the purpose and objective of the accounting practice appraisal, the analyst will estimate the fair market value (as the standard of value) of all tangible and intangible assets of Audits R. Us & Co., as of the valuation date. Initial analysis of the practice indicates a history of successful operations. Based on this, and given management's plans to sell the practice as an ongoing business, the analyst selects the individual asset valuation premise of value in continued use, as a going-concern business.

Exhibit 8.1 presents the GAAP-based statement of financial position of Audits R. Us & Co., as of December 31, 1996. Exhibit 8.1 then, is the basis working document that is the point of departure for an asset accumulation method accounting practice valuation.

Exhibit 8.2 presents the final summary of the asset accumulation method accounting practice valuation for Audits R. Us & Co. The exhibit presents both the historical-cost-based values for all recorded assets and liabilities of Audits R. Us & Co. (just slightly rearranged from the GAAP-based balance sheet) and the fair

ASSETS	
Current Assets	
Cash	$20,000
Accounts receivable	50,000
Prepaid expenses	20,000
Unbilled work in process	60,000
Total Current Assets	150,000
Noncurrent Assets	
Plant, property and equipment, at cost	
Land and buildings	170,000
Office furniture and fixtures	50,000
Computer equipment	30,000
Total plant, property and equipment	250,000
Less: accumulated depreciation	100,000
Net plant, property and equipment	150,000
Other noncurrent assets	
Note receivable from former employee	50,000
Total other noncurrent assets	50,000
TOTAL ASSETS	$350,000
LIABILITIES AND OWNER'S EQUITY	
Current Liabilities	
Accounts payable	40,000
Wages payable	20,000
Taxes payable	10,000
Accrued liabilities	30,000
Total Current Liabilities	100,000
Noncurrent Liabilities	
Mortgages payable	130,000
Total Noncurrent Liabilities	130,000
Owner's Equity	
Partners' capital	120,000
Total Owner's Equity	120,000
TOTAL LIABILITIES AND OWNER'S EQUITY	$350,000

Exhibit 8.1. Audits R. Us & Co., Statement of Financial Position as of December 31, 1996.

	At Historical Cost	At Fair Market Value
ASSETS		
Financial Assets		
Cash	$20,000	$20,000
Accounts receivable	50,000	50,000
Prepaid expenses	20,000	20,000
Unbilled work in process	60,000	60,000
Note receivable from former employee	50,000	20,000
Total Financial Assets	200,000	170,000
Tangible Real Estate		
Land and buildings	170,000	180,000
Less: accumulated depreciation	50,000	—
Net Tangible Real Estate	120,000	180,000
Tangible Personal Property		
Office furniture and fixtures	50,000	30,000
Computer equipment	30,000	10,000
Less: accumulated depreciation	50,000	—
Net Tangible Personal Property	30,000	40,000
Intangible Real Property		
Leasehold interests	0	20,000
Net Intangible Real Property	0	20,000
Intangible Personal Property		
Trademarks and trade names	0	20,000
Computer software	0	5,000
Client files and records	0	15,000
Trained and assembled workforce	0	15,000
Recurring client relationships	0	20,000
Net Intangible Personal Property	0	75,000
TOTAL ASSETS	$350,000	$485,000

(continued)

Exhibit 8.2. Audits R. Us & Co., Practice Valuation—Asset Accumulation Method as of December 31, 1996.

LIABILITIES AND OWNER'S EQUITY		
Current Liabilities		
Accounts payable	40,000	40,000
Wages payable	20,000	20,000
Taxes payable	10,000	10,000
Accrued liabilities	30,000	30,000
Total Current Liabilities	100,000	100,000
Noncurrent Liabilities		
Mortgages payable	130,000	120,000
Total Noncurrent Liabilities	130,000	120,000
TOTAL LIABILITIES	230,000	220,000
TOTAL LIABILITIES AND OWNER'S EQUITY	$350,000	$485,000
TOTAL OWNER'S EQUITY	$120,000	$265,000

Exhibit 8.2. *(continued)*

market values for all of the subject practice's assets and liabilities—tangible and intangible.

Based on the estimates of fair market value presented in Exhibit 8.2, it is possible to reach a valuation conclusion for each asset and liability and to describe a typical valuation approach to such an accounting practice. As the exhibit shows, the firm's cash balance remains at its historical cost value. The analyst should confirm whether or not the cash balance will be transferred to the new owner when the accounting practice is sold. Similarly, the accounts receivable assets remain at their historical cost value. This conclusion was reached after an assessment of the timing and collectibility of the receivables. Prepaid expenses likewise remain at their historical cost value. This estimate was reached by assessing the net realizable value of the prepaid expenses to the accounting practice. One more balance remains at historical cost: unbilled work in process. This estimate was based upon an analysis of the collectibility of the work-in-process accounts.

The note receivable from the former employee is revalued downward. Assume that some years ago this accounting practice extended a loan to one of its key employees. The decremental revaluation was based upon an analysis of the below-market interest rate on the note and of the former employee's erratic payment history on the note.

The real estate land and buildings are revalued upward. This appraisal of the properties' current market value is based upon a depreciated replacement cost analysis of the subject properties.

The office furniture and fixtures and computer equipment are revalued incrementally—that is, the current fair market value estimates for both asset categories exceed their (depreciated) historical cost. The depreciated replacement cost method would be a typical valuation method for the appraisal of these assets.

A leasehold interest is identified and capitalized on the valuation basis balance sheet. In this example, Audits R. Us & Co. enjoys a favorable rental advantage (i.e., below-market rental rates) on the branch office that it leases. The analyst has used the income approach to project and capitalize this favorable lease rate advantage and to conclude the fair market value of the leasehold interest. This favorable lease could be assigned to a new owner of the accounting practice.

The entire category of intangible personal property would not be recorded on a GAAP-based or historical-cost-based balance sheet. However, these intangible assets are identified and appraised for practice valuation purposes. The Audits R. Us & Co. trademarked advertising materials are an important intangible asset for the accounting firm. Firm management spends a great deal of time and money promoting the practice's slogan, "When it comes to audits, we look the other way." The firm advertises in local business journals, sends promotional announcements, sponsors booths at trade shows, and so forth.

The recreation cost method has been used to estimate the value of this intangible asset. The analyst has estimated the current cost required for the accounting firm to recreate its current level of consumer awareness, name recognition, and client loyalty. Then this estimated cost has been capitalized as the value of this intangible asset.

Computer software is an important intangible asset for Audits R. Us & Co. This proprietary tax return preparation computer software was developed in-house instead of being purchased. Therefore, the value of this computer software is not recorded on the GAAP-based balance sheet shown in Exhibit 8.1.

The analyst has used the sales comparison (or market) approach to estimate the value of this intangible asset as there are functionally similar systems available from a commercial software vendor. After consideration of the market value of a comparable commercial system and after including the costs of customization, installation, testing, and training, the analyst has concluded the market value of the Audits R. Us & Co. proprietary computer software.

Audits R. Us & Co. has valuable historical client work paper files. The value of these files has been estimated on a recreation cost basis—that is, the value of partner time and staff time required to recreate the information encompassed in the permanent client files.

Audits R. Us & Co. has a trained and assembled workforce that has worked together for years. The value of the trained and assembled workforce is the cost to recruit, hire, and train a replacement workforce of equivalent experience and expertise to the actual Audits R. Us & Co. workforce.

Last, Audits R. Us & Co. has valuable recurring client relationships. These recurring client relationships may be valued using an income approach.

The current liabilities of Audits R. Us & Co. have also been analyzed. Given the short-term nature of these monetary liabilities, the analyst has estimated their fair market value at their historical-cost carrying amounts.

The noncurrent liabilities have also been appraised. Given the term of these liabilities and their stated (or implied) interest rates, the analyst has estimated the fair market value of the bonds, notes, and debentures at their historical-cost carrying amounts.

The mortgage payable, however, has a substantial remaining term to maturity and has an interest rate considerably below current market rates. The analyst confirmed with the mortgage bank that they would allow Audits R. Us & Co. to pay off the mortgage at a discount—compared to the remaining outstanding principle balance. The analyst has estimated the amount of this discount and then has estimated the fair market value of the mortgage payable.

Finally, the analyst has summed the estimated fair market values for all tangible and intangible assets of Audits R. Us & Co., summed the estimated fair market values for all recorded and contingent liabilities of Audits R. Us & Co., and subtracted the total liability value from the total asset value. The remainder is the fair market value of the total owner's equity of Audits R. Us & Co., per the asset accumulation valuation method.

Advantages of the Asset Accumulation Method

As should be apparent from the above discussion, there are a number of advantages of the asset accumulation method of accounting practice valuation. First, the results of the asset accumulation valuation method are presented in the format of a traditional balance sheet financial statement. Anyone who has ever worked with basic financial statements should be familiar and comfortable with this format.

Second, this valuation method breaks the economic value of the subject accounting firm into its constituent components, making it possible to identify exactly which assets (tangible and intangible) contribute value to the accounting practice and how much value they contribute. Third, this valuation method is useful when structuring the sale of a practice. This method can immediately quantify the effects on the accounting practice value of many common seller questions, such as:

1. What if the seller retains the practice's cash on hand?
2. What if the seller retains (or leases back to the practice) the operating real estate facilities?
3. What if the seller personally retains title to some of the valuable assets of the practice?
4. What if the seller personally retains any or all of the debt instruments of the practice?

Fourth, this valuation method is useful to the seller when negotiating the sale of the practice. If the buyer offers a lower price than the asset accumulation method concludes, the seller can ask, "Since you're not willing to pay for all of the identified assets of the accounting practice, which of these assets do you want to exclude from the transaction?"

Fifth, this valuation method is useful to the buyer when negotiating the purchase of the practice. If the seller wants a higher price than the conclusions of the asset accumulation method, the buyer can ask, "What other identified assets are you willing to sell to me—in addition to what has already been appraised on this balance sheet—to justify the price you are asking?"

Sixth, after the sale transaction is consummated, this method of accounting practice valuation allows for a fast and reasonable allocation of the lump-sum purchase price among the individual assets acquired. This purchase price allocation is often required for both financial accounting purposes and tax accounting purposes. Depending upon the structure of the sale, many of the identified intangible assets may be subject to amortization cost recovery for federal income tax purposes.

Seventh, this valuation method is useful for financing the subject transaction. Typically, all categories of lenders (secured, unsecured, mezzanine, etc.) will want to know the value of the practice's individual assets—both tangible and intangible—before they will commit to finance the proposed deal. This accounting practice valuation method generally provides lenders with the information they need.

Eighth, this valuation method provides particularly useful support in the legal resolution of disputes. With the individual value components of the individual assets identified, measuring the impact of certain alleged actions (or lack of actions) on the value of the accounting firm is easy. This valuation method can also be used to allocate assets (as well as—or instead of—equity) in a stockholder/partner dissolution dispute or in a marital dissolution dispute.

Ninth, this valuation method can be used with virtually any standard of value or any premise of value. In other words, using the same comparative balance sheet format, analysts can value the same accounting practice under several alternative standards of value. Likewise, using the same comparative balance sheet format, analysts can value the same accounting practice under several alternative premises of value. Therefore, the impact of changing standards of value or premises of value can be immediately identified and quickly quantified.

Tenth, this valuation method requires the most rigorous analysis and thorough understanding of the subject practice operations on the part of the analyst. Such analyses can only help to enhance the quality of the valuation. Also, this valuation method generally requires much more active participation of the practice management in the valuation process. This active interest and participation can only help to enhance the quality of the accounting practice valuation.

Disadvantages of the Asset Accumulation Method

The primary disadvantage of the asset accumulation valuation method is that, if taken to its ultimate extreme, it could be quite expensive and time consuming. It also may necessitate involvement of appraisal specialists in several fields.

Also, as described in this chapter, capturing all the assets means the intangible as well as the tangible assets. Most intangible asset values depend especially heavily on income approaches. Therefore, when taken to its extreme, the asset accumulation valuation method may ultimately depend as much (or more) on income variables as on values of tangible assets, especially for accounting practices.

THE EXCESS EARNINGS METHOD

The excess earnings method of practice valuation is clearly an asset-based valuation method. As with the asset accumulation valuation method, the excess earnings method—also called the *formula method*—starts out with, and ends up with, the balance sheet for the subject accounting practice. Of course, the accounts on the subject balance sheet have been revalued to the appropriate standard of value.

The excess earnings valuation method requires an earnings capitalization to estimate the intangible value in the nature of goodwill of the subject accounting practice. Certainly, an earnings capitalization method is a form of the income approach to value. And, as was explained in the last few sections of this chapter, the income approach is one of the three traditional approaches (the others being the cost approach and the market, or sales comparison, approach) in the valuation of assets, on which the asset-based valuation approach is founded.

History of the Excess Earnings Method

The excess earnings method is sometimes called the *Treasury method* (or the *formula method*) because it originally appeared in a 1920 publication issued by the U.S. Treasury Department, ARM 34, which stands for Appeals and Review Memorandum, Number 34. It was adopted to estimate the value of the goodwill that breweries and distilleries lost because of prohibition.

Since then, both taxpayers and IRS agents have widely used (and misused) this method in the valuations of businesses and professional practices for gift and estate taxes and other tax-related purposes. Because it is well known and apparently simple, it has been widely adopted in one form or another for professional practice valuations.

In 1968 the Internal Revenue Service updated and restated the ARM 34 method with the publication of Revenue Ruling 68-609, which is reproduced in Appendix C. Revenue Ruling 68-609 is still in effect.

How It Works—A Step-by-Step Explanation

While there are several variations to the excess earnings valuation method, the typical steps can be summarized as follows:

1. Estimate the net tangible asset value for the subject accounting practice. Note that this value is typically for net tangible assets only and would not normally include intangible assets such as computer software, recurring client relationships, etc. However, as was explained above, the definition of *net tangible assets* may be expanded to include all identified tangible and intangible assets of the subject accounting practice.

   However, for purposes of simplicity and of strict conformity with the exact language of Revenue Ruling 68-609, only identified tangible assets will be considered here as part of net tangible assets based on this method.

2. Estimate a normalized level of economic income for the subject accounting practice.

3. Estimate an appropriate, or "fair," percentage rate of return on the net tangible asset value. Multiply the net tangible asset value from step 1 by that fair rate of return to estimate the amount of economic income attributable to the net tangible assets. Subtract that amount of fair return on assets from the normalized economic income estimate developed in step 2. The result of this step is called the *excess earnings:* that is, the amount of economic income above a fair return on the net tangible asset value of the subject accounting practice.

   Estimate an appropriate capitalization rate to apply to the excess earnings, which are presumably the level of earnings attributable to the intangible value in the nature of goodwill, instead of to the net tangible assets. The next step is to capitalize the excess earnings at that rate.

4. Add the values from steps 1 and 4.

Illustrative Example

Assume that the accounting practice of Andy Accountant, CPA, has a net tangible asset value of $20,000. Also assume that, after allowance for a reasonable salary for Andy, the practice earns about $8,000 per year.

In this example, the analyst engaged to appraise Andy's practice has calculated a rate of return on the net tangible assets of 15 percent. Assume that this capitalization rate has been derived in a manner consistent with the analyst's estimate of economic income. Further, the analyst will capitalize the indicated excess earnings at a 20 percent rate. (The issue of estimating the applicable rates is discussed later in the chapter.)

From these determinations, the indicated value of the Andy Accountant, CPA, practice has been computed as follows:

Net tangible asset value	$20,000
Normalized economic income	8,000
Earnings attributable to net tangible assets ($20,000 × .15) =	3,000
Excess economic earnings	5,000
Indicated value of excess earnings ($5,000 ÷ .20) = indicated value of the firm's intangible value in the nature of goodwill	25,000
Total value of the subject accounting practice (i.e., the value of the net tangible assets of $20,000 plus the indicated intangible value in the nature of goodwill of $25,000)	$45,000

Denunciation by the Internal Revenue Service

The IRS Appellate Conferee Valuation Training Program has denounced the naive application of ARM 34 or the excess earnings method of business and professional practice valuation. A valuation method denounced by its own promulgators yet among the most widely used business valuation methods certainly deserves some further consideration.

First, the Treasury Department did not initiate this valuation method to estimate the value of the total operating business entity; rather, this valuation method was developed specifically to estimate the value of the goodwill or other intangible value, if any (above the tangible asset value) of an operating business entity. However, since in estimating a total operating business value it is economically logical to add any intangible value identified by the excess earnings method to the firm's tangible values, this valuation method has become popular for estimating the value of a total entity.

Second, Revenue Ruling 68-609 contains many ambiguities and leaves many unanswered questions. Interpretations to the ambiguities and answers to the unanswered questions vary widely among valuation practitioners. We will discuss some of these ambiguities below.

Estimating Net Tangible Asset Value

Step 1 in the excess earnings method is to estimate a net tangible asset value. Revenue Ruling 68-609 does not define net tangible asset value, nor is it very specific with respect to the important question "net of what?"

Defining Tangible Asset Value

Revenue Ruling 68-609 offers absolutely no guidance as to either the appropriate standard or the appropriate premise of value that is intended in conjunction with the phrase "net tangible asset value." Does it mean replacement cost? Liquidation value? Market value?

Should Asset Value Adjustments Be Tax-Affected?

Because the purpose of the analysis is to estimate the value of the net tangible assets on a going-concern basis (on which a reasonable rate of return should be earned), the analyst normally does not make any adjustment to recognize the tax effect of unrealized gains or losses. However, there could be instances in a typical accounting practice valuation (e.g., substantial appreciation in owned real estate that the practice has put up for sale where a tax payment on the sale of the owned real estate is imminent) where a tax adjustment may be appropriate.

Treatment of Nonoperating Assets

There is general consensus among valuation practitioners that it is preferable to remove nonoperating and/or excess assets from the balance sheet (and the related revenue from the income statement) and to treat such items separately in the excess earnings valuation method.

Treatment of Real Estate Owned

Many valuation practitioners prefer to remove real estate of the subject accounting practice from the balance sheet and impute fair market rental expense on the income statement.

"Netted Out"

What is "netted out" in estimating tangible asset value? Depreciation? All liabilities? All current liabilities? All non-interest-bearing liabilities? Valuation practitioners generally agree that net tangible asset value should be net of all depreciation, amortization, and obsolescence. However, it often is not practical to measure all these items in terms of current economic values. In the simplest straight-equity application of the excess earnings method, all liabilities would be deducted in order to arrive at a net tangible asset value. However, the only mention of the netting of liabilities in Revenue Ruling 68-609 refers to taking out non-interest-bearing current liabilities. Furthermore, experienced valuation practitioners recognize that differences in leverage from one accounting practice to another can lead to distortions in valuation results derived from the excess earnings method.

Debt Valuation

Do you value debt at face value or at fair market value? It depends on when the debt is likely to be paid. If payment at face value is imminent (e.g., payment triggered by the very transaction for which the accounting practice valuation is being performed), then it is appropriate to value the debt at face value. But it appears that the debt will remain outstanding, then most valuation practitioners would prefer to value the debt at fair market value.

Estimating a Normalized Level of Earnings

Step 2 in the excess earnings valuation method is to estimate a normalized level of earnings. Revenue Ruling 68-609 does not make any attempt to define *earnings*. It does, however, make the key statement that the earnings "*should fairly reflect the probable future earnings*" (emphasis supplied). In suggesting the use of past years' earnings as a basis, it notes that abnormal years should be eliminated. Valuation practitioners also agree that nonrecurring items should be eliminated from any year used for earnings base calculations.

Treatment of Nonoperating Income
Consistent with removing nonoperating assets from the net tangible asset base, related nonoperating income should be removed form the earnings base.

Treatment of Equityholders' Compensation
Revenue Ruling 68-609 states, "If the business is a sole proprietorship or partnership, there should be deducted from the earnings of the business a reasonable amount for services performed by owner or partners engaged in the business." Valuation practitioners also concur that abnormal compensation should be adjusted to a normal level, generally taken to be the cost of comparable employees who would perform the same tasks as the accounting practice equityholders.

Definition of Earnings
As mentioned above, Revenue Ruling 68-609 is silent with respect to any definition of *earnings.* Is it net income? Net cash flow? Or some other measure of economic income?

    Some valuation practitioners believe that the variable best suited to represent earnings in the context of the excess earnings method is net cash flow to the practice equityholders. If net cash flow is used as the appropriate measure of earnings, then it is important to use an equity rate of return applicable to the variable being capitalized.

Appropriate Rate of Return on Net Tangible Assets

No one has totally and convincingly refuted the position taken by the IRS stating that any arbitrary rate of earnings as a normal return on net tangible assets cannot be demonstrated to have a reasonable basis. Nevertheless, some ways of looking at the problem of estimating a fair rate of return on net tangible assets could be helpful.

Valuation practitioners generally agree that the appropriate percentage rate of return on net tangible assets in the excess earnings method depends on the asset mix in each individual practice valuation case. Assets that are highly liquid, low in risk, and/or readily acceptable as loan collateral require lower rates of return than assets less liquid, more risky, and/or less acceptable as loan collateral.

Appropriate Capitalization Rate for Excess Earnings

Net tangible assets provide a measure of safety since they can usually be liquidated if earnings fail to materialize as expected. Like many other intangible assets, goodwill, on the other hand, generally has no liquidation value in the absence of earnings since its value typically lies in its ability to generate economic income. Therefore, the risk attached to the intangible portion of the assets would seem to be greater and demand a higher rate of return.

In general, accounting practice buyers are not willing to pay cash up front for more than one to five years' worth of earnings from accounting practice goodwill— sometimes even less. The length of expected future earnings from goodwill for which buyers are willing to pay depends primarily on the perceived persistence of those earnings in the future, independent of further investment of time and effort to perpetuate them.

One way to develop a capitalization rate to apply to excess earnings is to think in terms of converting the number of years' worth of expected future excess earnings the investor would be willing to pay for in terms of cash up front into a capitalization rate. The capitalization rate in this scenario is simply the reciprocal of the number of years' expected excess earnings for which the buyer would be willing to pay cash up front. For example, if the typical buyer would pay the cash equivalent of four years' excess earnings, then the calculation would be

$$1 \div 4 = 25\%$$

The following table presents capitalization rates for excess earnings based on assumed tolerances of accounting practice buyers for a range of payback periods (the length of time the accounting practice buyer is willing to accept to recover the initial cash outlay).

Payback Period (in years)	Capitalization Rate (%)
1	100
2	50
3	33.33 ...
4	25
5	20

Negative Goodwill

The excess earnings method is used to value the earnings, if any, over and above a reasonable rate of return on the net tangible assets. But what if the earning power is less than a reasonable rate of return on the net tangible assets? Such a circumstance could indicate negative goodwill; it could be an indication that the value of the overall accounting practice is less that the value of its net tangible assets.

Common Errors in Applying the Excess Earnings Method

The excess earnings method is widely misused in professional practice valuation. Some of the errors most commonly encountered are discussed in the following sections.

Failure to Allow for Equityholders' Salaries

As noted in Revenue Ruling 68-609, "If the business is a sole proprietorship or partnership, there should be deducted from the earnings of the business a reasonable amount for services performed by the owner or partners engaged in the business." Unfortunately, accounting practice valuations performed by the excess earnings method often do not include a reasonable allowance for compensation to the equityholders of the accounting practice. This error results in an overstatement of the true economic earnings, which in turn leads to an overstatement of the value of the accounting practice.

Failure to Use Realistic Normalized Earnings

The excess earnings method is valid to the extent that it depends on a reasonable estimate of normalized earnings. As noted in Revenue Ruling 68-609, "The past earnings to which the formula is applied should fairly reflect the probable future earnings."

This valuation method is often naively applied to the latest year's earnings, or to some simple or weighted average of recent years' earnings, without regard to whether or not the earnings base used reflects fairly the probable future earnings. Such a naive use of a historical earnings base usually results in an undervaluation or an overvaluation of the subject accounting practice.

Using Book Values of Assets

The book value of assets usually represents the acquisition cost of assets less any depreciation recorded for financial accounting and/or income tax purposes. The longer the accounting practice has held the assets, the less likely it is that the book value will reasonably approximate any kind of economic value.

Net tangible asset value used in the excess earnings method should reflect an informed judgment about the value of the tangible assets. Understatement of the value of the net tangible assets results in a high capitalization rate being applied to too large a portion of the total earnings, which leads to an undervaluation of the total accounting practice—or to an overvaluation if the net tangible asset value is overstated.

Errors in Estimating Appropriate Capitalization Rates

The estimation of the appropriate capitalization rate is critical to the validity of the result of the excess earnings valuation method. One approach to the estimation of the rates was suggested in an earlier section. Another, clearly erroneous approach that recurs in the selection of the rates is to use the rates suggested in the revenue ruling itself.

The ruling, written in 1968, suggests rates of 8 to 10 percent on tangible assets, with 15 to 20 percent applied to the excess earnings. However, the ruling states that "the percentage of return . . . should be the percentage prevailing in the industry involved at the date of the valuation. . . . The above rates are used as examples and are not appropriate in all cases. . . . The capitalization rates are dependent upon the facts pertinent thereto in each case." Both the wording of the ruling and common sense indicate that the specific rates mentioned in the ruling are merely examples and that the actual capitalization rates to use in a given accounting practice valuation depend on the facts and circumstances appropriate at the time of the valuation.

SUMMARY

The asset-based accounting practice valuation approach can be performed either on a discrete asset valuation basis or on a collective asset valuation basis. The first part of this chapter discussed the asset accumulation method, an individual asset valuation method within the asset-based approach. The second part of this chapter discussed the excess earnings method, a collective asset valuation method within the asset-based approach.

Among asset-based practice valuation methods, the asset accumulation valuation method is commonly used. The theoretical underpinning of this method is simple: the value of the subject accounting practice is the value of the practice assets (tangible and intangible) less the value of the practice liabilities (recorded and contingent). Basically, this method recognizes that all of the economic value of an accounting practice has to come from—and be identified back with—the productive assets of the practice.

The asset accumulation valuation method can be applied on a collective basis, where all of the economic value of the accounting firm greater than the tangible value is aggregated and called *goodwill*. A common implementation of this valuation method is the capitalized excess earnings method. The asset accumulation valuation method can also be applied on a discrete basis, where all of the accounting firm's tangible and intangible assets are individually identified and appraised.

The intangible assets of an accounting firm may contribute substantial economic value, or they may contribute little or no economic value. They may even contribute negative economic value, which is recognized as economic obsolescence or as a decrease in the value of the tangible assets of the accounting firm. Again, the ultimate application of an asset-based valuation method requires a structured, rigorous, and comprehensive valuation analysis of all of the assets of the subject accounting practice.

The excess earnings method dates back to the period of Prohibition. The Internal Revenue Service's current position on this valuation method is embodied in Revenue Ruling 68-609. The Internal Revenue Service says that the method "may be used in determining the value of intangible assets of a business only if there is not a better basis for making the determination." In spite of this lack of enthusiasm on the part of the Internal Revenue Service, the excess earnings valuation method is one of the most widely used—and misused—methods of professional practice valuation.

9

VALUATION OF FRACTIONAL
BUSINESS INTERESTS

DEFINITION OF A FRACTIONAL INTEREST

Once an accountant adds a partner or other co-owner to the practice, the appraisal issue of immediate importance is the value of an ownership interest that represents less than 100 percent control of the subject accounting firm. Any ownership interest representing less than the value of the practice as a whole is generally called a *fractional* interest.

Because most accountants practice in a partnership, the focus of this chapter will be on the valuation of fractional interests in partnerships. Nonetheless, the same concepts and applications will apply to limited liability companies and to other corporate forms.

REASONS TO APPRAISE A FRACTIONAL INTEREST

Establishing the value for a fractional interest takes on some importance at several points in the business life of an accounting practice. An ownership interest might be acquired as part of the founding of a partnership, by admission as a partner in a growing firm, or through merger with or acquisition of another practice. In all such cases, the initial buy-in price should reflect the value of the ownership interest at the acquisition date.

After the entry value is established, the next most important event that requires a valuation is the exit value of a fractional interest. Exit values can be driven by both voluntary and involuntary events. Voluntary events can include the resignation of a partner moving on to another accounting firm or the planned retirement of a partner. Involuntary events include termination of the equityholder through death, permanent disability, dismissal, or the dissolution of an accounting practice due to financial distress or personal conflicts among the owners.

Beyond the transaction-driven reasons for a fractional interest practice valuation, there are a number of "score-keeping" reasons to estimate a value for a fractional ownership interest. Some valuations are tax-driven, as when reportable gains on a sale are needed for income taxes or when date-of-death values are required for estate taxes. Other fractional interest appraisals are planning-driven, as are valuations of accruing partnership ownership interests for the younger partners buying into a firm, for personal financial or estate tax planning, or for annual buy-sell agreement updates. Other reasons for estimating the value of an accounting practice fractional interest can include marital dissolution and marital estate settlement (see Chapter 14 for a further discussion of this topic).

GENERALLY ACCEPTED FRACTIONAL INTEREST VALUATION METHODS

The methods for valuing a fractional interest in an accounting practice can be divided into three major categories. The first starts with the value of the entire accounting practice and then allots to the fractional interest a value proportional to its ownership share in the overall practice, which for this purpose is considered a homogeneous economic unit. The second category proceeds from the economic features of the specific fractional business interest and then builds up a value based on an economic analysis of each identifiable right and feature. The third estimates the value of the fractional interest by comparing it to other fractional interests. Two of these fractional interest valuation methods are described below.

Allocation of Overall Practice Value

Perhaps the most common method of appraising the value of a fractional interest is to estimate the value of the overall accounting practice and then to distribute a proportional part of this overall value to the subject fractional interest. The most common allocation procedure—though not the most conceptually correct one—is simply to take the pro rata portion of the overall accounting practice value and assume that it is equal to the value of the subject fractional interest.

The preferred allocation procedure is to recognize the differences in control and marketability between the fractional business interest and the overall accounting practice. Appraisals of fractional interest value that follow this preferred procedure apply successive valuation discounts for the relative lack of control and the relative lack of marketability associated with the fractional interest. The identification and quantification of such valuation discounts are discussed in the next chapter.

Often the accounting firm's buy-sell or partnership agreement will set forth the rights that each fractional business interest holder may have relative to control and salability of the ownership interest. In some cases, as when a supermajority vote is required for equityholders to implement firm actions, a minority ownership interest in the practice can take on additional potential value.

Build-up of Practice Fractional Interest Value

Another accepted method of estimating the value of a fractional interest in an accounting practice is to examine the rights and features attributable to the subject fractional ownership interest and then to classify how those rights and features affect the assignment of underlying asset and liability values. This may require an entirely different discount rate or economic valuation of the practice's net assets (under those respective income approach and asset-based approach methods) than would the discount rate or total asset value appropriate for the valuation of the accounting firm as a whole.

To illustrate this process, consider the case of a 20 percent partner in a professional accounting firm with an existing buy-sell agreement that is binding for the subject value. Suppose this partner withdraws from the partnership to take a job as controller with a client firm. Under this valuation method, the partner's rights under the buy-sell agreement may include the following factors that drive the value of the fractional ownership interest:

1. *Book value of partnership capital account or adjusted net asset value of all tangible assets.* Return of the pro rata portion of the partner's share of the net tangible assets of the partnership, adjusted for their estimated current fair market values on either a going-concern basis or on an orderly disposition basis.

   Some fractional ownership interest buy-out agreements have been struck at the book value of the accounting firm's assets—based on the concept that a partner will buy into the firm believing that book value represents fair market value (even though it does not) and that, therefore, he or she should cash out under the same value assumption.

2. *Discounted value of accounts receivable for cases supervised by the partner.* The exiting owner's interest in outstanding accounts receivable for the accounting firm may be discounted to reflect both collectibility and the time horizon over which the expected collections will occur.

3. *Discounted value of work-in-process on cases brought in by the exiting partner.* The exiting owner's interest in a percentage of the work to be billed on that partner's clients' cases, may also be discounted for the time value of money over the expected time period necessary for the work performance and the collection of the fees.

4. *Noncompete and other restrictions.* If a partner leaves and takes existing clients with him or her, some basis for payment to the subject accounting firm's other owners may be necessary.

5. *Other income continuation provisions.* Payment of income to spouses at the death of partner is not unusual. To the extent such payments may be regarded as a return of, or a return on, a fractional practice ownership interest investment, then they must be considered part of the ownership interest's value.

SUMMARY

Appraisals of fractional ownership interests in accounting practices are conducted for numerous reasons. There are three common methods for estimating the value of such fractional ownership interests:

1. An allocation of the overall value of the subject accounting practice, less any appropriate valuation discounts for lack of control, lack of marketability, etc.
2. The build-up method of valuation.
3. Valuation by comparison with other minority interests.

We have discussed in detail the application of the first two methods. We have not discussed the third method here, because it is merely a micro-application of the market approach, which is discussed in Chapter 7. Any of these three valuation methods may be used to estimate a reasonable valuation conclusion for a fractional ownership interest in an accounting practice.

10

IDENTIFICATION AND QUANTIFICATION OF VALUATION DISCOUNTS AND PREMIUMS

One of the final—yet most important—steps in the valuation of an accounting practice is the identification and quantification of any appropriate valuation discounts and premiums. Among the many types of valuation discounts and premiums, the most common value adjustments that apply to accounting practices are (1) the discount for lack of control (also called the *discount for minority interest*) and (2) the discount for lack of marketability. These two valuation discounts involve separate although somewhat interrelated concepts.

The concept of a discount for minority interest refers to that interest's degree of control in a closely held accounting practice as compared to a controlling interest. The concept of a discount for lack of marketability refers to the liquidity of the security interests of the subject accounting practice—that is, how quickly and certainly an ownership interest can be converted to cash at the equityholder's discretion.

As with all valuation discounts and premiums, the discounts for lack of control and lack of marketability are meaningless until their bases have been defined. Since a valuation discount for minority interest reflects lack of control, the base from which the discount is subtracted is its proportionate share of the overall accounting practice value, including all rights of control. Since a valuation discount for lack of marketability reflects lack of liquidity, the base from which the discount is subtracted is the value of an equity interest that is otherwise comparable but enjoys superior liquidity.

These two valuation discounts are interrelated. For example, both minority interests and controlling interests suffer from a lack of marketability—but in differing degrees. Given its absolute lack of control, a minority ownership interest is clearly harder to sell than a controlling ownership interest. However, even controlling ownership interests suffer to some extent from a lack of marketability. One would expect that it would take at least several months to sell the overall accounting practice, and perhaps considerably longer.

The following sections provide an outline of the theory and rationale supporting these two common valuation discounts, as well as a summary of several of the primary empirical studies that attempt to quantify these discounts as they actually occur in the transactional markets.

CONTROLLING VERSUS NONCONTROLLING INTEREST: DISCOUNT FOR MINORITY INTEREST

The value of a fractional ownership interest in an accounting practice may be equal to, more than, or less than the value of a pro rata share of the entire practice. While this principle is widely accepted among valuation professionals, it often comes as a surprise to a minority equityholder in a professional practice.

Certain valuation approaches provide indications of the value on an overall accounting practice (i.e., controlling ownership interest) basis; other approaches provide indications of value on a minority ownership interest basis. The appraiser must reconcile these differing value indications to arrive at one that is consistent with the purpose and objective of his or her assignment. The adjustment from an overall accounting practice value to a minority ownership interest basis is most often made by applying a minority interest discount.

Theory and Rationale

Control rights, if any, are one of the most important factors affecting the value of an accounting practice. The premium for ownership control—or the discount associated with a lack of ownership control—depends primarily on an equityholder's ability to exercise any or all of a variety of the legal rights typically associated with control ownership. As this ability varies from one situation to another, the value of a minority ownership interest is not necessarily a pro rata percentage of the value of the overall accounting practice. The reverse is also true, of course.

By definition, the holder of a minority ownership interest lacks control and has little or no voice in the affairs of accounting practice management. Controlling interest equityholders, on the other hand, have the opportunity to exercise these common prerogatives:

1. Appoint management committee
2. Determine management compensation and perquisites
3. Set policy and change business practices of the firm
4. Acquire or liquidate assets
5. Select people with whom to do business and award contracts
6. Make acquisitions

7. Liquidate, dissolve, sell out, or recapitalize the practice

8. Hire and fire employees; set employee compensation levels

9. Admit partners; set partner compensation levels

10. Change the articles of partnership agreement and bylaws

This list makes it clear that a controlling equityholder in an accounting practice enjoys some valuable rights denied to a minority equityholder. However, particularly in an accounting practice, many factors may limit a majority equityholder's exercise of the prerogatives normally associated with ownership control and thus the value accruing to the majority position. At the same time, a minority interest investment may not be totally bereft of control factors. For example, a minority equityholder may be in a position to cast crucial swing votes and, in some measure, influence important practice policies.

A willing buyer contemplating the purchase of a minority ownership interest from a willing seller will consider the disadvantages that arise from a lack of control. Therefore, regardless of the overall accounting practice value, one would not expect a willing buyer to purchase a minority ownership interest except at a (sometimes substantial) discount from its pro rata share of the overall accounting practice value.

Empirical Evidence

One appropriate method for quantifying minority interest discounts is to examine stock tender offers. Fellows and Painter have articulated the conceptual basis for such analysis by pointing out that

> in fact, there are only differing degrees of control; when control is entirely absent, there is only its absence. . . . A minority discount, then, is a corollary of a majority premium and depends on the latter for its validity. A discount for lack of control is only appropriate if the amount discounted already includes a majority premium.[1]

Thus, objective and established evidence of the appropriate discount for minority ownership interests has been the study of cash tender offers. By looking at premiums offered during a tender for control of a company with publicly held shares, the valuation difference between controlling and noncontrolling security ownership interests can be approximated.

In studies performed by Willamette Management Associates it was found that control premiums vary widely, with the median being approximately 30 to 40 percent

---

[1]M. L. Fellows and W. M. Painter, "Valuing Close Corporations for Federal Wealth Transfer Taxes: A Statutory Solution to the Disappearing Wealth Syndrome," *Stanford Law Review* 30 (May 1978): 895–933.

	Price Premium Offered		
Year	Mean (%)	Median (%)	Base
1985	37.1	27.7	331
1986	38.2	29.9	333
1987	38.3	30.8	237
1988	41.9	30.9	410
1989	41.0	29.0	303
1990	42.0	32.0	175
1991	35.1	29.4	137
1992	41.0	34.7	142
1993	38.7	33.0	173
1994	41.9	35.0	260
1995	44.7	29.2	324

Source: *Mergerstat Review* (Los Angeles: Houlihan Lokey Howard & Zukin, 1996), 22. Reprinted with permission.

Exhibit 10.1. *Mergerstat Review,* Price Premiums.

over the average public market price in the months just prior to the tender offer announcement. The high end of the range was a premium of over 100 percent, and the low end of the range was a discount of about 10 percent—both clearly indicating special factors involved. Mathematically, a premium for ownership control of 30 to 40 percent is equivalent to a discount for minority ownership interest of about 23 to 29 percent.

Currently, the most comprehensive resource for evidence of actual market control premiums (and their opposites, minority ownership interest discounts) is the annual *Mergerstat Review.*[2] As reported on page 22 of the 1996 edition, the median price premium paid over market price in publicly traded company acquisitions was 29.2 percent in 1995. A control price premium of 29.2 percent is mathematically equivalent to a minority ownership interest price discount of 23 percent. Exhibit 10.1 presents a 10-year summary of acquisition price premiums, as calculated by *Mergerstat Review.*

Mergerstat Review for 1996 also presents price premium data grouped by the industry classification of the selling company. For example, on pages 58 and 59 *Mergerstat Review* presents information on 82 transactions involving companies in the banking and finance industry classification in 1995. The average price premium paid in these 82 transactions was 49.9 percent. A price premium of 49.9 percent is mathematically equivalent to a discount for lack of control of approximately 33.3 percent.

[2]*Mergerstat Review* (Los Angeles: Houlihan Lokey Howard & Zukin, annual).

Also, in court cases deciding appropriate valuation discounts for minority owner-ship interests, there is a wide range of accepted discounts. However, the mode for mi-nority ownership interest valuation discounts tends toward 35 percent.

MARKETABLE VERSUS NONMARKETABLE INTEREST: DISCOUNT FOR LACK OF MARKETABILITY

With regard to marketability, fractional ownership interests in an accounting practice have some fundamental similarities to ownership interests in closely held corpora-tions. The common stock of a closely held corporation is less valuable than the oth-erwise similar stock of a publicly traded corporation because the publicly traded common shares are more quickly and certainly convertible into cash. The market pays a premium for liquidity and, conversely, demands a discount for lack of liquid-ity. Consequently, accounting practices and fractional ownership interests that lack ready marketability generally are worth less than otherwise comparable practices or fractional interests that are readily marketable.

Marketability, or the lack thereof, is a critical issue in the valuation of accounting practices, and the quantification of marketability discounts has been the subject of many empirical research studies, including a series of unpublished studies conducted by Willamette Management Associates. While these empirical studies largely con-cern closely held corporations, they may be applied by analogy to the analysis of marketability in the fractional ownership interests of accounting firms.

Empirical Research

Sophisticated investors have long known that common stock prices are highly de-pendent on marketability. However, only since the late 1960s have analysts at-tempted to isolate and quantify the effect of marketability factors on security pricing. Research attempting to quantify valuation discounts for lack of marketability gener-ally falls into two fields of analysis: (1) empirical studies of transactions in the re-stricted stock of publicly traded companies and (2) empirical studies of private trans-actions in stock of companies that subsequently had initial public offerings.

Restricted-Stock Studies

Through a private placement, a publicly traded corporation may sell unregistered se-curities. Such "restricted" stock is identical in all respects to its publicly traded coun-terpart, except that it is restricted from trading in the public market for some time. (Securities and Exchange Commission Rule 144 generally requires a two-year hold-ing period, after which the stock may be freely traded.) Purchasers of restricted stock consistently require a discount from the price of the restricted stock's unrestricted publicly traded counterpart.

Nearly every private placement of publicly traded stock since the late 1960s has been studied for evidence of discounts for lack of marketability. Through these studies, a strong base of empirical evidence has been developed from which to quantify the appropriate valuation discounts for lack of marketability.

Exhibit 10.2 summarizes the overall conclusions of several well-known restricted-stock studies. The valuation discounts associated with the individual transactions examined in these 10 studies ranges from 0 percent to over 90 percent. However, the studies consistently indicate average price discounts for the restricted stock of publicly traded corporations—compared to its freely tradable counterpart—of approximately 35 percent.

It is important to note that this indicated valuation discount is based upon transactions in stock that will be freely tradable in a relatively short period of time. One would expect a higher valuation discount to reflect the greater lack of marketability of a fractional ownership interest in an accounting practice (which may never have a public market).

Initial-Public-Offering Studies

A second line of evidence quantifying valuation discounts for lack of marketability is found in studies of initial public offerings (IPOs). The scope of these IPO studies

Study	Years Covered in Study	Average Price Discount (%)
SEC Overall Average	1966–1969	25.8
SEC Nonreporting OTC Companies	1966–1969	32.6
Milton Gelman	1968–1970	33.0
Robert E. Moroney	1969–1972	35.6
Robert R. Trout	1968–1972	35.6
J. Michael Maher	1968–1973	35.4
Standard Research Consultants	1978–1982	45.0
Willamette Management Associates	1981–1984	31.2
William L. Silber	1981–1988	33.8
FMV Opinions, Inc.	1979–1992	23.0

Source: Shannon P. Pratt, Robert F. Reilly, and Robert P. Schweihs, *Valuing a Business: The Analysis and Appraisal of Closely Held Companies,* 3d ed. (Burr Ridge, Ill.: Irwin Professional Publishing, 1996), 343. Reprinted with permission.

Exhibit 10.2. Summary of Restricted-Stock Studies.

includes transactions in the stock of closely held corporations that subsequently completed an initial-public stock offering. The implied valuation discount is generally calculated as the difference between the price at which a company's stock was issued in the IPO and the price at which the company's stock traded in arm's-length transactions prior to the IPO (when the company was closely held).

The IPO studies add to the evidence presented by the restricted stock studies and assist the appraiser in estimating the appropriate valuation discounts for lack of marketability. Two well-recognized studies, which examine IPOs for evidence of lack of marketability valuation discounts, are outlined below.

Baird Studies John Emory of Robert W. Baird & Co. has conducted a series of seven studies that examine transactions in closely held stock in the five-month period preceding a company's IPO. Each of the Baird studies has been published in *Business Valuation Review.*[3]

The Baird studies included transactions involving direct arm's-length sales of common stock as well as options to purchase common stock. According to one study:

> In most cases, the transactions included were stated to have been at fair market value and all ultimately would have had to be able to withstand [SEC], IRS, or judicial review, particularly in light of the subsequent public offerings.[4]

Taken together, the Baird studies identified valuation discounts for lack of marketability in a general range of 40 to 45 percent.

Willamette Management Associates Studies In addition to the restricted stock study mentioned previously, Willamette Management Associates annually conducts a study of completed IPOs in an attempt to quantify the price differential between publicly traded and closely held securities attributable to marketability.

As with the Baird studies, the Willamette Management Associates studies calculate the difference between the price at which a closely held company's stock traded and the price at which the company's stock was subsequently offered to the public. Every effort is made to include only those transactions conducted on an arm's-length basis, as though the parties were unrelated and without any semblance of conflict of interest.

At the time of writing, the empirical studies have covered the years 1975 through 1993. For each of these years, every successfully completed IPO has been reviewed to identify arm's-length transactions that occurred within the 36 months prior to the

---

[3]Published quarterly by the American Society of Appraisers.

[4]John D. Emory, "The Value of Marketability as Illustrated in Initial Public Offerings of Common Stock, January 1994 through June 1995," *Business Valuation Review* (December 1995), 155–160.

IPO. The studies also incorporate certain adjustments in an effort to minimize the effects of changing earnings levels within a company as well as within that company's industry.

Based upon the totality of data compiled in these studies, the indicated valuation discounts for lack of marketability generally fall into a range of 40 to 55 percent. Exhibit 10.3 summarizes the historical results of the Willamette Management Associates studies on lack of marketability valuation discounts.

Summary of Empirical Evidence

The restricted stock studies discussed previously indicate quite consistently an average valuation discount for lack of marketability of approximately 35 percent. Further, the two IPO studies discussed above provide convincing support for a somewhat greater valuation discount for lack of marketability of approximately 45 percent.

This apparent discrepancy in conclusions of the two types of studies is both rational and predictable. Restricted securities are only temporarily removed from their liquid public market (typically less than two years). However, closely held stock does not have

Time Period	Number of Companies Analyzed	Number of Transactions Analyzed	Median Discount (%)
1975–1978	17	31	54.7
1979	9	17	62.9
1980–1982	58	113	55.5
1984	20	33	74.4
1985	18	25	43.2
1986	47	74	47.5
1987	25	40	43.8
1988	13	19	51.8
1989	9	19	50.5
1990	17	23	48.5
1991	27	34	31.8
1992	36	75	52.4
1993	51	110	53.3

Source: Willamette Management Associates.

Exhibit 10.3. Summary of Discounts for Private-Transaction P/E Multiples Compared to Public-Offering P/E Multiples Adjusted for Changes in Industry P/E Multiples.

this pending access to the public market, and will probably never enjoy such liquidity. Therefore, the valuation discounts based upon the IPO studies would be expected to more closely represent the actual valuation discount for lack of marketability demanded by an actual investor when investing in the shares of a closely held company.

Factors Affecting Marketability

When selecting an appropriate valuation discount for lack of marketability, several factors affect the valuation discount that would be appropriate in certain situations, including, but not limited to, the following:

Size of the Firm
Several of the empirical studies referred to above note a negative relationship between a company's market value and the indicated discount for lack of marketability. Similarly, companies that trade over-the-counter have historically exhibited greater discounts than companies trading on the larger stock exchanges (i.e., NYSE and ASE). By analogy, small accounting firms may deserve a higher valuation discount for lack of marketability.

Restrictions
Provisions that restrict the sale, transfer, or ownership of the practice ownership interests—including buy-sell agreements, rights of first refusal, stock purchase agreements, or built-in capital gains—can increase the lack of marketability of a fractional ownership interest. From this it is evident that accounting practice fractional ownership interests that are restricted may deserve a higher discount for lack of marketability. The effect of transferability restrictions on the selection of valuation discounts for lack of marketability is discussed in greater detail later in this chapter.

Put Options
Mandatory put options, such as those often attached to fractional ownership interests in many accounting firms, provide an equityholder with the legal right to sell his interest at an agreed-upon price (typically defined as fair market value). Such options add liquidity to otherwise unmarketable ownership interests. Thus, accounting practice fractional ownership interests that possess a put option may deserve a lower valuation discount for lack of marketability.

Size of Ownership Interest
As previously mentioned, controlling ownership interests and minority ownership interests in accounting practices are affected by marketability in distinct ways. For

example, while both interests are subject to marketability considerations, the appropriate valuation discount for lack of marketability for a 100 percent controlling interest in the practice is likely to be somewhat less than that for a 3 percent minority interest. As a result, accounting firm controlling ownership interests may deserve a lower valuation discount for lack of marketability.

Prospects of a Merger

The likelihood of a future merger for the practice may cause a reduction in the valuation discount for lack of marketability. Conversely, the lack of any impending merger may be cause for an increased discount. In accounting firms, the controlling partners will often want very much to maintain independent ownership. Accordingly, equity interests in accounting firms with legitimate prospects of a future merger may deserve a lower valuation discount for lack of marketability.

Summary and Conclusion

This section has summarized a great deal of empirical evidence quantifying valuation discounts for lack of marketability. As with all valuation issues, appraisers must give careful consideration to the specific facts and circumstances surrounding the subject accounting practice in selecting an appropriate valuation discount for lack of marketability.

Consideration of Transferability Restrictions

As previously mentioned, restrictions on transferability can play a significant role in the estimation of an appropriate valuation discount for lack of marketability. The specific purposes and objectives of restrictive agreements vary widely. For fractional ownership interests of an accounting practice, however, two common objectives include: (1) the ability to regulate ownership transition and future equity transactions and (2) the ability to effectively fix equity value for estate tax and other purposes.

If properly drafted, transferability restrictions in the accounting firm's bylaws, articles of incorporation, or partnership agreement can sometimes render the appraised fair market value of the practice meaningless. The three primary types of restrictive agreements are described below.

Buy-Sell Agreements

Buy-sell agreements commonly have the form of a legal contract between shareholders/partners stating that upon any transfer of equity interests, the interests must be purchased by the other shareholders/partners. Often, the applicable transfer of ownership interests occurs upon death, disability, or retirement.

Stock Purchase Options

Stock purchase options are a type of restrictive agreement that provides a shareholder/partner or firm with the option, in certain instances, to purchase another shareholder/partner's ownership interest at a specified price. This type of agreement is often used in estate planning. Typically the option price will be based upon a formula price (i.e., book value) where the option price was equivalent to fair market value on the date of issuance.

Restrictions on Sale

Restrictive sale agreements are often characterized as a *right of first refusal* since in certain instances they provide the accounting firm and its equityholders with a senior right to purchase a selling equityholder's fractional ownership interest. In a typical situation, an equityholder who receives a purchase offer must first tender his interest to the accounting firm or other equityholders at the offered price. Thereby, the accounting firm has the option to match any offer and thus to preserve the restricted ownership.

DISCOUNTS AND PREMIUMS
FOR OTHER NONSYSTEMATIC RISK FACTORS

While valuation discounts for minority interest and for lack of marketability are perhaps the most common of the valuation discounts and premiums, several other valuation discounts and premiums exist that reflect nonsystematic risk factors affecting accounting practices. A brief description of several other valuation discounts and premiums follows.

Key-Person Discount

Analysts are frequently asked to estimate the value of an accounting practice ownership interest in the estate of a recently deceased key partner of the firm. In this situation, it is often reasonable for the appraiser to consider the possibility that the loss of this key partner may have some negative affect on the subject accounting practice.

The valuation discount that may be appropriate to reflect the loss of a key individual depends on several factors. Typically, one of the most important factors is the extent of the deceased partner's actual duties, responsibilities, and contributions to the practice. Often, the key partner's primary contribution is in the form of long-standing client relationships and general industry know-how.

Another important factor to be considered by the analyst is the ability of the accounting firm's other partners to assume the duties of the vacant position. Other important factors include the compensation necessary to replace the partner, the reaction of clients and competitors upon learning of the loss, and the amount of any proceeds from life insurance.

A discount for the loss of a key individual can be incorporated into the valuation conclusion by several methods. However, it is most common to deduct a percentage discount from the overall conclusion of the accounting practice value, as one would a discount for marketability.

Swing Block Premium

Often the owner of a minority interest in an accounting practice has little or no voice in firm affairs and is generally at the whim of the controlling interest equityholder. However, in certain instances a minority interest may hold a strategic position with the ability to cast a decisive vote on firm issues. Where this is the case, the subject minority ownership interest may deserve a swing block premium. (When control basis valuation approaches have been used, the analyst may prefer simply to apply a reduced discount rather than a full discount countered by a subsequent swing block premium.)

To illustrate, assume that Cain and Able & Co., CPAs, is capitalized with 100 partner units and has three equityholders. Two brothers, each owing 45 units, are involved in a bitter dispute regarding the direction of the firm. An unrelated third accountant owns the remaining 10 units. It is clear that the two brothers are at odds and do not intend to vote together on important firm issues. As a result, the 10 percent minority interest is a swing block—it holds the power to break the stalemate between the two 45 percent partners and effectively decide a partnership vote. In consequence, the per unit value of the 10 percent ownership interest is likely to be equivalent to, or possibly greater than, the per unit value of either 45 percent ownership interest.

Voting Premium/Discount

For accounting firms with both voting and nonvoting partners (i.e., two classes of equity interest), the premium associated with the possession of voting rights and the discount associated with the lack thereof are among the most difficult variables of their type to quantify. Of course, the per unit value of an accounting practice's nonvoting interests is clearly somewhat lower than the per unit value of that firm's voting interests, all other things being equal.

The primary factor affecting the magnitude of the voting discount or premium is ownership control—the degree to which voting rights affect an equityholder's operational authority in the subject accounting firm. Where ownership control is an issue, voting rights become more valuable.

In publicly traded companies that have both voting and nonvoting common stock outstanding, the nonvoting stock typically trades at discounts of approximately 3 to 10 percent from the price of the company's voting stock. Clearly, for very small minority ownership interests—such as those typically trading in the public exchanges—the market places relatively little value on voting rights. The market recognizes, however, that the dynamics and scale of fractional ownership interests in accounting firms are not always comparable. In certain instances, no valuation discount may be appropriate for nonvoting shares. In other instances—for example, where the voting units are concentrated in the hands of a small group of controlling partners—a significant valuation discount for nonvoting shares may be appropriate for a very small minority interest.

Practice-Specific Discount/Premium

A valuation discount or premium for practice-specific factors reflects unsystematic risk—that is, risk not due to the market (systematic risk) but rather in most part to the individual accounting firm and its risk environment. For example, if an analyst has valued an accounting firm by comparison with guideline merged firms, a valuation discount or a premium may appropriately reflect the subject firm's position relative to the guideline firms'. Alternatively, in the income approach the analyst may find it appropriate to adjust the selected discount rate to reflect certain risk factors specific to the subject accounting practice and not likely reflected in the market data from which the discount rate was derived.

Accounting practice–specific factors that may influence the selection of a valuation discount or premium can include:

1. Diversification, or the lack thereof (product line, geographical territory, industry specialization, etc.)
2. Depth of management
3. Size (revenues, assets, market value, employees, etc.)
4. Industry cyclicality
5. Leverage
6. Access to additional capital

Typically, the accounting practice–specific risk discount or premium is incorporated in the selection of valuation multiples or in the calculation of a present value discount rate or capitalization rate rather than being applied to the final conclusion of value.

SEQUENCING OF DISCOUNTS AND PREMIUMS

Most valuation discounts and premiums are applied to the final indication of value. However, the analyst needs to use caution as not all valuation discounts may be appropriate for all valuation approaches.

To illustrate, assume that the analyst, in estimating a minority ownership value, has arrived at indications of value from the income approach and the market approach. A valuation discount for minority ownership interest is applicable to the market approach estimate but may not be applicable to the income approach estimate (depending on how the income approach has been applied). However, the valuation discount for lack of marketability is applicable to both indications of value.

When more than one valuation discount or premium is to be applied, it is important to apply them in the proper sequence. A common mistake is to add together two valuation discounts prior to their application. For example, when an analyst has selected a valuation discount for minority interest of 25 percent and a valuation discount for lack of marketability of 40 percent, it is not appropriate simply to sum the discounts and apply an overall valuation discount of 65 percent to the indication of value.

The valuation discounts must be applied in sequence. In this example, the correct application of the two valuation discounts will result in an overall valuation discount of 55 percent, not 65 percent.

ILLUSTRATIVE EXAMPLE

To demonstrate the appropriate application (i.e., sequencing) of valuation discounts for minority interest and for lack of marketability, suppose that an analyst has been asked to estimate the fair market value of a minority ownership interest in the practice of A, B, C & Co., CPAs. Using generally accepted valuation methods, the analyst has arrived at three indications of value for the subject practice fractional ownership interest, shown in Exhibit 10.4 on a per unit basis.

Each of these three accounting practice valuation approaches has produced an indication of value on a control ownership basis. Since the analyst has been asked to estimate the fair market value of a minority ownership interest, each of these three valuation approaches must be adjusted.

Using the empirical evidence presented earlier in this chapter, the analyst estimates that a valuation discount of 25 percent is appropriate to adjust the three valua-

Valuation Approach	Indicated Value per Unit	Value Basis— Ownership Interest
Market approach	$55.00	Marketable, control
Income approach	$53.00	Marketable, control
Asset-based approach	$50.00	Marketable, control

Exhibit 10.4. A, B, C & Co., CPAs, Preliminary Valuation of Minority Ownership Interest.

Valuation Approach	Indicated Value per Unit	Value Basis— Ownership Interest
Market approach	$41.25	Marketable, minority
Income approach	$39.75	Marketable, minority
Asset-based approach	$37.50	Marketable, minority

Exhibit 10.5.   A, B, C & Co., CPAs, Adjusted Valuation of Minority Ownership Interest.

tion approaches to a minority ownership interest basis. Applying this valuation discount to the three valuation approaches results in adjusted indications of value for the subject fractional ownership interest shown in Exhibit 10.5 on a per unit basis.
As shown in Exhibit 10.5, each of the three practice valuation approaches is now expressed on a marketable, minority ownership interest basis.

At this point, it would be appropriate to synthesize these three indications of value into a single value. For simplicity's sake, suppose that the analyst gives each indication equal weight (33 percent) and concludes a unit value of $39.50 on a marketable, minority ownership interest basis. However, since the subject accounting firm is, obviously, closely held, this value indication must be adjusted to a nonmarketable basis.

Again drawing upon the empirical evidence presented earlier in this chapter, the analyst estimates that a valuation discount of 40 percent is appropriate to adjust the value indication to a nonmarketable basis. Applying this valuation discount results in a conclusion of the fair market value, on a nonmarketable, minority ownership interest basis, of $23.70 per equity unit.

SUMMARY

Many appraisal problems involve the estimation of the value of a fractional ownership interest in an accounting practice—either together with or independent from the overall valuation of the subject accounting practice. This chapter discussed several common methods used in the identification and quantification of valuation discounts and premiums.

After consideration of any appropriate valuation discounts or premiums, the analyst is ready to complete the valuation process by performing the valuation synthesis and concluding the final value estimate.

11

VALUATION SYNTHESIS AND CONCLUSION

This chapter takes up the final step in the accounting practice valuation process. Therefore, it is, effectively, a review of all the procedures, data, analyses, and analyst inputs needed to reach the final value estimate. The topics discussed are:

1. How to conduct a thorough and effective review of the appraisal work
2. How to reconcile different value estimates developed from the different valuation approaches into one estimate of the single, most probable, price the subject accounting practice will bring under the market conditions at the time of the appraisal and in conformance with a client's instructions, legal considerations, and the contingent and limiting conditions used by the analyst
3. Why much of the accepted dogma concerning the applicability or appropriateness of the various valuation approaches is not true for every situation
4. How to develop a supportable and defensible estimate of the most probable price an accounting practice ownership interest will bring, using knowledge of the subject accounting practice being appraised, the data being used, and an understanding of the theory behind the various valuation approaches

THE RECONCILIATION PROCESS

During the reconciliation process, it is important for the analyst to review all the steps of the accounting practice valuation. As a first step in this reconciliation process, the analyst should review the appraisal assignment and answer the question, "Did I accomplish what I set out to accomplish?" A review of the appraisal assignment should consider:

1. The purpose and objective of the appraisal
2. The accounting practice ownership interest to be appraised

3. The bundle of legal rights to be appraised
4. The date of the appraisal
5. The definition of value to be estimated
6. The premise of value to be assumed

RECONCILING VALUE INDICATIONS

The appraisal is performed to answer a client's question about the value of an accounting practice. To answer this question, the analyst goes through the valuation process. Yet even within the same valuation approach, different methods will typically result in different indications of value. For example, it is quite likely that there will be different indicated values resulting from two different income approach methods (e.g., from a direct capitalization method versus a yield capitalization method). Hence the process of reconciliation, in which the alternative valuation conclusions are analyzed and synthesized to produce a final value estimate for the subject accounting practice.

THE REVIEW PROCESS

Before reaching a final value estimate, the analyst should review the entire accounting practice appraisal for appropriateness and accuracy. Some of the items to be considered in this review process include the following:

1. Validity—was the appraisal verified and transcribed correctly?
2. Pertinence—is the analysis pertinent to the appraisal problem? Does the appraisal help the reader arrive at the same value conclusion? Is it just fluff? Have you overlooked any data that could be used in the valuation?
3. Consistency—are the same numbers used throughout the appraisal? Is the same description of the accounting practice business interest subject to appraisal in all sections of the report?
4. Quantity of data—is there enough data to perform a meaningful valuation analysis?
5. Quality of data—are the "comparable" accounting practice sale transactions really comparable? Are the data believable?

As a next step, the analyst should review the quantitative and qualitative analytical methods used in the accounting practice valuation. Some of the factors to consider include the following:

1. Appropriateness—are the methods and procedures employed by the analyst the best to measure the reaction of the marketplace? Are the methods and pro-

cedures appropriate in light of (*a*) the definition of value sought? (*b*) the legal bundle of ownership interests appraised? (*c*) the limiting conditions (if any) imposed?

2. Logic—are the techniques applied logically? Do they lead to meaningful conclusions related to the expected purpose and use of the appraisal?

3. Consistency—are the techniques employed consistently? Do they use reasonable and consistent amounts of data? Is rounding employed consistently throughout the appraisal?

The analyst continues by checking for simple arithmetic accuracy. In this regard, there are two simple suggestions:

First, check for math errors yourself

Second, have someone else check your math

Prior to reaching the final value estimate, the analyst should conduct a simple review of the overall presentation of the analysis prepared so far. This review of the presentation will:

1. Check the spelling and grammar of the analysis

2. Check the neatness of the presentation (it does count!)

3. Check the overall completeness and readability of thinking, reporting, and presentation—the bases for the client's impression of the analyst's acuity and of the validity of the value conclusions

RELATIONSHIP OF THE REVIEW PHASE TO THE VALUATION PROCESS

The considerations and calculations in each valuation approach must be consistent with the purpose and use of the appraisal. Likewise, the data used and the assumptions made must be consistent in all parts of the valuation process.

The definition of the appraised value and its relation to each step in the valuation process should be reexamined in the reconciliation process. The relationship between non-arm's-length arrangements and atypical market conditions—either for the guideline practice transactions analyzed or for any proposed subject practice transaction—should be reconciled and explained in relation to the final value estimate.

RECONCILIATION CRITERIA

The analyst weighs the relative significance, applicability, and defensibility of each value indication and relies most heavily on the valuation approach most appropriate to the nature of the particular accounting practice appraisal. Some of the criteria to use in this reconciliation of the various valuation approaches are listed below.

Appropriateness

1. Weigh the strengths and weaknesses of each valuation approach as it applies to the particular accounting practice subject to appraisal.
   - Market approach—applicable to all mature accounting practices providing that there are adequate transactional data available
   - Asset-based approach—works well when the analyst can identify and quantify the value of the subject accounting practice's intangible assets
   - Income approach—may be utilized when reliable financial projections are available
2. Use the criteria of appropriateness to judge the relevance of each comparable accounting practice transaction analyzed and each significant valuation adjustment made.

Accuracy

The accuracy of an estimate is measured by the analyst's confidence in the reliability of the data, in the calculations of each valuation approach, and in the adjustments made to the guideline or comparable transactions. To this end, the guideline or comparable transaction adjusted values are examined for:

1. The number of adjustments
2. The net adjustments
3. The gross adjustments

Quality and Quantity of Evidence

Appropriateness and accuracy affect the quality of the market evidence used in the appraisal. Both factors must also be studied in relation to the quantity of market evidence used in the appraisal.

FINAL VALUE ESTIMATE

Either of the following types of final value estimates may be appropriate, given the purpose and objective of the accounting practice valuation:

1. A point estimate, the single figure typically used to state the accounting practice final value estimate
2. A range of value, within which the accounting practice indicated value is said to fall—reported either as the sole conclusion of value or in conjunction with a point estimate

A range of values may provide useful additional information to help a client reach an investment or other business decision, and it is intrinsic to the analyst's reasoning process, anyway.

VALUATION CONCLUSION

The final estimate should generally be a number within the final range of values indicated by the various valuation approaches used in the analysis. The final value estimate may be one of those indicated values, the result of the valuation approach relied on most heavily, or another number within the indicated range.

It is generally inappropriate simply to average in order to arrive at a final value estimate. A simple arithmetic mean implies that all of the valuation approaches have equal validity and equal weight; this is usually not the case. The final value conclusion for the subject accounting practice should be derived from the analyst's best judgment of all of the factors considered and from the impartial weighing of the market evidence.

PRESENTATION OF VALUATION CONCLUSION

The final factors to consider in the presentation of the valuation conclusion are discussed below.

Probability Range

An analyst may report a probability range to suggest the confidence level associated with the concluded value estimate. For example, different capitalization rates may be applied to an estimated economic income stream to suggest projected accounting practice values under different scenarios.

Rounding

All final estimates are opinions, albeit impartial, expert, and well reasoned. Analysts do not wish to impute to the value estimate a degree of precision that it does not and cannot possess. Therefore, all final value opinions should be rounded appropriately according to the magnitude of the numbers and the degree of confidence associated with the opinion.

1. Generally, rounding should occur at the end of each valuation approach.
2. Rounding should reflect the number of significant digits implicit in the observed market transaction pricing.
3. Value estimates may be rounded up or down, depending upon the degree of conservatism that is appropriate.

SUMMARY

The final accounting practice value estimate is ultimately based upon the experience and judgment of the analyst. However, the valuation process should be presented in such a way as to lead the reader to the same value estimate conclusion reached by the analyst. Accordingly, all qualitative and quantitative data and analyses should be presented in the appraisal, and all judgments and thought processes should be documented. In this way the reader of the accounting practice appraisal should be able to understand—and recreate—exactly how the analyst reached the final valuation conclusion.

12

ACCOUNTING PRACTICE VALUATION REPORTING STANDARDS

This chapter will present the following topics related to the preparation and issuance of accounting practice valuation reports:

1. An overview of the appraisal reporting process
2. USPAP appraisal reporting standards
3. The form, format, and content of various common types of appraisal reports, as categorized by USPAP
4. The documentation and retention requirements of USPAP
5. The confidentiality requirements of USPAP

DEFINITION OF THE APPRAISAL REPORT

An appraisal report is broadly defined to be any communication, written or oral, of an appraisal. This definition encompasses the document transmitted to the client upon completion of an appraisal assignment. An appraisal report should lead the reader from the definition of the appraisal problem through the analysis and the relevant descriptive data to a specific value conclusion.

The length, type, and content of accounting practice appraisal reports may be dictated by

1. The client
2. Regulatory requirements
3. The courts
4. The type of accounting practice ownership interest being appraised
5. The nature of the appraisal problem

APPRAISAL REPORTING STANDARDS

The *Uniform Standards of Professional Appraisal Practice* dictates minimum standards to be applied in all types of appraisal reports. USPAP states that each written or oral appraisal report must

1. Clearly and accurately set forth the appraisal in a manner that will not be misleading
2. Contain sufficient information to enable the person(s) who receive or rely on the report to understand it properly
3. Clearly and accurately disclose any extraordinary assumption or limiting condition that directly affects the appraisal, and indicate its impact on the concluded value

Written Appraisal Report Standards

In accounting practice valuations, USPAP also requires that each written appraisal report must

1. Identify and describe the practice and the practice ownership interest being appraised
2. Identify the bundle of legal rights being appraised
3. State the purpose of the appraisal
4. Define the type of value to be estimated
5. Set forth the effective date of the appraisal and the date of the report
6. Describe the extent of the process of collecting, confirming, and reporting data
7. Set forth all assumptions and limiting conditions that affect the analyses, opinions, and conclusions
8. Set forth the information considered, the appraisal procedures followed, and the reasoning that supports the analyses, opinions, and conclusions
9. Set forth the appraiser's opinion of the highest and best use of the practice ownership interest being appraised when such an opinion is necessary and appropriate
10. Explain and support the exclusion of any of the usual valuation approaches
11. Set forth any additional information that may be appropriate to show compliance with, or clearly identify and explain permitted departure from, the requirements of all USPAP Standards
12. Include a signed certification in accordance with USPAP Standards Rule 2-3

Oral Reports

For accounting practice valuations, USPAP provides the following guidance with regard to the preparation and issuance of an oral appraisal report:

1. An appraiser may make an oral report when the circumstances or the needs of the client do not permit or warrant a written report.
2. Expert testimony in depositions or in court is considered to be an oral report.
3. To the extent that it is possible and appropriate, oral reports *must* address the substantive matters set forth in Standards Rule 2-2.
4. Each oral report should include a description of the subject accounting practice and ownership interest and the facts, assumptions, conditions, and reasoning on which the conclusion is based.
5. After communicating an oral report, the appraiser should keep on file all notes and data relating to the assignment and a complete memorandum on the analysis, conclusion, and opinion.

Limited Reports

For accounting practice valuations, USPAP also provides the following guidance with regard to the preparation and the issuance of a limited appraisal report:

1. Sometimes, by prior agreement with the client, an appraiser submits the results of the accounting practice appraisal in a limited report.
2. Although these reports are abbreviated, they still must conform in all respects to the *Uniform Standards of Professional Appraisal Practice.*
3. The Departure Provision of the USPAP standards specifies which elements of the appraisal report may be omitted under certain circumstances.
4. Other elements of the appraisal report are binding requirements and may not be omitted.
5. The most common types of limited appraisal reports are
   a. Letter reports
   b. Form reports

Letter Reports

USPAP considers a letter report to be a type of limited report, and it provides the following guidance:

1. Under the *Uniform Standards of Professional Appraisal Practice,* a letter report must comply with all the reporting requirements.

2. A letter report should indicate that all significant data and other information that support the analyses, opinions, and conclusions in the report have been retained in the appraiser's files.

3. A statement regarding the limited nature of the report must also be included.

4. The client should be informed that many regulatory agencies and third-party users of appraisal reports do not accept letter reports.

Form Reports

USPAP considers a form report to be a type of limited report, and it provides the following guidance:

1. Form reports meet the needs of many financial institutions, insurance companies, and government agencies.

2. Form reports must qualify as limited reports under the conditions set forth in USPAP.

3. Some forms may not conform to the USPAP reporting standards and, then, additional material must be included.

4. Certain forms do not contain a certification statement that complies with these standards and, therefore, supplementary material must be added.

5. A form appraisal report is unacceptable if the appraiser fails to

   a. Consider the purpose of the report, the value definition, and the assumptions and conditions inherent in the report

   b. Question the client about any engagement criteria that conflict with proper appraisal practice

   c. Review the report before signing it

Narrative Reports

Narrative valuation reports are the most complete type of appraisal report. They reflect the appraiser's ability to interpret relevant data and select valuation methods and procedures appropriate for estimating a specifically defined value.

The appraiser should bear in mind that the narrative valuation report is his or her representative, and the quality and presentation of the report will reflect on the appraiser's competence and reputation. The presentation of narrative valuation reports will be better if

1. The paper, cover, and binding are of good quality

2. The report is professionally typed and printed

3. Graphics and charts are carefully prepared

4. Illustrations have been placed on pages facing the material being discussed
5. The contents are designed for maximum communication
6. The sections are clearly labeled and identified in the table of contents
7. Superfluous material has been eliminated
8. The writing is clear and easy to read
9. Technical jargon and slang are avoided

ELEMENTS OF THE APPRAISAL

Every narrative valuation report of an accounting practice appraisal should explicitly address the following topics:

1. The contingent and limiting conditions
2. The purpose and use of the appraisal
3. The definition of value estimated
4. The date of the value estimate and the date of the valuation report
5. The accounting practice ownership rights being appraised
6. The scope of the appraisal—that is, the extent of the process of collecting, confirming, and reporting of data; the scope of the appraisal will vary according to the nature of the accounting practice ownership interest being appraised.

RETENTION OF APPRAISAL REPORTS AND FILES

The record-keeping section of the Ethics Provision of USPAP states:

An appraiser must prepare written records of appraisal, review, and consulting assignments—including oral testimony and reports—and retain such records for a period of at least five (5) years after preparation or at least two (2) years after final disposition of any judicial proceeding in which testimony was given, whichever period expires last. The written records of the assignment are the workfile.[1]

1. Written records include true copies of written reports, written summaries of oral testimony and reports, and all data required by the USPAP Standards.

[1]*Uniform Standards of Professional Appraisal Practice* (Washington, DC: The Appraisal Foundation, 1996), 3.

2. Written records also include information stored on electronic or magnetic files.
3. All supporting notes, documentation, and file memorandums should likewise be retained.

USPAP CONFIDENTIALITY PROVISIONS

The confidentiality section of the Ethics Provision of USPAP addresses the privileged nature of the appraiser-client relationship. It states:

> An appraiser must not disclose confidential factual data obtained from a client or the results of an assignment prepared for a client to anyone other than, (1) the client and persons specifically authorized by the client, (2) such third parties as may be authorized by due process of law, and (3) a duly authorized professional peer review committee.[2]

SUMMARY

When all is said and done, the appraisal report is the final product of the accounting practice valuation process. It must convince the reader of the quality, completeness, and accuracy of the valuation analyses and of the reasonableness of the valuation conclusions.

The *Uniform Standards of Professional Appraisal Practice* provides significant guidance for accounting practice valuation reporting standards. Appraisers should be familiar with these standards, with regard both to the form and content of appraisal reports and to work paper files and confidentiality requirements. The title page and table of contents of the 1996 edition of USPAP are included in Appendix E.

[2]Ibid.

13

EXAMPLE OF AN ACCOUNTING PRACTICE VALUATION

The illustrative example of Stall, DeLay, & Hindre, CPAs, is a case contrived to illustrate the application of some commonly used accounting practice valuation methods and procedures. It is not based upon an actual accounting practice. Rather, this hypothetical example synthesizes and abstracts characteristics of many small accounting practices that the authors have analyzed over the years.

The objective of this example is to show one possible way of valuing an accounting practice and then organizing and presenting the accounting practice valuation in a written appraisal report.

DESCRIPTION OF THE ASSIGNMENT

We were retained by the three partners to provide our opinion of the fair market value of their collective 100 percent equity interest in the accounting firm partnership known as Stall, DeLay & Hindre, CPAs (SD&H). This practice has been approached by a large national firm to see if the three partners want either to sell or to merge their practice.

Since we are considering a possible sale, we will value a marketable, controlling interest in SD&H in fee simple interest. Further, we will value the subject 100 percent ownership interest under the premise of value in continued use, as a going-concern business enterprise. In our opinion, this valuation premise represents the highest and best use of the subject ownership interest.

The objective of the appraisal is to estimate the fair market value of a 100 percent equity interest in Stall, DeLay & Hindre, CPAs, as of December 31, 1996. The purpose of the appraisal is to provide an independent valuation opinion to assist the practice equityholders in their evaluation of an offer price to buy their practice.

DESCRIPTION OF THE PRACTICE

Stall, DeLay & Hindre is an accounting and tax consulting partnership located in Farout, Montana. There are three general partners of the firm, with Mr. Stall owning a 60 percent interest and the other two name partners each holding a 20 percent interest.

Mr. Stall started the firm in 1973 as a sole practitioner. Messrs. DeLay and Hindre both joined the firm in 1985. In 1991 Messrs. DeLay and Hindre were promoted and became equity owners. Based upon our investigation, the event that provided Messrs. DeLay and Hindre with equity ownership is not considered to represent a fair market value transaction.

Currently, all three partners work a 40-hour week, on average, with peak time being put in during the normal tax season. This level of effort is down from Mr. Stall's previous weekly rate of between 60 to 80 hours five years ago. All three partners have an established network of contacts in the local business community.

Because of its regional location, SD&H provides most of its tax and related accounting and advisory services to the gas and oil industry. In addition to at least one Big Six accounting firm and three other regional firms, SD&H competes with approximately 50 other local accounting practices similar in size. Thus, competition for accounting and tax services in the firm's local service area is significant.

Historically, the practice has been supported by a concentration of services in the tax area. For the calendar year ended December 31, 1996, approximately 75 percent of the firm's revenues were attributable to tax-related services, with over 60 percent of these services resulting from services performed for individual taxpayers. For the same period, approximately 10 percent of the calendar year's revenues were attributable to audit services, and approximately 12 percent were attributable to corporate compilation and bookkeeping services.

Accounting firms that derive a larger proportion of their revenue from audit services tend to fall in the higher end of the range of transaction-based valuation pricing multiples because audit revenue is usually seen as being more predictably cyclic than tax services. Since most SD&H revenues are attributable to services more vulnerable to competition, more risk is associated with its revenue stream than would be with revenues generated by audit-related services.

SOURCES OF INFORMATION

In preparing this appraisal report, we have reviewed the following documents:

1. Annual compiled financial statements prepared internally by SD&H for the fiscal years ending December 31, 1992, through December 31, 1996
2. Federal income tax returns for the partnership for the same period

3. Federal individual income tax returns for all three partners for the years 1991 through 1995

4. A copy of the lease agreement between the partnership and Professional Accounting Building, Inc., for the space that houses the subject firm

5. Depreciation schedules for furniture, fixtures, and equipment owned by the accounting practice

6. The partnership agreement, including all modifications up to the valuation date

7. A schedule of the workforce in place, including historical billing activity per professional

8. A summary of client relationships, emphasizing the 100 top clients, by fees, over the previous five years and including a brief description of the work paper files for each

Mr. Peter Prann, our associate, toured the offices of the subject accounting practice and interviewed each partner as well as the firm's controller. For economic data we used *Greater Farout Economic Profile* and *Business Profile,* both published by the Farout Area Commerce and Trade Organization; *Regional Economic Update for Farout,* published by Third National Bank; and information from the *Montana Business Quarterly.*

Summaries of the financial statements for SD&H covering calendar years 1992 through 1996 are presented in Exhibits 13.1 and 13.2.

AREA ECONOMIC PROFILE

For the third year in a row, Montana's economy has increased. During the 1980s, the state experienced short periods of economic stability or even slight growth, but this trend reversed as the 1990s began.

In 1995 Montana's nonfarm labor income increased 1.7 percent, compared to a decline in the comparable measure for the United States as a whole. While the data are not final yet, 1996 looks even better at 5.1 percent growth for Montana's nonfarm labor income versus 3.0 percent for the United States. However, once the negative impacts of 1996 mine closures and wood products industry cutbacks have been tallied, Montana's overall growth rate for the year is expected to drop to 1.2 percent, according to *Montana Business Quarterly.*

In Farout, Montana, local economic conditions have improved in the 1990s as well. Nonfarm labor income began outpacing total basic labor income in 1995, the result of Farout's boom in construction, health care, and business services, industries traditionally considered derivative rather than basic. The *Montana Business Quarterly* expects real economic growth of 1 percent per year for Farout between 1997 and 1999.

STALL, DELAY & HINDRE, CPAS
COMMON-SIZE BALANCE SHEETS

	As of December 31					As of December 31				
	1996 ($)	1995 ($)	1994 ($)	1993 ($)	1992 ($)	1996 (%)	1995 (%)	1994 (%)	1993 (%)	1992 (%)
ASSETS										
Current Assets										
Cash & cash equivalents	10,000	9,000	8,000	7,000	6,000	1.9	1.9	1.9	1.8	1.7
Client accts. receivable	240,000	216,000	194,000	175,000	158,000	45.3	45.3	45.3	45.5	45.7
Work in progress	120,000	108,000	97,000	87,000	78,000	22.6	22.6	22.7	22.6	22.5
Prepaid expenses	40,000	36,000	32,000	29,000	26,000	7.5	7.5	7.5	7.5	7.5
Total Current Assets	410,000	369,000	331,000	298,000	268,000	77.4	77.4	77.3	77.4	77.5
Fixed Assets, Cost										
Furniture & fixtures	120,000	108,000	97,000	87,000	78,000	22.6	22.6	22.7	22.6	22.5
Computer equipment	60,000	54,000	49,000	44,000	40,000	11.3	11.3	11.4	11.4	11.6
Leasehold improvements	40,000	36,000	32,000	29,000	26,000	7.5	7.5	7.5	7.5	7.5
Net Fixed Assets	220,000	198,000	178,000	160,000	144,000	41.5	41.5	41.6	41.6	41.6
Accum. depreciation	(100,000)	(90,000)	(81,000)	(73,000)	(66,000)	(18.9)	(18.9)	(18.9)	(19.0)	(19.1)
Total Fixed Assets, Net	120,000	108,000	97,000	87,000	78,000	22.6	22.6	22.7	22.6	22.5

(continued)

Exhibit 13.1. Summary of Common-Size Balance Sheets for Stall, Delay & Hindre, CPAs, 1992 through 1996.

STALL, DELAY & HINDRE, CPAS
COMMON-SIZE BALANCE SHEETS

| | As of December 31 | | | | | As of December 31 | | | | |
	1996 ($)	1995 ($)	1994 ($)	1993 ($)	1992 ($)	1996 (%)	1995 (%)	1994 (%)	1993 (%)	1992 (%)
Other Assets										
Leasehold Interest	—	—	—	—	—	—	—	—	—	—
Trained and assembled workforce	—	—	—	—	—	—	—	—	—	—
Client work papers	—	—	—	—	—	—	—	—	—	—
Client relationships	—	—	—	—	—	—	—	—	—	—
Goodwill	—	—	—	—	—	—	—	—	—	—
Accumulated amortization	—	—	—	—	—	—	—	—	—	—
Total Other Assets	—	—	—	—	—	—	—	—	—	—
Total Assets	530,000	477,000	428,000	385,000	346,000	100.0	100.0	100.0	100.0	100.0

(continued)

Exhibit 13.1. *(continued)*

STALL, DELAY & HINDRE, CPAS
COMMON-SIZE BALANCE SHEETS

	As of December 31					As of December 31				
	1996 ($)	1995 ($)	1994 ($)	1993 ($)	1992 ($)	1996 (%)	1995 (%)	1994 (%)	1993 (%)	1992 (%)
LIABILITIES AND EQUITY										
Current Liabilities										
Notes payable	40,000	35,000	31,000	28,000	25,000	7.5	7.3	7.3	7.3	7.2
Contracts payable	20,000	18,000	16,000	14,000	13,000	3.8	3.8	3.7	3.6	3.8
Accounts payable	25,000	23,000	21,000	19,000	17,000	4.7	4.8	4.9	4.9	4.9
Salaries payable	10,000	9,000	8,000	7,000	6,000	1.9	1.9	1.9	1.8	1.7
Accrued liabilities	25,000	23,000	21,000	19,000	17,000	4.7	4.8	4.9	4.9	4.9
Total Current Liabilities	120,000	108,000	97,000	87,000	78,000	22.6	22.6	22.7	22.5	22.5
Partners' Capital	410,000	369,000	331,000	298,000	268,000	77.4	77.4	77.3	77.5	77.5
TOTAL LIABILITIES AND EQUITY	530,000	477,000	428,000	385,000	346,000	100.0	100.0	100.0	100.0	100.0

Source: Internally prepared financial statements.

Exhibit 13.1. *(continued)*

STALL, DELAY & HINDRE, CPAS
COMMON-SIZE INCOME STATEMENTS

	Fiscal Years Ending December 31					Fiscal Years Ending December 31				
	1996 ($)	1995 ($)	1994 ($)	1993 ($)	1992 ($)	1996 (%)	1995 (%)	1994 (%)	1993 (%)	1992 (%)
Client Revenues	1,250,000	1,125,000	1,013,000	912,000	821,000	100.0	100.0	100.0	100.0	100.0
Operating Expenses										
Partners' salaries	350,000	315,000	284,000	256,000	230,000	28.0	28.0	28.0	28.1	28.0
Associates' salaries	250,000	225,000	203,000	183,000	165,000	20.0	20.0	20.0	20.0	20.1
Staff salaries	80,000	72,000	65,000	59,000	53,000	6.4	6.4	6.4	6.4	6.5
Taxes & insurance	150,000	135,000	122,000	110,000	99,000	12.0	12.0	12.0	12.0	12.1
Depr. & amort.	15,000	14,000	13,000	12,000	11,000	1.2	1.2	1.3	1.3	1.3
Rents	80,000	72,000	65,000	59,000	53,000	6.4	6.4	6.4	6.4	6.5
Office expenses	25,000	23,000	21,000	19,000	17,000	2.0	2.0	2.1	2.1	2.1
Other misc. expenses	25,000	23,000	21,000	19,000	17,000	2.0	2.0	2.1	2.1	2.1
Total Operating Expenses	975,000	879,000	794,000	717,000	645,000	78.0	78.1	78.4	78.6	78.6
Pretax Income	275,000	246,000	219,000	195,000	176,000	22.0	21.9	21.6	21.4	21.4

Source: Internally prepared financial statements.

Exhibit 13.2. Summary of Common-Size Income Statements for Stall, Delay & Hindre, CPAs, 1992 through 1996.

185

ACCOUNTING INDUSTRY PROFILE

The Department of Labor projects a 60 percent increase in jobs within the accounting industry by the year 2005. This would reverse the recent trend of accounting staff reductions.

The "urge to merge" in the accounting industry has, at least temporarily, subsided. Conflicts of interests and the seemingly constant announcements about accountant professional liability have cooled the recent merger fever. Limited liability partnerships and limited liability corporations may solve the profession's current litigation problem.

Larger education commitments are required of incoming accounting professionals. The quality and availability of future accountants and the ultimate threat of litigation are the two major hazards facing the accounting industry.

Industry specialization and service line specialization are expected to be the dominant trends in the profession for the foreseeable future.

VALUATION METHODOLOGY

We considered all three generally accepted approaches to accounting practice valuation.

Market Approach

In using this valuation approach, we analyzed the SD&H practice by service line in order to choose the comparability criteria we would use to select a sample database of guideline practice sale transactions and valuation pricing multiples.

Income Approach

Under this valuation approach, the value of the subject accounting practice is estimated as the present value of the economic income expected to be generated by the practice and distributed to the equityholders of the firm over the next five years. For this purpose, economic income is considered to be net operating income less depreciation, less net working capital requirements, less incremental investments in capital expenditures. Our valuation model includes an estimate of the labor expense for the partners—as if they were employees of the firm—without including partner profit distributions.

The valuation analysis is performed on a pretax basis because the partnership itself is not a taxpayer. To calculate the prospective economic income we took the revenues we expected the practice to generate between 1997 and 2002 and added to this number the residual value of the practice at the end of this discrete projection period. In this analysis we concluded that the appropriate present value discount rate is the pretax cost of equity capital for the subject practice because the partnership has no outstanding long-term debt.

Asset-Based Approach

In this approach the value of the subject accounting practice is estimated to be the fair market value of all of the firm's assets less the current value of all of its liabilities. In using this valuation approach, a fair market value–based balance sheet is prepared instead of a GAAP-based historical cost balance sheet. In the case of SD&H, we identified and appraised the following intangible assets, leasehold interest, a trained and assembled workforce, client work paper files, client relationships, and goodwill.

After considering these three valuation approaches and applying our experience and professional judgment, we synthesized the indications of value into a final value conclusion for SD&H.

VALUATION PROCEDURES

After executing an engagement agreement, we developed a detailed engagement work plan that included a request of the client for information and task assignments for the appraisal team members. We researched accounting industry trends and conditions and local economic factors and conditions that affect SD&H.

The firm's historical financial performance was summarized. We analyzed their historical trends and prepared common-size statements. Financial and operational ratios were calculated. With the assistance of the accounting firm's management, prospective financial projections were prepared.

We then applied the three traditional accounting practice valuation approaches.

Market Approach

Relevant valuation pricing multiples were derived from an analysis of transactions involving accounting practices with characteristics similar to SD&H. The practice sale transactions identified and relied upon are all mature accounting practices with a focus on tax services. These practices are similar to the SD&H practice, and each guideline market transaction closed (was consummated) within a reasonably recent period of time. This market approach valuation analysis is summarized in Exhibit 13.3.

The indicated value using this valuation approach is $1,100,000.

STALL, DELAY & HINDRE, CPAS
MARKET APPROACH
FAIR MARKET VALUE AS OF DECEMBER 31, 1996

Guideline Practice Sale Transactional Data

Guideline Market Transactions	Confirmed Sale Price	Guideline Practice		Indicated Transactional Pricing Multiples	
		Last Year Revenues	Last Year Pretax Income	Price/ Revenues	Price/ Pretax Income
1. Sole proprietor CPA practice in Deadwood, Montana, sold in July 1996—practice is principally personal tax and write-up work	$ 300,000	$ 360,000	$ 75,000	0.83 times	4.0 times
2. Sale of three-partner CPA practice in Nowhere, Montana, sold in August 1996—practice is principally commercial tax work	1,000,000	1,100,000	250,000	0.91 times	4.0 times
3. Sale of two-partner CPA practice in Leftbehind, Montana, sold in December 1996—practice is 50% (nonaudit) accounting and 50% personal and commercial tax work	650,000	700,000	160,000	0.93 times	4.1 times
Indicated Valuation Multiples: Mean				0.89 times	4.0 times
Median				0.91 times	4.0 times

(continued)

Exhibit 13.3. Summary of Market Approach Valuation Analysis for Stall, Delay & Hindre, CPAs.

STALL, DELAY & HINDRE, CPAS
MARKET APPROACH
FAIR MARKET VALUE AS OF DECEMBER 31, 1996

Analysis of the Subject Practice

Stall, Delay & Hindre, CPAs	Market Approach Valuation Analysis	
	Last Year Revenues	Last Year Pretax Income
Subject Practice Financial Fundamentals	$1,250,000	$ 275,000
Selected Market-Derived Valuation Pricing Multiples	.90 times	4.0 times
Indications of Value	1,125,000	1,100,000
Overall Indication of Value (Rounded)	$1,100,000	

Exhibit 13.3. *(continued)*

189

Income Approach

Our projection of economic income was prepared based upon our interviews with the management of SD&H, on our analysis of the historical results of the firm's operations, and on our analysis of the local competitive environment for accounting practices. Economic income is presented on a pretax basis, and we used a pretax present value discount factor.

Our projection of economic income took into consideration a hypothetical salary expense for the partners and thus only measures the partners' ownership interest. This income valuation approach analysis is summarized on Exhibit 13.4.

The indicated value using this valuation approach is $1,300,000.

STALL, DELAY & HINDRE, CPAS
INCOME APPROACH
FAIR MARKET VALUE AS OF DECEMBER 31, 1996

| Economic Income | (in $000s) | | | | | Residual |
Projection Variable	Year 1	Year 2	Year 3	Year 4	Year 5	Value
Total Net Client Revenues	1,400	1,500	1,600	1,700	1,800	
Pretax Income	280	300	320	340	360	
Less: increase in net working capital	20	30	40	50	50	
Less: increase in capital expenditures	30	30	30	40	40	
Plus: depreciation expenses	16	18	20	22	26	
Equals: net cash flow (pretax)	246	258	270	272	296	1,184
Times: present value discount factor (at 20% present value discount rate)	0.909	0.757	0.631	0.526	0.438	0.402
Present value of net cash flow	224	195	170	143	130	476
Total present value of net cash flow	1,338					
Indicated fair market value (rounded)	1,300					

Exhibit 13.4.   Summary of Income Approach Valuation Analysis for Stall, Delay & Hindre, CPAs.

Asset-Based Approach

The fair market value of financial assets is typically the same as their net realizable value. To analyze the fixed assets of SD&H, we reviewed and relied upon an appraisal of the furniture, fixtures, equipment, and leasehold improvements conducted by the Hokum Appraisal Company.

Identifying and valuing the intangible assets of a subject accounting practice is a complex procedure. Intangible assets are generally created by the owners of the accounting practice and are not recorded on the historical-cost-based balance sheet.

The value of the leasehold interest is the present value of the advantageous rent situation, because SD&H has a contract rent for the next five years that is $6 per square foot below the prevailing market rental rate for similar professional office space. The leasehold interest is presented in Exhibit 13.5.

The trained and assembled workforce of SD&H was valued by consideration of the costs a hypothetical willing buyer would incur to recruit, hire, and train a workforce of comparable experience and expertise. An analysis of the fair market value of the SD&H workforce is given as Exhibit 13.6.

The client work paper files were valued using a similar cost avoidance method. In this case, we estimated the cost to recreate the work paper files for recurring audit, bookkeeping, and tax clients (see Exhibit 13.7). Since clients normally return to the same accounting firm, their historical and permanent accounting and tax files are

---

STALL, DELAY & HINDRE, CPAS
LEASEHOLD INTEREST
FAIR MARKET VALUE AS OF DECEMBER 31, 1996

Net size of leased office space	6,000 square feet
Current market rent for comparable space	$ 18.00 per square foot
Current contract rent	$ 12.00 per square foot
Favorable leasehold advantage per square foot (#2 − #3)	$ 6.00 per square foot
Total annual favorable leasehold advantage (#4 × #1)	$36,000
Number of years remaining in lease term	5.0 years
Appropriate before-tax present value discount rate	20.0%
Present value of annuity factor at 20% for 5 years	2.99
Present value of favorable leasehold advantage (#8 × #5)	$107,640
Fair market value of leasehold interest (rounded)	$110,000

Exhibit 13.5. Estimate of Present Value of Stall, Delay & Hindre's Five-Year Lease on Office Space.

STALL, DELAY & HINDRE, CPAS
TRAINED AND ASSEMBLED WORKFORCE
FAIR MARKET VALUE AS OF DECEMBER 31, 1996

| Category of Employee | Total Annual Compensation ($) | Percent of Annual Compensation to | | | | Replace-ment Cost ($) |
		Recruit (%)	Hire (%)	Train (%)	Total (%)	
Professional Staff	250,000	10	10	30	50	125,000
Paraprofessional Staff	40,000	10	—	20	30	12,000
Support Staff	40,000	10	—	10	20	8,000
Total Cost to Recruit, Hire, & Train Replacement Workforce						$145,000
Fair Market Value of Trained and Assembled Workforce (Rounded)						$150,000

Exhibit 13.6.   Estimate of Present Value of Stall, Delay & Hindre's Workforce.

STALL, DELAY & HINDRE, CPAS
CLIENT WORK PAPER FILES
FAIR MARKET VALUE AS OF DECEMBER 31, 1996

Type of Client	Number of Clients	Hours to Recreate Permanent File	Cost Per Hour ($)	Cost to Recreate Each Client File ($)	Cost to Recreate All Client Files ($)
Recurring Audit	30	10.0	40.00	400	12,000
Recurring Bookkeeping	60	5.0	30.00	150	9,000
Recurring Tax—Corporate	100	2.0	30.00	60	6,000
Recurring Tax—Individual	200	1.0	20.00	20	4,000
Total Cost to Recreate Client Work Paper Files					$31,000
Fair Market Value of Client Work Paper Files (Rounded)					$30,000

Exhibit 13.7.   Estimate of Present Value of Stall, Delay & Hindre's Work Paper Files for Recurring Clients.

valued using an estimate of the hours required to recreate the permanent file times the cost per hour of using professional staff and clerical workers to recreate them.

To estimate the value of the client relationships we first analyzed the firm's historical client turnover; and found that client relationships have historically lasted five years. With that figure we were able to estimate the average remaining life of existing client relationships and the projected net income from the current clients and their contribution margin (note that future clients are associated with the practice goodwill). Exhibit 13.8 shows how further adjustments were made to these figures. Net earnings were converted into a projection of economic income after adjusting for the net financial assets (working capital) attributable to the increase in net client fees.

The net earnings from the client relationships was reduced by a fair return on all of the assets employed in the service of these clients. Finally, we estimated the present value of the economic income over the expected remaining life of the client rela-

---

STALL, DELAY & HINDRE, CPAS
CLIENT RELATIONSHIPS
FAIR MARKET VALUE AS OF DECEMBER 31, 1996

(in $000s)

Projection Variable		Year 1	Year 2	Year 3	Year 4	Year 5
Net Client Revenues (from Current Clients Only)		1,313	1,378	1,447	1,519	1,595
×	Contribution margin	20.0%	20.0%	20.0%	20.0%	20.0%
=	Contribution	263	276	289	304	319
−	Increase in net financial assets	10	11	11	12	12
−	Return on assets employed	142	142	142	142	142
=	Economic income	111	123	136	150	165
×	Present value factor at 20% present value discount rate (mid-year convention)	0.909	0.757	0.631	0.526	0.438
=	Present value of economic income	100	93	86	79	72
	Total present value of economic income					431
	Fair Market Value of Client Relationships (Rounded)					$430

Exhibit 13.8. Estimate of Present Value of Stall, Delay & Hindre's Client Relationships as Projected for Five Years.

tionships. The present value of the projected economic income represents the value of the recurring client relationships to SD&H.

As shown in Exhibit 13.9, the value of the goodwill of the practice was estimated by applying a capitalized excess earnings method. First, we calculated the fair market value of the net assets of the practice (i.e., total identified tangible and intangible asset value less current value of liabilities). Next, we estimated a fair return on the practice net assets by applying the firm-specific weighted-average return on capital to the net assets of the subject practice.

The excess income is the difference between the actual net income and the calculated fair return on net assets. We capitalized the excess income as annuity in perpetuity, using the firm-specific present value discount rate. The capitalized excess income represents the intangible value in the nature of goodwill of SD&H.

Under the asset-based approach, the fair market value of the equity of the subject accounting firm is equal to the difference between the fair market value of the firm's assets less the current value of the firm's liabilities. This asset-based approach valuation analysis is summarized in Exhibit 13.10.

The indicated value using this valuation approach is $1,200,000.

STALL, DELAY & HINDRE, CPAS
INTANGIBLE VALUE IN THE NATURE OF GOODWILL
FAIR MARKET VALUE AS OF DECEMBER 31, 1996

Fair Market Value of Identified Assets	
Financial assets	$410,000
Tangible real and personal property	170,000
Intangible assets (excluding goodwill)	720,000
Total (Rounded)	1,300,000
− Total current value of short-term liabilities	120,000
= Net fair market value of identified assets	1,180,000
× Present value discount rate	× 20%
= Fair return on net assets	236,000
Net Income	240,000
Excess Earnings (i.e., Actual Net Income Less Fair Return on Net Assets)	$4,000
Capitalized as an Annuity in Perpetuity (at 20% capitalization rate)	× 5.00
Fair Market Value of the Intangible Value in the Nature of Goodwill	$20,000

Exhibit 13.9.   Estimate of Present Value of Stall, Delay & Hindre's Intangible Value in the Nature of Goodwill Using a Capitalized Excess Earnings Method.

STALL, DELAY & HINDRE, CPAS
ASSET-BASED APPROACH
FAIR MARKET VALUE AS OF DECEMBER 31, 1996

	At Historical Cost	At Fair Market Value
ASSETS		
Current Assets		
Cash & cash equivalents	$10,000	$10,000
Client accounts receivable	240,000	240,000
Work-in-progress	120,000	120,000
Prepaid expenses	40,000	40,000
Total Current Assets	410,000	410,000
Fixed Assets		
Furniture & fixtures	120,000	100,000
Computer equipment	60,000	40,000
Leasehold improvements	40,000	30,000
Gross Fixed Assets	220,000	170,000
Less: accumulated depreciation	(100,000)	
Total Fixed Assets, Net	120,000	170,000
Intangible Assets		
Leasehold interest (see Exhibit 13-5)	—	110,000
Trained & assembled workforce (see Exhibit 13-6)	—	150,000
Client work paper files (see Exhibit 13-7)	—	30,000
Client relationships (see Exhibit 13-8)	—	430,000
Intangible value in the nature of goodwill (see Exhibit 13-9)	—	20,000
Total Intangible Assets	—	740,000
TOTAL ASSETS	$530,000	$1,320,000
LIABILITIES AND OWNERS' EQUITY		
Current Liabilities		
Notes payable	40,000	40,000
Contracts payable	20,000	20,000
Accounts payable	25,000	25,000
Salaries payable	10,000	10,000
Accrued liabilities	25,000	25,000
Total Current Liabilities	120,000	120,000
Partners' Capital	410,000	1,200,000
TOTAL LIABILITIES AND OWNER'S EQUITY	$530,000	$1,320,000

Exhibit 13.10. Summary of Asset-Based Approach Valuation Analysis for Stall, Delay & Hindre, CPAs.

VALUATION SYNTHESIS AND CONCLUSION

We relied upon the three accounting practice valuation approaches described above to reach our opinion of value. The indicated values from the three valuation approaches are as follows:

Market approach	$1,100,000
Income approach	$1,300,000
Asset-based approach	$1,200,000

To arrive at our final opinion of the fair market value of the subject accounting practice, we assigned slightly greater weight to the market approach and to the asset-based approach. This weighting was based upon our review of the quantity and quality of available data and of our degree of confidence in each valuation analysis in this particular appraisal.

Based upon the valuation procedures described above and in our considered opinion, the fair market value of 100 percent of the owners' equity of Stall, DeLay & Hindre, as of December 31, 1996, is

$1,200,000

14

SPECIAL PRACTICE VALUATION TOPICS

This chapter will discuss the following special topics related to accounting practice valuations:

1. Practice valuation in marital dissolutions
2. Practice valuation in estate planning
3. Valuation of limited liability companies and limited liability partnerships
4. Other special valuation topics

PRACTICE VALUATION IN MARITAL DISSOLUTIONS

Divorce is stressful not only to the accountant experiencing the breakup of his or her marriage but often to the accountant's firm as well. An accountant's ownership interest in a practice typically becomes an element in considerations of the divorcing couple's equitable division of the assets in the marital estate—and in considerations of spousal support.

One distinguishing feature of the valuation of accounting practices (and, indeed, of many professional practices) for divorce purposes is the variation of allowable valuation methods among courts in different states. This variation of allowable valuation methods arises from two major reasons.

First, laws, divorce court ruling precedents, and local custom vary widely from state to state. Judges sometimes vary the emphasis they place on certain valuation issues. As a result, statutes that claim fair market value as the standard of value in equitable divisions may be less pertinent to the actual application of appraisal methods than the views of the court that will be judging the appraiser's work. Unfortunately, very few states provide much detail in their statutes regarding the appropriate standard of value or the acceptable valuation methods to be used to estimate professional practice values in a divorce.

The second and perhaps more important reason for the variation of allowable valuation methods in divorce proceedings is that divorce courts are courts of equity. Each judge is trying to achieve a rough balance of all of the economic interests of the two parties within the broad framework of the laws.

In most states all property acquired during a marriage is presumed to be marital property unless it can clearly be proven by one side or the other to have been owned previous to the marriage or to have been acquired by gift or inheritance.

A critical issue that arises in each state is whether a professional license is personal property or marital property. In some cases, reinvesting partnership income in a partnership interest predating the marriage creates both a marital and a nonmarital component of ownership in that interest. Professionals often have unusual property issues of this type arise during their divorce litigation, including the value of professional degrees, professional licenses, and intellectual property (such as software or books) developed in connection with their professional practice.

In the case of professional accountants, income issues (which may affect both support and alimony) and property issues (which relate to the equitable division of the marital estate) can be intermingled in the valuation of the accounting practice. Valuation practitioners must guard against the continual potential for overlap, double-counting, or duplication of value when both a professional license and professional practice are involved in a determination of support and division of property in divorce.[1]

Another issue commonly seen in marital dissolution appraisals is the necessity to prepare valuations as of multiple dates. Typically, a marital dissolution appraisal may require a valuation of the subject accounting practice ownership interest as of the couple's marriage date (to measure the appreciation of value during the marriage), as of their date of separation, as of the date the divorce action was formally filed, and, lastly, as of the date of the divorce trial.

Because emotions tend to run high between the divorcing parties, appraisers sometimes have to deal with lack of cooperation in obtaining even basic financial data, outright concealment of monies, and the lack of willingness of parties to compromise on reasonable grounds.

PRACTICE VALUATION IN ESTATE PLANNING

The objectives of estate planning for the professional accounting practice are to provide:

- The lowest sustainable fair market value for transfer purposes
- A nondisruptive process to transfer ownership interests from the original equityholder to the logical successor owner(s)

---

[1]For further discussion on this special issue in valuation, see Ronald L. Brown, ed., *Valuing Professional Practices and Licenses: A Guide for the Matrimonial Practitioner,* 2d ed. (Englewood Cliffs, N.J.: Prentice-Hall Law and Business, 1993).

In this special context an appraisal may be needed for

- Buy-sell agreements
- Determination of appropriate life insurance coverage
- Gift values
- Estate tax values, both as of the date of death and as of the alternate value date (i.e., six months after date of death)
- Post–estate tax settlement distributions of the subject business interests to beneficiaries

Requests for estate-planning valuations from professional accounting practices most commonly concern buy-sell agreements. Because of the skilled labor–intensive nature of accounting practices, they typically do not have multiple family members practicing together. For this reason, the buy-sell agreement often functions as the exit vehicle for the accounting practice ownership interest rather than as an estate value minimization device.

Buy-sell agreements can be designed to accomplish the following objectives:

- Identify situations that will trigger the buy-sell agreement—including death, disability, retirement, divorce, and dismissal or other irreconcilable dissension among the owners
- Provide a definitive mechanism to obtain liquidity for a departing equity-holder's ownership interest at a stated and fair provision for estimating the value
- Help the accounting practice continue as a going concern by providing a fair method to fund the buyout of the departing owner's equity interest without unduly disrupting the financial stability of the firm
- Prevent the ownership interest from being sold or transferred to any party not acceptable to the other remaining accounting practice owners
- Set a binding price respected by the Internal Revenue Service for estate, gift and income tax purposes—and by courts for other purposes, such as divorce and fundamental owner disagreement
- Coordinate the personal and business estate and financial planning of the accounting practice owners and of any family members involved in the accounting practice

The most common issues addressed in estate-planning valuations in general, and buy-sell agreements in particular, are the value of fractional interests in relation to the value of entire accounting firms (see Chapter 9).

VALUATION OF LIMITED LIABILITY COMPANIES AND LIMITED LIABILITY PARTNERSHIPS

An emerging issue in accounting practice valuation is the relatively recent phenomenon of new forms of enterprise organization, the limited-liability company (LLC) and the limited-liability partnership (LLP). LLCs first emerged in 1977 in Wyoming, while the LLP first came into being in Texas in 1991. As of this writing, all states with the exception of Vermont and Hawaii have passed LLC-enabling laws, and over 36 states have passed legislation providing for the formation of LLPs.

In the general partnership typical of many accounting practices, all partners' practice and personal assets are exposed to the liabilities created by the actions of any single partner. In the LLC only the practice assets are basically still at risk when another owner is sued for malpractice. In the LLP the partner(s) accused of malpractice still has (or have) personal exposure.

LLCs and LLPs differ in other ways as well. LLP owners retain joint and several liability for ordinary business debts such as lease payments and bank loans. The Internal Revenue Service has issued formal Revenue Ruling positions that treat LLCs as partnerships (provided they meet certain criteria) but as yet has provided only the limited assurance of a Private Letter Ruling to LLPs. Also, because LLPs are so new, most of the 14 states that do not now allow the formation of LLPs also do not yet legally recognize the legitimacy of LLPs formed in other states to practice and retain their liability shield within their borders. On the other hand, LLCs are typically more expensive to set up and to maintain.

In several states the issue of an accounting practice within either an LLC or LLP is moot because professionals such as attorneys and accountants are essentially barred from utilizing such forms of organization. Critics of both LLCs and LLPs for professionals also express the fear that any limitation of joint liability will also limit the energy other owners will put into supervising or, ultimately, defending a partner accused of wrongdoing.

The valuation of LLC and LLP ownership interests depends on the same or similar factors that go into the valuation of a professional corporation for a general or limited partnership:

1. An examination of the associated bundle of rights and obligations that come with an ownership interest is the base for departure.
2. An examination of the business risks and returns is necessary.
3. Baseline values for the net assets (tangible and intangible) and the baseline net income potential of the firm need to be analyzed.

Adjustments for relative lack of control and for relative lack of marketability also will be applied.

The key valuation differences for LLCs and LLPs arise from the increased legal, tax, and business uncertainties associated with these forms of organization, as discussed above. The marketability rules in each state for partnership and incorporated enterprises are relatively well understood. LLCs and LLPs, particularly fractional interests, may not even be marketable until state securities regulators decide which procedures apply to such interests. The additional delay and uncertainty appear to argue for a higher valuation discount for relative lack of marketability.

INTERNATIONAL ISSUES

The accounting profession is increasingly international, as are the securities markets. Partnerships involving exclusive affiliations with foreign firms may have special competitive advantages and costs that affect the baseline level of net income and, therefore, the accounting practice valuation. In addition, the provision for foreign citizen partners or owners may require the consideration both of a more complex capital structure and of marketability problems.

TRANSFER PRICING ISSUES

Accounting firms are increasingly involved in rendering other services beyond taxation and audit functions. As a result, valuing separate lines of business within a firm may become a relevant appraisal issue. The allocation of costs and transfer pricing of services of personnel and equipment and information will probably become a more important issue internally and, in the case of accounting firm mergers, externally for accounting practices.

SPECIAL PROFESSION-RELATED INTANGIBLE AND INTELLECTUAL PROPERTY VALUATIONS

Because computer support, information databases, and know-how have become so important to the accounting profession, the value of computer software or written procedures and data compilations on a stand-alone basis will also become a greater issue of concern to accountants. These issues are particularly meaningful in dissolution or damages disputes arising from defecting partners or from former employees accused of stealing what are regarded as proprietary intangible assets or intellectual properties of the accounting practice.

Appendix A

ACCOUNTING PRACTICE VALUATION BIBLIOGRAPHY

Berkowitz, Richard K. "Putting a Price Tag on Your Company." *Nation's Business* (January 1992): 29–32.

"Capitalization of Excess Earnings for Talent-Based Personal Service Business: Case Report." *FAIR$HARE: The Matrimonial Law Monthly* (February 1996): 13.

Cenker, William, and Robert Bloom. "Valuation of Accounting Practice and Goodwill." *Journal of Accounting Education* (Fall 1990): 311–319.

Cheifetz, A.J. "A Practical Guide to Determining the Value of a Professional Practice." *Taxation for Accountants* (February 1982): 102–105.

Cohrs, Denis A. "Guidelines for Purchasing an Accounting Practice." *Practical Accountant* (August 1989): 16–18.

Coker, Robert L. "Some Practical Tips on Buying or Merging an Accounting Practice." *Practical Accountant* (March 1981): 17–25.

Fairchild, Bruce H., and Keith W. Fairchild. "How to Value Personal Service Practices." *Practical Accountant* (August 1989): 27–30; 32–40.

Feeney, Charles F. "Buying and Selling an Accounting Practice." *CPA Journal* (January 1977): 53–56.

———. "Purchase of an Accounting Practice." *Michigan CPA* (September/October 1978): 45–47.

Gallagher, Robert J. "How to Value an Accounting Practice." *Asset* [Missouri Society of CPAs] (31 August 1990): 3, 14.

Gold, Michael H. "Considerations in the Purchase and Sale of an Accounting Practice." *New York Certified Public Accountant* (April 1970): 314–321.

Goodman, Beverly. "Appraisers Find Band of Gold in Dissolving Ties that Bind Business Appraisers." *Accounting Today* (7 August 1995): 3–6.

Hanan, Martin D. "Placing the Correct Value on an Accounting Practice." *WG&L Accounting News* (Fall 1987): 3–4.

Israel, Seymour M. "Providing for the Split-Up of an Accounting Firm." *Practical Accountant* (July/August 1979): 29–32.

Jarrow, Sidney F. "How to Successfully Merge Your Accounting Practice." *Practical Accountant* (December 1986): 70–77.

Johnson, John. "The Valuation of Future Enhanced Earnings and the Theory of Merger." *FAIR$HARE: The Matrimonial Law Monthly* (May 1995): 7–15.

Keane, Simon M., and Institute of Chartered Accountants of Scotland. "A Survey of the Valuation Practices of Professional Accounting Firms." *Accounting and Business Research* (Spring 1993): 188–189.

Kennedy, R. M. "Valuation of Goodwill in an Accounting Practice." *Chartered Accountant in Australia* (September 1986): 61–64.

Lang, Stuart S. "Buying, Merging, or Selling an Accounting Practice." *Practical Accountant* (November 1983): 87–95.

Lavine, A. "Selling Out: How Do You Value a Small to Midsized Financial Planning Practice for Sale or Disposition." *Financial Planning* (May 1987): 123–124.

Lippitt, Jeffrey W., and Nicholas J. Mastracchio, Jr. "The Value of CPA Firms, Firm Multiples, and Owner Compensation." *CPA Journal* (May 1993): 26–28.

Maccarrone, Eugene T., and Martha S. Weisel. "The CPA License at Divorce." *CPA Journal* (March 1992): 22–27.

Mastracchio, Nicholas J., Jr. "How to Value a Professional Practice." *Practical Accountant* (December 1985): 22–26.

Nielsen, Gordon L. "The Purchase of an Accounting Practice: Making the Right Choice." *Journal of Accountancy* (February 1984): 76–81.

Nielsen, Gordon L., and Dennis H. Hudson. "How to Value an Accounting Practice." *National Public Accountant* (February 1987): 26–29.

Pearson, Claude M. "Using 'Streamlined' Arbitration to Resolve Valuation Disputes for an Accounting Partnership." *Practical Accountant* (September 1987): 116–117.

Reilly, Robert F. "How Much Is Your Practice Worth?" *Today's CPA* (May/June 1991): 27–37.

Reilly, Robert F., and Robert P. Schweihs. "Valuation of Accounting Practices." *Ohio CPA Journal* (Autumn 1990): 19–26.

———. "Valuation of Accounting Practices: What's It Worth?" *National Public Accountant* (February 1991): 20–29.

Sandfort, James D., and Carl W. Gilmore. "Valuation of Leases as Property in Divorce Proceedings." *American Journal of Family Law* (Winter 1995): 191–200.

Schultz, Clayton G. "What's a Professional Practice Really Worth?" *CA Magazine* (June 1983): 36–40.

Scott, Robert R., Jr. "Practice Valuation: Thumb Rules and Common Sense." *Journal of Accountancy* (December 1992): 74–77.

Schnepper, Jeff A. "Valuing the Professional Practice." *National Public Accountant* (June 1988): 20–26.

Semanik, Michael K., and John H. Wade. "When Planning to Sell Your Firm." *Nation's Business* (July 1994): 38–40.

Smith, Charles M. "Valuation of An Accounting Firm—Is Your Practice Worth What You Think?" *Connecticut CPA Quarterly* (September 1992): 22.

Strischek, Dev. "How to Determine the Value of a Firm." *Management Accounting* (January 1983): 42–49.

Tibergien, Mark C. "How to Value a Financial Planning Practice." *Personal Financial Planning* (July/August 1991): 22–28.

Torres, Paul D. "The Valuation of Professional Accounting Practices—Guidelines for Buyers and Sellers." *National Public Accountant* (April 1978): 28–32.

Towey, John F. "Valuing a CPA Practice." *Management Accounting* (September 1988): 32.

Wallace, Pauline. "The Role of the Forensic Accountant." *Australian Accountant* (February 1992): 46–49.

Wentworth, David F. "Valuing an Accounting Practice." Parts 1 and 2. *Practicing CPA* (March 1982; April 1982): 1–2, 6; 7–8.

Wright, John E. "On Buying and Selling a Practice." *Journal of Accountancy* (January 1982): 38, 40.

Appendix B

GENERAL VALUATION BIBLIOGRAPHY

Articles

Alerding, R. James, Jr. "IRS Valuation Methods Lag behind Business Practice." *Taxation for Accountants* (July 1992): 4–9.

Angelini, James P.; Chet Hickox; and Joseph P. Matoney. "Covenants Not to Compete and Goodwill: Under Post-TRA Law, the Seller and Buyer Are No Longer Such Natural Antagonists." *Tax Adviser* (August 1988): 576–580.

Annin, Michael. "The Right Tools Can Simplify Company Valuation." *Accounting Today* (November 1995): 14, 35.

Arneson, George S. "Minority Discounts beyond Fifty Percent Can Be Supported." *Taxes* (February 1981): 97–107.

Basi, Bart A., and Mike Crane. "Amortization of Intangible Assets Separate from Goodwill." *Oil & Gas Tax Quarterly* (December 1993): 273–286.

Beauchene, Scott L.; James G. Rabe; and Jeffrey S. Tarbell. "Estimating Valuation Discounts for Family Limited Partnerships—A Review of Empirical Pricing Evidence." *Willamette Management Associates Insights* (Autumn 1995): 18–20.

Berkowitz, Richard K., and Joseph A. Blanco. "Putting a Price Tag on Your Company." *Nation's Business* (January 1992): 29–31.

Bielinski, Daniel W. "The Comparable-Company Approach: Measuring the True Value of Privately Held Firms." *Corporate Cashflow Magazine* (October 1990): 64–66.

Black, Fischer. "A Simple Discounting Rule." *Financial Management* (Summer 1988): 7–11.

Blue, Ian; Pamela Meneguzzi; and Stephen R. Cole. "Business Valuation: Creature from the Green Lagoon." *CA Magazine* (July 1992): 42–44, 47.

Blumberg, Grace Ganz. "Identifying and Valuing Goodwill at Divorce." *Law and Contemporary Problems* (Spring 1993): 217–272.

Bogdanski, John A. "Contractual Allocations of Price in Sales of Businesses." *Journal of Corporate Taxation* (Summer 1988): 99–137.

———. "Closely Held Businesses and Valuation: Dissecting the Discount for Lack of Marketability." *Estate Planning* (February 1996): 91–95.

Bolten, Steven E. "Discounts for Stocks of Closely Held Corporations." *Trusts and Estates* (December 1990): 47–48.

Brooks, Jeb, and Nicholas T. Rhinelander. "Understanding the Principles Involved in Partnerships." *Trusts and Estates* (February 1990): 44–48.

Brooks, Robin C. "The Valuation of Trademarks and Trade Names Using an Income Approach." *Willamette Management Associates Valuation Insights* (Winter 1992): 1–3.

Campbell, Brian. "Evaluating the Goodwill of a Business Entity." *American Journal of Family Law* (Winter 1992): 243–245.

Caudill, William H., and James T. Budyak. "New IRS Position on Valuation May Result in Reduced Marital and Charitable Deductions." *Journal of Taxation* (September 1993): 176–179.

Cenker, William J., and Carl J. Monastra. "The Basics of Business Valuation in Divorce Settlements." *Practical Accountant* (January 1990): 18–26.

Cleaver, K., and P. Ormrod. "Contracts, Regulations and Company Accounting—The Impact of Intangible Assets." *Journal of Business Law* (January 1992): 39–46.

Colborn, Asli F. "Estimating a Firm's Continuing Value." *Business Valuation Review* (December 1991): 157–162.

Connell, John R., and William H. Vincent. "Valuing Pension Benefits in Divorce: Look before You Leap." *Journal of Accountancy* (January 1994): 98–100.

Coolidge, H. Calvin. "Fixing Value of Minority Interest in Business: Actual Sales Suggest Discounts as High as 70%." *Estate Planning* (Spring 1975): 138–141.

Craig, Thomas, and Timothy Hoerr. "Recasting Income Statements in Valuations of Closely Held Businesses." *Business Valuation Review* (September 1993): 134–139 .

Curtis, Andrew M. "Discounting Minority Stock Interests in Closely Held Corporations: When and How Much?" *Journal of Taxation of Estates and Trusts* (Spring 1991): 26–30.

Dandekar, Manoj P., and Robert F. Reilly. "The Valuation of Goodwill." *Willamette Management Associates Valuation Insights* (Spring 1993): 7–12.

Dant, Thomas W., Jr. "Courts Increasing Amount of Discount for a Minority Interest in a Business." *Journal of Taxation* (August 1975): 104–109.

Doering, James A. "The Amortization of Intangibles: Before and after Section 197." *Taxes* (October 1993): 621–635.

Driscoll, Barrie K., and Stephen C. Gerard. "A Round for Buyers on Depreciation of Intangible Assets." *Mergers and Acquisitions* (July/August 1993): 22–25.

Dukes, William P., and Oswald D. Bowlin. "Valuation of Closely Held Firms." *Business Valuation Review* (December 1990): 127–137.

Fenton, Edmund D., Jr.; Lucinda VanAlst; and Patricia Isaacs. "The Determination and Valuation of Goodwill." *Tax Adviser* (September 1991): 602–612.

Field, Irving M. "A Review of the Principles of Valuation." *ASA Valuation* (June 1986): 2–10.

Fiflis, Ted J. "Accounting for Mergers, Acquisitions, and Investments in a Nutshell: The Interrelationships of, and Criteria for, Purchase or Pooling, the Equity Method, and Parent-Company-Only and Consolidated Statements." *Business Lawyer* (November 1981): 89–140.

Fiore, Nicholas J. "All in the Family: Determining the Value of a Minority Interest in Stock in a Closely Held Corporation." *Journal of Accountancy* (September 1991): 14.

———. "Valuing Closely Held Businesses." *Journal of Accountancy* (April 1990): 10.

Fishman, Jay E. "The Alternate Market Comparison Approach in Valuing Closely Held Enterprises." *FAIR$HARE: The Matrimonial Law Monthly* (October 1988): 7–8.

———. "The Problem with Rules of Thumb in the Valuation of Closely Held Entities." *FAIR$HARE: The Matrimonial Law Monthly* (December 1984): 13–15.

———. "Reasonable Owner's Compensation; Survey Data; Single Contract; Historical Data." *FAIR$HARE: The Matrimonial Law Monthly* (February 1995): 13–16.

Fishman, Jay E.; Shannon P. Pratt; J. Clifford Griffith; and D. Keith Wilson. "Premiums and Discounts in Business Valuations." Parts 1 and 2. *FAIR$HARE: The Matrimonial Law Monthly* (May and June 1992): 11–17; 14–16.

Flesher, Dale L. "Using ESOPs to Solve Succession Problems." *Journal of Accountancy* (May 1994): 45–48.

Fox, Jeffery D. "Closely Held Business Valuations: The Uninformed Use of the Excess Earnings/Formula Method." *Taxes* (November 1982): 832–836.

Frumkes, Melvyn B. "Unique Valuation Problems in Equitable Distribution Cases." *American Journal of Family Law* (Spring 1990): 1–13.

Gallinger, George W., and Glenn A. Wilt, Jr. "The Excess Earnings Model's Necessary Assumptions." *ASA Valuation* (February 1988): 74–78.

Gibbs, Larry W. "Do You Speak Tax, Mr. Appraiser? Evaluating the Appraiser and the Appraisal Report after 1990." *Institute on Estate Planning* (University of Miami, 1993): 15-1–15-120.

Graham, Michael D. "Selection of Market Multiples in Business Valuation." *Business Valuation Review* (March 1990): 8–12.

Greenstein, Brian R. "The Depreciation of Customer-Based Intangible Assets after Newark Morning Ledger." *Journal of Corporate Taxation* (Winter 1994): 315–325.

Gregory, Michael A. "Why Appraisers Should Be Concerned with Standards." *Business Valuation Review* (March 1994): 33–35.

Harper, John S., Jr. "Minority Shareholders: It's the Cash You Get that Counts: Discounting Expected Future Cash Distributions to Determine the Fair Market Value of a Minority Ownership Interest in a Partnership Corporation." *Tax Management Estates, Gifts, and Trusts Journal* (November/December 1990): 215–221.

Harris, James Edward. "Minority and Marketability Discounts: Are You Taking Enough?" *Probate and Property* (January/February 1990): 6–11.

Herpe, David A. "Climate for Valuation Discounts Remains Good despite IRS Obstinacy." *Trusts and Estates* (January 1995): 16–20.

Higgins, Mark C. "The Valuation of Family Limited Partnerships." *Trusts and Estates.* (September 1995): 66–78.

Hitchner, James R. "Valuation of Closely Held Businesses: Estate and Gift Tax Issues." *Tax Adviser* (July 1992): 471–479.

Hitchner, James R., and Kevin J. Rudd. "The Use of Discounts in Estate and Gift Tax Valuations." *Trusts and Estates* (August 1992): 49–56, 60.

Hochberg, R. Mark. "Valuing a Closely Held Business: IRS Guidelines." *Financial World* (20 July 1993): 71.

Hoeppner, James B. "Closely Held Business Interests—Valuation Strategies." *Tax Adviser* (April 1990): 218–220.

Horsman, Steven E. "Minority Interest Discounts on Gifts among Family Members." *Trusts and Estates* (July 1987): 54–55.

Jaeger, David G. "Supreme Court Decides Newark Morning Ledger Co." *Taxes* (July 1993): 406–413.

Kalcheim, Michael W., and Norah M. Plante. "Professional Goodwill in Divorce after *Zells.*" *Illinois Bar Journal* (December 1991): 624–626.

Kaltman, Todd A. "Capitalization Using a Mid-Year Convention." *Business Valuation Review* (December 1995): 178–182.

Kaplan, Steven P., and Egon Fromm. "The Impact of Taxes on the Value of Close Corporations." *Estate Planning* (May/June 1992): 137–142.

Keligian, David L., "Appraisal Issues Now Require Greater Attention for Tax Planning to Be Effective." *Journal of Taxation* (February 1994): 98–103.

Kelsey, David. "The Real Bottom Line in Divorce." *National Public Accountant* (November 1991): 28–30.

Kimball, Curtis R., and Robert F. Reilly. "Kinder, Gentler Gift and Estate Tax Valuation Rules Offer Planning Possibilities." *Journal of Taxation of Estates and Trusts* (Fall 1991): 27–33.

Kuga, Mark W. "Tax Court Determines Reasonableness of Owner's Compensation Based upon 'Independent Investor's' Return on Equity Test." *Willamette Management Associates Insights* (Winter 1994): 1–4.

Lanzilotti, R. F., and A. K. Esquibel. "Measuring Damages in Commercial Litigation: Present Value of Lost Opportunities." *Journal of Accounting Auditing, and Finance* (Spring 1990): 125–144.

Larson, James A., and Jeffrey P. Wright. "Key Person Discount in Small Firms: Fact or Fiction?" *Business Valuation Review* (March 1996): 4–12.

Lauer, Eliot, and Bernard V. Preziosi, Jr. "A Fair Share for Minority Shareholders." *New York Law Journal* (1 June 1992): 7.

LeClair, Mark S. "Valuing the Closely-Held Corporation: The Validity and Performance of Established Valuation Procedures." *Accounting Horizons* (September 1990): 31–42.

Ledereich, Leonard, and Joel G. Siegel. "What's a Business Worth? Valuation Methods for Accountants." *National Public Accountant* (February 1990): 18–22.

Levy, Marc D.; Ellen MacNeil; and Barbara J. Young. "Supreme Court's Decision on Amortizing Intangibles Removes One Barrier." *Journal of Taxation* (July 1993): 4–10.

Longenecker, Ruth R. "A Practical Guide to Valuation of Closely Held Stock." *Trusts and Estates* (January 1983): 32–41.

Mackles, Glenn R. "15-Year Amortization of Purchased Intangible Assets—Some Winners, Some Losers." *Journal of Taxation* (December 1993): 332–337.

Maher, J. Michael. "An Objective Measure for a Discount for a Minority Interest and a Premium for a Controlling Interest." *Taxes* (July 1979): 449–454.

Mard, Michael J. "Dividing a Non-divisible General Partnership." *FAIR$HARE: The Matrimonial Law Monthly* (April 1989): 3–7.

Mercer, Z. Christopher. "Should 'Marketability Discounts' Be Applied to Controlling Interests of Private Companies?" *Business Valuation Review* (June 1994): 55–65.

Mezzullo, Louis A. "Buy-Sell Agreements after Chapter 14." *Trusts and Estates* (June 1994): 49–59.

Millon, Thomas J. "Revenue Reconciliation Act of 1993 Allows Amortization of Acquired Goodwill and Other Purchased Intangible Assets." *Willamette Management Associates Valuation Insights* (Autumn 1993): 17–20.

Nath, Eric W. "Control Premiums and Minority Interest Discounts in Private Companies." *Business Valuation Review* (June 1990): 39–46.

"The Opinion of the College on Defining Standards of Value." *ASA Valuation* (June 1989): 65–72.

Osteryoung, Jerome S. and Derek Newman. "Key Person Valuation Issues for Private Businesses." *Business Valuation Review* (September 1994): 115–119.

Parkman, Allen. "The Treatment of Professional Goodwill in Divorce Proceedings." *Family Law Quarterly* (Summer 1984): 213–223.

Pennell, Jeffrey N. "Wealth Transfer Tax Valuation Conundrums." *Trusts and Estates* (January 1995): 20–25.

Peterson, Renno L. "A Guide to Valuing the Closely Held Business." *Practical Accountant* (April 1989): 34–39.

Phelps, Mary Brooke. "Valuation of Closely Held Stock." *Tax Advisor* (December 1995): 723.

Phillips, John R., and Neill W. Freeman. "Do Privately-Held Controlling Interests Sell for Less?" *Business Valuation Review* (September 1995): 102–113.

Pissott, Linda. "The Amortization of Customer-Based Intangibles: The 'Separate and Distinct from Goodwill' Requirement and H.R. 3035's Proposal for Change." *Tax Lawyer* (Summer 1992): pp. 1031–1043.

Pope, Ralph A. "Evaluating Pension Benefits in Divorce." *Journal of Accountancy* (August 1993): 62–66.

Pratt, Shannon P. "Valuing a Minority Interest in a Closely Held Company." *Practical Accountant* (June 1986): 60–68.

Randisi, Martin P. "Comparable Company Method of Valuing a Closely Held Business." *FAIR$HARE: The Matrimonial Law Monthly* (January 1991): 3–5.

Rayburn, William B.; Dennis S. Tosh; and Roger King. "*Uniform Standards of Professional Appraisal Practice:* Implications for the Financial Community." *Appraisal Journal* (January 1993): 90–99.

Reilly, Robert F. "The Identification of Intangible Assets for Bankruptcy and Reorganization Purposes." *Willamette Management Associates Insights* (Winter 1994): 5–7.

———. "Pricing and Structuring the Sale of a Closely Held Corporation." *The Ohio CPA Journal* (December 1995): 13–15.

———. "The Valuation of Computer Software." *ASA Valuation* (March 1991): 34–54.

———. "The Valuation of Intangible Assets for Bankruptcy and Reorganization Purposes." *Willamette Management Associates Insights* (Spring 1994): 3–7.

———. "What Financial Advisors Need to Know about Business Valuation and Security Analysis Services." *The Corporate Growth Report* (January 1992): 11–15.

———, and Robert P. Schweihs. "How the Buy/Sell Agreement Smoothes a Shift in Control." *Mergers and Acquisitions* (January/February 1991): 52–57.

Schilt, James H. "Challenging Standard Business Appraisal Methods." *Business Valuation News* (December 1984): 4–14.

Schweihs, Robert P. "Litigation Support, Valuation-Related Dispute Resolution, and Expert Witness Services." *ABI Bankruptcy Journal* (September 1993): 16, 19, 22.

———. "The Use and Misuse of CAPM in Property Tax Valuation." *Journal of Property Tax Management* (Fall 1994): 51–60.

———, and Robert F. Reilly. "The Valuation of Intellectual Properties." *Licensing Law and Business Report* (May/June 1988): 1–12.

Sherman, Lawrence F. "Valuation of Preferred Capital Stock for Business Enterprises." *Valuation* (March 1994): 72–83.

Shishido, Zenichi. "The Fair Value of Minority Stock in Closely Held Corporations." *Fordham Law Review* (October 1993): 65–110.

Shayne, Mark. "A Reexamination of Revenue Ruling 68–609." *FAIR$HARE: The Matrimonial Law Monthly* (July 1992): 5–8.

Siciliano, Peter J., and Mark Jones. "Business Valuation for the Nonspecialist: Finding the Best Value." *Practical Accountant* (September 1991): 70f.

Stevens, Michael G. "Accountants Caught in a Tug of War." *Practical Accountant* (March 1994): 18–24.

Trieschmann, James S.; E. J. Leverett; and Peter J. Shedd. "Valuing Common Stock for Minority Stock and ESOP in Closely Held Corporations." *Business Horizons* (March/April 1988): 63–69.

Turner, Mark A. "Accounting for Inventory in a Reorganization or Liquidation." *Management Accounting* (February 1993): 29–32.

Wagner, Michael J. "How Do You Measure Damages? Lost Income or Lost Cash Flow?" *Journal of Accountancy* (February 1990): 28–33.

———. "Opportunities in Litigation Services." *Journal of Accountancy* (June 1992): 70–73.

Walburn, Allen. "Depreciation of Intangibles: An Area of the Tax Law in Need of Change." *San Diego Law Review* (Spring 1993): 453–483.

Wall, Patricia S., and Lee Sarver. "Appraiser's Liability: An Overview." *National Public Accountant* (December 1992): 42–46.

Wertlieb, Mark; Judy Scarabello; and Tracy L. Curran. "The Amortization of Purchased Intangible Assets." *Tax Adviser* (September 1993): 583–590.

Wilhoite, Charles and James G. Rabe. "Valuation Differences between Big Businesses and Small Businesses." *Willamette Management Associates Insights* (Autumn 1995): 6–11.

Wise, Richard M. "The CA's Role in Valuations: An Inside-out Perspective." *CA Magazine* (28 September 1984): 28–40.

Wolosky, Howard W. "Depreciating Customer Bases after *Newark*." *Practical Accountant* (July 1993): 34–39.

Books

Babcock, Henry A. *Appraisal Principles and Procedures.* Washington, D.C.: American Society of Appraisers, 1980.

Bonbright, James C. *The Valuation of Property.* Vols. 1 and 2. 1937. Reprint: Charlottesville, Va.: The Michie Company, 1965.

Burke, Frank M. *Valuation and Valuation Planning for Closely Held Businesses.* Englewood Cliffs, N.J.: Prentice-Hall Law & Business, 1987.

Copeland, Thomas E. *Valuation: Measuring and Managing the Value of Companies.* New York: John Wiley & Sons, 1996.

Dewing, Arthur Stone. *The Financial Policy of Corporations.* 5th ed. Vols. 1 and 2. New York: Ronald Press, 1953.

Fishman, Jay E.; Shannon P. Pratt; J. Clifford Griffith; and D. Keith Wilson. *Guide to Business Valuations.* 6th ed. Fort Worth, Tex.: Practitioners Publishing, 1996.

Florio, Nicholas M. *Business Asset Valuation: Allocation and Recovery of Investment in Business Acquisitions.* Boston: Little, Brown, 1995.

Goldberg, Barth H. *Valuation of Divorce Assets.* St. Paul, Minn.: West Publishing, 1984 [updated in 1987].

IRS Valuation Guide for Income, Estate, and Gift Taxes: Valuation Training for Appeals Officers. Chicago: Commerce Clearing House, 1994.

Miles, Raymond C. *Basic Business Appraisal.* New York: John Wiley & Sons, 1984.

Palepu, Krishna G. *Business Analysis and Valuation: Using Financial Statements: Text and Cases.* Cincinnati: South-Western College Publishing, 1996.

Pratt, Shannon P.; Robert F. Reilly; and Robert P. Schweihs. *Valuing a Business: The Analysis and Appraisal of Closely Held Companies.* 3d ed. Burr Ridge, Ill.: Irwin Professional Publishing, 1996.

————. *Valuing Small Businesses and Professional Practices.* 2d ed. Burr Ridge, Ill.: Irwin Professional Publishing, 1993.

Pratt, Shannon P.; Robert F. Reilly; Robert P. Schweihs; and Jay E. Fishman. *Business Valuation Videocourse.* Videotape and course handbook. New York: American Institute of Certified Public Accountants, 1993, updated 1996.

Rigby, James S., Jr. *Performing Business Valuations.* San Diego: Harcourt Brace & Co., 1994.

Smith, Gordon V. *Corporate Valuation—A Business and Professional Guide.* New York: John Wiley & Sons, 1988.

Smith, Gordon V., and Russell L. Parr. *Valuation of Intellectual Property and Intangible Assets.* New York: John Wiley & Sons, 1989.

Trugman, Gary R. *Conducting a Valuation of a Closely Held Business.* New York: American Institute of Certified Public Accountants, 1993.

Uniform Standards of Professional Appraisal Practice. Annual. Washington, D.C.: The Appraisal Foundation.

West, Thomas L., and Jeffrey D. Jones, eds. *Handbook of Business Valuation.* New York: John Wiley & Sons, 1992.

Yegge, Wilbur M. *A Basic Guide for Valuing a Company.* New York: John Wiley & Sons, 1996.

Zukin, James H., ed. *Financial Valuation: Businesses and Business Interests.* New York: Warren, Gorham & Lamont, 1990 [supplemented annually with yearbook currently edited by Robert F. Reilly and Robert P. Schweihs].

Appendix C

RELEVANT REVENUE RULINGS

REVENUE RULING 59–60

SECTION 2031.—DEFINITION OF GROSS ESTATE

26 CFR 20.2031-2: Valuation of stocks and bonds. Rev. Rul. 59–60
(Also Section 2512.)
(Also Part II, Sections 811 (k), 1005, Regulations 105, Section 81.10)

> In valuing the stock of closely held corporations, or the stock of corporations where market quotations are not available, all other available financial data, as well as all relevant factors affecting the fair market value must be considered for estate tax and gift tax purposes. No general formula may be given that is applicable to the many different valuation situations arising in the valuation of such stock. However, the general approach, methods, and factors which must be considered in valuing such securities are outlined.
>
> Revenue Ruling 54–77, C.B. 1954-1, 187, superseded.

SECTION 1. PURPOSE.

The purpose of this Revenue Ruling is to outline and review in general the approach, methods and factors to be considered in valuing shares of the capital stock of closely held corporations for estate tax and gift tax purposes. The methods discussed herein will apply likewise to the valuation of corporate stocks on which market quotations are either unavailable or are of such scarcity that they do not reflect the fair market value.

SEC. 2. BACKGROUND AND DEFINITIONS.

.01 All valuations must be made in accordance with the applicable provisions of the Internal Revenue Code of 1954 and the Federal Estate Tax and Gift Tax Regulations. Sections 2031(a), 2032 and 2512(a) of the 1954 Code (sections 811 and 1005 of the 1939 Code) require that the property to be included in the gross estate, or made the subject of a gift, shall be taxed on the basis of the value of the property at the time of death of the decedent, the alternate date if so elected, or the date of gift.

.02 Section 20.2031-1(b) of the Estate Tax Regulations (section 81.10 of the Estate Tax Regulations 105) and section 25.2512-1 of the Gift Tax Regulations (section 86.19 of Gift Tax Regulations 108) define fair market value, in effect, as the price at which the property would change hands between a willing buyer and a willing seller when the former is not under any compulsion to buy and the latter is not under any compulsion to sell, both parties having reasonable knowledge of relevant facts. Court decisions frequently state in addition that the hypothetical buyer and seller are assumed to be able, as well as willing, to trade and to be well informed about the property and concerning the market for such property.

.03 Closely held corporations are those corporations the shares of which are owned by a relatively limited number of stockholders. Often the entire stock issue is held by one family. The result of this situation is that little, if any, trading in the shares takes place. There is, therefore, no established market for the stock and such sales as occur at irregular intervals seldom reflect all of the elements of a representative transaction as defined by the term "fair market value."

SEC. 3. APPROACH TO VALUATION.

.01 A determination of fair market value, being a question of fact, will depend upon the circumstances in each case. No formula can be devised that will be generally applicable to the multitude of different valuation issues arising in estate and gift tax cases. Often, an appraiser will find wide differences of opinion as to the fair market value of a particular stock. In resolving such differences, he should maintain a reasonable attitude in recognition of the fact that valuation is not an exact science. A sound valuation will be based upon all the relevant facts, but the elements of common sense, informed judgment and reasonableness must enter into the process of weighing those facts and determining their aggregate significance.

.02 The fair market value of specific shares of stock will vary as general economic conditions change from "normal" to "boom" or "depression," that is, according to the degree of optimism or pessimism with which the investing public regards the future at the required date of appraisal. Uncertainty as to the stability or continuity of the future income from a property decreases its value by increasing the risk of loss of earnings and value in the future. The value of shares of stock of a company with very uncertain future prospects is highly speculative. The appraiser must exercise his judgment as to the degree of risk attaching to the business of the corporation which issued the stock, but that judgment must be related to all of the other factors affecting value.

.03 Valuation of securities is, in essence, a prophesy as to the future and must be based on facts available at the required date of appraisal. As a generalization, the prices of stocks which are traded in volume in a free and active market by informed persons best reflect the consensus of the investing public as to what the future holds for the corporations and industries represented. When a stock is closely held, is traded infrequently, or is traded in an erratic market, some other measure of value must be used. In many instances, the next best measure may be found in the prices at which the stocks of companies engaged in the same or a similar line of business are selling in a free and open market.

SEC. 4. FACTORS TO CONSIDER.

.01 It is advisable to emphasize that in the valuation of the stock of closely held corporations or the stock of corporations where market quotations are either lacking or too scarce to be recognized, all available financial data, as well as all relevant factors affecting the fair market value, should be considered. The following factors, although not all-inclusive are fundamental and require careful analysis in each case:

(a)   The nature of the business and the history of the enterprise from its inception.

(b)   The economic outlook in general and the condition and outlook of the specific industry in particular.

(c)   The book value of the stock and the financial condition of the business.

(d)   The earning capacity of the company.

(e)   The dividend-paying capacity.

(f)   Whether or not the enterprise has goodwill or other intangible value.

(g)   Sales of the stock and the size of the block of stock to be valued.

(h)   The market price of stocks of corporations engaged in the same or a similar line of business having their stocks actively traded in a free and open market, either on an exchange or over-the-counter.

.02 The following is a brief discussion of each of the foregoing factors:

(a)   The history of a corporate enterprise will show its past stability or instability, its growth or lack of growth, the diversity or lack of diversity of its operations, and other facts needed to form an opinion of the degree of risk involved in the business. For an enterprise which changed its form of organization but carried on the same or closely similar operations of its predecessor, the history of the former enterprise should be considered. The detail to be considered should increase with approach to the required date of appraisal, since recent events are of greatest help in predicting the future; but a study of gross and net income, and of dividends covering a long prior period, is highly desirable. The history to be studied should include, but need not be limited to, the nature of the business, its products or services, its operating and investment assets, capital structure, plant facilities, sales records and management, all of which should be considered as of the date of the appraisal, with due regard for recent significant changes. Events of the past that are unlikely to recur in the future should be discounted, since value has a close relation to future expectancy.

(b)   A sound appraisal of a closely held stock must consider current and prospective economic conditions as of the date of appraisal, both in the national economy and in the industry or industries with which the corporation is allied. It is important to know that the company is more or less successful than its competitors in the same industry, or that it is maintaining a stable position with respect to competitors. Equal or even greater significance may attach to the ability of the industry with which the company is allied to compete with other industries. Prospective competition which has not been a factor in prior years should be given careful attention. For example, high profits due to the novelty of its product and the lack of competition often lead to increasing competition. The public's appraisal of the future prospects of competitive industries or of competitors within an industry may be indicated by price trends in the markets for commodities and for securities. The loss of the manager of a so-called "one-man" business may have a depressing effect upon the value of the stock of such business, particularly if there is a lack of trained personnel capable of succeeding to the management of the enterprise. In valuing the stock of this type of business, therefore, the effect of the loss of the manager on the future expectancy of the business, and the absence of management succession potentialities are pertinent factors to be taken into consideration. On the other hand, there may be factors which offset, in whole or in part, the loss of the manager's services. For instance, the nature of the business and of its assets may be such that they will not be impaired by the loss of the manager. Furthermore, the loss may be adequately covered by life insurance, or competent management might be employed on the basis of the consideration paid for the former manager's services. These, or other offsetting factors, if found to exist, should be carefully weighed against the loss of the manager's services in valuing the stock of the enterprise.

(c) Balance sheets should be obtained, preferably in the form of comparative annual statements for two or more years immediately preceding the date of appraisal, together with a balance sheet at the end of the month preceding that date, if corporate accounting will permit. Any balance sheet descriptions that are not self-explanatory, and balance sheet items comprehending diverse assets or liabilities, should be clarified in essential detail by supporting supplemental schedules. These statements usually will disclose to the appraiser (1) liquid position (ratio of current assets to current liabilities); (2) gross and net book value of principal classes of fixed assets; (3) working capital; (4) long-term indebtedness; (5) capital structure; and (6) net worth. Consideration also should be given to any assets not essential to the operation of the business, such as investments in securities, real estate, etc. In general, such nonoperating assets will command a lower rate of return than do the operating assets, although in exceptional cases the reverse may be true. In computing the book value per share of stock, assets of the investment type should be revalued on the basis of their market price and the book value adjusted accordingly. Comparison of the company's balance sheets over several years may reveal, among other facts, such developments as the acquisition of additional production facilities or subsidiary companies, improvement in financial position, and details as to recapitalizations and other changes in the capital structure of the corporation. If the corporation has more than one class of stock outstanding, the charter or certificate of incorporation should be examined to ascertain the explicit rights and privileges of the various stock issues including: (1) voting powers, (2) preference as to dividends, and (3) preference as to assets in the event of liquidation.

(d) Detailed profit-and-loss statements should be obtained and considered for a representative period immediately prior to the required date of appraisal, preferably five or more years. Such statements should show (1) gross income by principal items; (2) principal deductions from gross income including major prior items of operating expenses, interest and other expense on each item of long-term debt, depreciation and depletion if such deductions are made, officers' salaries, in total if they appear to be reasonable or in detail if they seem to be excessive, contributions (whether or not deductible for tax purposes) that the nature of its business and its community position require the corporation to make, and taxes by principal items, including income and excess profits taxes; (3) net income available for dividends; (4) rates and amounts of dividends paid on each class of stock; (5) remaining amount carried to surplus; and (6) adjustment to, and reconciliation with, surplus as stated on the balance sheet. With profit and loss statements of this character available, the appraiser should be able to separate recurrent from nonrecurrent items of income and expense, to distinguish between operating income and investment income, and to ascertain whether or not any line of business in which the company is engaged is operated consistently at a loss and might be abandoned with benefit to the company. The percentage of earnings retained for business expansion should be noted when dividend-paying capacity is considered. Potential future income is a major factor in many valuations of closely held stocks, and all information concerning past income which will be helpful in predicting the future should be secured. Prior earnings records usually are the most reliable guide as to the future expectancy, but resort to arbitrary five- or ten-year averages without regard to current trends or future prospects will not produce a realistic valuation. If, for instance, a record of progressively increasing or decreasing net income is found, then greater weight may be accorded the most recent years' profits in estimating earning power. It will be helpful, in judging risk and the extent to which a business is a marginal operator, to consider deductions from income and net income in terms of percentage of sales. Major categories of cost and expense to be so analyzed include the consumption of raw materials and supplies in the case of manufacturers, processors and fabricators; the cost of purchased merchandise in the case of merchants; utility services; insurance; taxes; depletion or depreciation; and interest.

(e)   Primary consideration should be given to the dividend-paying capacity of the company rather than to dividends actually paid in the past. Recognition must be given to the necessity of retaining a reasonable portion of profits in a company to meet competition. Dividend-paying capacity is a factor that must be considered in an appraisal, but dividends actually paid in the past may not have any relation to dividend-paying capacity. Specifically, the dividends paid by a closely held family company may be measured by the income needs of the stockholders or by their desire to avoid taxes on dividend receipts, instead of by the ability of the company to pay dividends. Where an actual or effective controlling interest in a corporation is to be valued, the dividend factor is not a material element, since the payment of such dividends is discretionary with the controlling stockholders. The individual or group in control can substitute salaries and bonuses for dividends, thus reducing net income and understating the dividend-paying capacity of the company. It follows, therefore, that dividends are less reliable criteria of fair market value than other applicable factors.

(f)   In the final analysis, goodwill is based upon earning capacity. The presence of goodwill and its value, therefore, rests upon the excess of net earnings over and above a fair return on the net tangible assets. While the element of goodwill may be based primarily on earnings, such factors as the prestige and renown of the business, the ownership of a trade or brand name, and a record of successful operation over a prolonged period in a particular locality, also may furnish support for the inclusion of intangible value. In some instances it may not be possible to make a separate appraisal of the tangible and intangible assets of the business. The enterprise has a value as an entity. Whatever intangible value there is, which is supportable by the facts, may be measured by the amount by which the appraised value of the tangible assets exceeds the net book value of such assets.

(g)   Sales of stock of a closely held corporation should be carefully investigated to determine whether they represent transactions at arm's length. Forced or distress sales do not ordinarily reflect fair market value nor do isolated sales in small amounts necessarily control as the measure of value. This is especially true in the valuation of a controlling interest in a corporation. Since, in the case of closely held stocks, no prevailing market prices are available, there is no basis for making an adjustment for blockage. It follows, therefore, that such stocks should be valued upon a consideration of all the evidence affecting the fair market value. The size of the block of stock itself is a relevant factor to be considered. Although it is true that a minority interest in an unlisted corporation's stock is more difficult to sell than a similar block of listed stock, it is equally true that control of a corporation, either actual or in effect, representing as it does an added element of value, may justify a higher value for a specific block of stock.

(h)   Section 2031(b) of the Code states, in effect, that in valuing unlisted securities the value of stock or securities of corporations engaged in the same or a similar line of business which are listed on an exchange should be taken into consideration along with all other factors. An important consideration is that the corporations to be used for comparisons have capital stocks which are actively traded by the public. In accordance with section 2031(b) of the Code, stocks listed on an exchange are to be considered first. However, if sufficient comparable companies whose stocks are listed on an exchange cannot be found, other comparable companies which have stocks actively traded in on the over-the-counter market also may be used. The essential factor is that whether the stocks are sold on an exchange or over-the-counter there is evidence of an active, free public market for the stock as of the valuation date. In selecting corporations for comparative purposes, care should be taken to use only comparable companies. Although the only restrictive requirement as to comparable corporations specified in the statute is that their lines of business be the same or similar, yet it is obvious that consideration must be given to other relevant factors in order that the most valid comparison possible will be obtained. For illustration, a corporation having one or more issues of preferred stock, bonds or debentures in addition to its common stock should not be considered to be directly comparable to one having only common stock outstanding. In like manner, a company with a declining business and decreasing markets is not comparable to one with a record of current progress and market expansion.

SEC. 5. WEIGHT TO BE ACCORDED VARIOUS FACTORS.

The valuation of closely held corporate stock entails the consideration of all relevant factors as stated in section 4. Depending upon the circumstances in each case, certain factors may carry more weight than others because of the nature of the company's business. To illustrate:

(a)   Earnings may be the most important criterion of value in some cases whereas asset value will receive primary consideration in others. In general, the appraiser will accord primary consideration to earnings when valuing stocks of companies which sell products or services to the public; conversely, in the investment or holding type of company, the appraiser may accord the greatest weight to the assets underlying the security to be valued.

(b)   The value of the stock of a closely held investment or real estate holding company, whether or not family owned, is closely related to the value of the assets underlying the stock. For companies of this type the appraiser should determine the fair market values of the assets of the company. Operating expenses of such a company and the cost of liquidating it, if any, merit consideration when appraising the relative values of the stock and the underlying assets. The market values of the underlying assets give due weight to potential earnings and dividends of the particular items of property underlying the stock, capitalized at rates deemed proper by the investing public at the date of appraisal. A current appraisal by the investing public should be superior to the retrospective opinion of an individual. For these reasons, adjusted net worth should be accorded greater weight in valuing the stock of a closely held investment or real estate holding company, whether or not family owned, than any of the other customary yardsticks of appraisal, such as earnings and dividend paying capacity.

SEC. 6. CAPITALIZATION RATES.

In the application of certain fundamental valuation factors, such as earnings and dividends, it is necessary to capitalize the average or current results at some appropriate rate. A determination of the proper capitalization rate presents one of the most difficult problems in valuation. That there is no ready or simple solution will become apparent by a cursory check of the rates of return and dividend yields in terms of the selling prices of corporate shares listed on the major exchanges of the country. Wide variations will be found even for companies in the same industry. Moreover, the ratio will fluctuate from year to year depending upon economic conditions. Thus, no standard tables of capitalization rates applicable to closely held corporations can be formulated. Among the more important factors to be taken into consideration in deciding upon a capitalization rate in a particular case are: (1) the nature of the business; (2) the risk involved; and (3) the stability or irregularity of earnings.

SEC. 7. AVERAGE OF FACTORS.

Because valuations cannot be made on the basis of a prescribed formula, there is no means whereby the various applicable factors in a particular case can be assigned mathematical weights in deriving the fair market value. For this reason, no useful purpose is served by taking an average of several factors (for example, book value, capitalized earnings and capitalized dividends) and basing the valuation on the result. Such a process excludes active consideration of other pertinent factors, and the end result cannot be supported by a realistic application of the significant facts in the case except by mere chance.

SEC. 8. RESTRICTIVE AGREEMENTS.

Frequently, in the valuation of closely held stock for estate and gift tax purposes, it will be found that the stock is subject to an agreement restricting its sale or transfer. Where shares of stock were acquired by a decedent subject to an option reserved by the issuing corporation to repurchase at a certain price, the option price is usually accepted as the fair market value for estate tax purposes. See Rev. Rul. 54–76, C.B. 1954-1, 194. However, in such case the option price is not determinative of fair market value for gift tax purposes. Where the option, or buy and sell agreement, is the result of voluntary action by the stockholders and is binding during the life as well as at the death of the stockholders, such agreement may or may not, depending upon the circumstances of each case, fix the value for estate tax purposes. However, such agreement is a factor to be considered, with other relevant factors, in determining fair market value. Where the stockholder is free to dispose of his shares during life and the option is to become effective only upon his death, the fair market value is not limited to the option price. It is always necessary to consider the relationship of the parties, the relative number of shares held by the decedent, and other material facts to determine whether the agreement represents a bonafide business arrangement or is a device to pass the decedent's shares to the natural objects of his bounty for less than an adequate and full consideration in money or money's worth. In this connection see Rev. Rul. 157 C.B. 1953-2, 255, and Rev. Rul. 189, C.B. 1953-2, 294.

SEC. 9. EFFECT ON OTHER DOCUMENTS.

Revenue Ruling 54–77, C.B. 1954-1, 187, is hereby superseded.

Revenue Ruling 68-609

The "formula" approach may be used in determining the fair market value of intangible assets of a business only if there is no better basis available for making the determination; A.R.M. 34, A.R.M. 68, O.D. 937, and Revenue Ruling 65-192 superseded.

SECTION 1001.—DETERMINATION OF AMOUNT OF AND RECOGNITION OF GAIN OR LOSS

26 CFR 1.1001-1: Computation of gain or loss.   Rev. Rul. 68-609[1]
(Also Section 167; 1.167(a)-3.)

The purpose of this Revenue Ruling is to update and restate, under the current statute and regulations, the currently outstanding portions of A.R.M. 34, C.B. 2, 31 (1920), A.R.M. 68, C.B. 3, 43 (1920), and O.D. 937, C.B. 4, 43 (1921).

The question presented is whether the "formula" approach, the capitalization of earnings in excess of a fair rate of return on net tangible assets, may be used to determine the fair market value of the intangible assets of a business.

The "formula" approach may be stated as follows:

A percentage return on the average annual value of the tangible assets used in a business is determined, using a period of years (preferably not less than five) immediately prior to the valuation date. The amount of the percentage return on tangible assets, thus determined, is deducted from the average earnings of the business for such period and the remainder, if any, is considered to be the amount of the average annual earnings from the intangible assets of the business for the period. This amount (considered as the average annual earnings from intangibles), capitalized at a percentage of, say, 15 to 20 percent, is the value of the intangible assets of the business determined under the "formula" approach.

The percentage of return on the average annual value of the tangible assets used should be the percentage prevailing in the industry involved at the date of valuation, or (when the industry percentage is not available) a percentage of 8 to 10 percent may be used.

The 8 percent rate of return and the 15 percent rate of capitalization are applied to tangibles and intangibles, respectively, of businesses with a small risk factor and stable and regular earnings; the 10 percent rate of return and 20 percent rate of capitalization are applied to businesses in which the hazards of business are relatively high.

The above rates are used as examples and are not appropriate in all cases. In applying the "formula" approach, the average earnings period and the capitalization rates are dependent upon the facts pertinent thereto in each case.

SOURCE: Rev. Rul. 68-609, 1968-2. C.B. 327.

The past earnings to which the formula is applied should fairly reflect the probable future earnings. Ordinarily, the period should not be less than five years, and abnormal years, whether above or below the average, should be eliminated. If the business is a sole proprietorship or partnership, there should be deducted from the earnings of the business a reasonable amount for services performed by the owner or partners engaged in the business. See *Lloyd B. Sanderson Estate* v. *Commissioner,* 42 F. 2d 160 (1930). Further, only the tangible assets entering into net worth, including accounts and bills receivable in excess of accounts and bills payable, are used for determining earnings on the tangible assets. Factors that influence the capitalization rate include (1) the nature of the business, (2) the risk involved, and (3) the stability or irregularity of earnings.

The "formula" approach should not be used if there is better evidence available from which the value of intangibles can be determined. If the assets of a going business are sold upon the basis of a rate of capitalization that can be substantiated as being realistic, though it is not within the range of figures indicated here as the ones ordinarily to be adopted, the same rate of capitalization should be used in determining the value of intangibles.

Accordingly, the "formula" approach may be used for determining the fair market value of intangible assets of a business only if there is no better basis therefor available.

See also Revenue Ruling 59–60, C.B. 1959-1, 237, as modified by Revenue Ruling 65–193, C.B. 1965-2, 370, which sets forth the proper approach to use in the valuation of closely-held corporate stocks for estate and gift tax purposes. The general approach, methods, and factors, outlined in Revenue Ruling 59–60, as modified, are equally applicable to valuations of corporate stocks for income and other tax purposes as well as for estate and gift tax purposes. They apply also to problems involving the determination of the fair market value of business interests of any type, including partnerships and proprietorships, and of intangible assets for all tax purposes.

A.R.M. 34, A.R.M. 68, and O.D. 937 are superseded, since the positions set forth therein are restated to the extent applicable under current law in this Revenue Ruling. Revenue Ruling 65–192, C.B. 1965-2, 259, which contained restatements of A.R.M. 34 and A.R.M. 68, is also superseded.

---

[1]Prepared pursuant to Rev. Proc. 67-6, C.B. 1967-1, 576.

Appendix D

RECENT COURT CASE DEVELOPMENTS INVOLVING ACCOUNTING PRACTICES

Bolan v. Bolan, 796 SW2d 358 (Ark. App. 1990)

The husband's solo accounting practice was found to have decreased in value during the course of the marriage. *Bolan* v. *Bolan* simply deferred to the trial judge who concluded that the valuation approach presented by the husband's expert was "more reasoned," although the specifics were not set forth. The wife's expert testified that the proper method was to multiply gross income by a factor of 1.5. He said that this method was an industry rule of thumb for valuing small businesses, particularly CPA firms. The husband and his expert testified that a more appropriate formula was to multiply annual earnings by three. The gross income of the practice in 1983 was $232,119, with net income of $64,378. In 1988, the gross income was $264,910, while net income for that year was $42,014. The use of wife's method placed the value of the firm at $348,178.50 at the time of the marriage, and $397,365 at the time of the divorce, the difference resulting in an increased value of $49,186.50 during the marriage. Conversely, the method used by husband reflected a decrease in value of $67,042. After reviewing this conflicting evidence, the lower Court found that the business had decreased in value, which was affirmed.

Bostwick v. Bostwick, CN89-7038, 1991 Del. Fam. Ct. LEXIS 4 (Mar. 8, 1991)

This divorce case involves the valuation of a husband's interest in a closely held accounting firm. Husband was a senior member and a 50 percent stockholder. The wife's valuation expert contended that goodwill should be added to the adjusted value of the tangible assets for an accurate appraisal of the accounting firm. The husband's expert contended that goodwill did not exist, and the value of his interest should be limited to 50 percent of the adjusted value of the tangible assets. The Court concluded that no goodwill value should be attached to the firm. Of special note in this case is the Court's opinion that, "Courts have simply not received . . . the kind of real expertise in analyzing the concept of professional goodwill that would be conducive to well-reasoned and enlightened opinions on the subject." The Court doubted the two experts' expertise in the field of professional practice evaluation.

Butler v. Butler, 541 Pa. 364; 663 A.2d 148 (1995)

In this case, the husband's employment as a partner in a CPA firm was subject to a 50 percent shareholder agreement. The lower Court allowed the inclusion of goodwill in the total value of the firm. However, the Supreme Court of Pennsylvania established that because of the shareholder agreement, the husband would not be able to realize any value attributable to the going-concern or goodwill of the firm should he leave the firm. Citing precedent, the Court overruled the lower court's opinion by stating that "where such goodwill is attributable solely to an individual's attributes it cannot be viewed as a value of the business a whole." The Court remanded the matter for a revaluation of the husband's partnership interest, but affirmed the Superior Court's order vacating the Trial Court's order of equitable distribution.

Gerard v. *Gerard,* 825 SW2d 21 (Mo. App. 1992)

The valuation of the wife's solo accounting practice as its tangible assets and receivables, less debts ($8,297), was affirmed by a Missouri appellate court which concluded that no goodwill existed. Gerard v. Gerard found a reasonable basis for this conclusion because there was conflicting expert testimony. The husband's expert found goodwill because of sales (purportedly with a goodwill component) in another city. (These sales all had noncompete clauses, the value of which Missouri does not include as goodwill.) The wife's expert disputed that the cities were comparable, adding that a solo practice where the wife was located was not marketable without a covenant not to compete and that there had been no sales in that city in the past eight to nine years.

Guzman v. *Guzman,* 827 SW2d 445 (Tex. App. Corpus Christi 1992)

Where the goodwill of the husband's solo CPA practice did not exist independently of the husband's professional ability, this goodwill could not be divided upon divorce. *Guzman* explained that only goodwill in a professional corporation that existed independently of a professional's personal skills may be subject to division.

McCabe v. *McCabe,* CS91-3090, 1995 Del. Fam. Ct. LEXIS 5 (May 9, 1995)

In this case involving resolution of the division of a marital estate and other ancillary matters, the central issues addressed by the Court were the valuations of the parties' interest in the husband's accounting firm and a TCBY franchise. Husband was the co-owner of an accounting firm, and the husband and wife owned a 50 percent interest in a TCBY franchise. The wife's expert used the "formula approach" to argue that a value should be placed on the firm's client list and other intangibles in addition to the book value of the accounting firm. The husband's expert argued that goodwill is nonexistent in closely held professional practices where the services are rendered by the principals and the clients rely on the principals' individual expertise. The Court stated that, while a client list may have value, it is valueless without a covenant not to compete. In addition, the Court stated that the issues in this particular case did not lend themselves to the method of valuation argued by the wife's expert.

Marriage of Leff, 499 NE2d 1042 (Ill. App. 2 Dist. 1986)

An Illinois appellate court affirmed, assigning a zero value to the husband's 50 percent interest in his accounting practice. *Marriage of Leff* explained that the wife had failed to offer any evidence as to the value of the business, save for a loan application, even though she clearly had attempted to gather such evidence. The Court concluded that her failure to offer such evidence under these circumstances created the presumption that the evidence would have been unfavorable to her position. The Court also relied on the fact that the Trial Court had equated the value of the husband's interest in the business with its income potential to him, and considered that value in apportioning the parties' assets and in determining maintenance and child support.

Marriage of Sedlock, 849 P2d 1243 (Wash. App. Div. 1 1993)

Valuing the husband's interest in his accounting practice at approximately $170,000, a compromise figure between the figures used by the parties' two experts, was affirmed by a Washington appellate court. The wife's expert valued the interest at $262,000, the husband's expert at $100,000. The Court noted that both experts were credible. However, the opinion did point out that there were some logical inconsistencies in the Trial Court's "hybrid" approach to these valuation issues which "would likely shock both expert witnesses." Nevertheless, the Court concluded that, where a trial court determines that the true value of an asset lies somewhere between the values testified to by "expert A" and "expert B," the Trial Court may adopt a "compromise" figure: "To rule otherwise would be to place the appellate courts in the position of weighing expert testimony, a position we decline to take."

Rice v. Rice, 634 NYS2d 761 (N.Y. App. 1995)

The Supreme Court of New York concurred that the Trial Court properly rejected the husband's argument that the value of his partnership interest in a big six accounting firm be limited to the balance of his capital account. The Court stated that the husband's contention ignores his status as a "continuing and productive partner in an ongoing enterprise." The Court agreed with the wife's expert that the capitalization of excess earnings formula was an appropriate method of valuing the husband's interest. However, the Court held that the expert's valuation was excessive. The Court concluded that "substituting a rate of 2 for the rate of 3 employed by the wife's expert ... " produces a value of the husband's partnership interest of $350,750.

Williams v. Williams, 667 So. 2d 915 (Fla. App. 1996)

This appeal deals with the review of the lower Court's valuation of an accounting practice for purposes of equitable distribution. The Appellate Court held that the Lower Court erred in assigning a value for goodwill to the practice. The evidence in the case failed to show the existence of goodwill. Furthermore, The husband's expert stated that "no one would buy the practice without a noncompete clause." The Court confirmed that the lack of a noncompete clause "is telling evidence of a lack of goodwill."

Appendix E

UNIFORM STANDARDS OF PROFESSIONAL APPRAISAL PRACTICE TABLE OF CONTENTS*

UNIFORM STANDARDS OF PROFESSIONAL APPRAISAL PRACTICE

1996 EDITION

Appraisal Standards Board

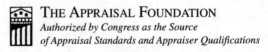

THE APPRAISAL FOUNDATION
*Authorized by Congress as the Source
of Appraisal Standards and Appraiser Qualifications*

TABLE OF CONTENTS

UNIFORM STANDARDS OF PROFESSIONAL APPRAISAL PRACTICE

INTRODUCTION

STANDARDS AND STANDARDS RULES

STATEMENTS ON APPRAISAL STANDARDS

Appendix F

BUSINESS VALUATION STANDARDS OF THE AMERICAN SOCIETY OF APPRAISERS*

In 1996 the Business Valuation Committee of the American Society of Appraisers issued a new standard: BVS-VII Valuation Discounts and Premiums. The previous BVS-VII (Comprehensive, Written Business Valuation Report) becomes BVS-VIII. However, as of this writing, the American Society of Appraisers has not published a new set of the standards with the new BVS-VII included. Therefore, we have provided in this Appendix the full set of standards as it stood before the issuance of the new BVS-VII (Valuation Discounts and Premiums) and at the end of the Appendix have included the newly issued standard.

*ASA Business Valuation Standards, American Society of Appraisers, ©1992, 1994, 1996. Reprinted with permission.

American Society of Appraisers

Business Valuation Standards©

This release of the approved Business Valuation Standards of the American Society of Appraisers contains all standards approved through January 23, 1994, and are to be used in conjunction with the Uniform Standards of Professional Appraisal Practice (USPAP) of The Appraisal Foundation and the Principles of Appraisal Practice and Code of Ethics of the American Society of Appraisers.

It contains the following sections, with the effective approval date of each:

Item	Title	Effective Date	Page
PREAMBLE		September 1992	
		Revised January 1994	
BUSINESS VALUATION STANDARDS			
BVS-I	General Requirements For	January 1992	
	Developing A Business Valuation	Revised June 1993	
		Revised January 1994	
BVS-II	Financial Statement Adjustments	September 1992	
		Revised January 1994	
BVS-III	Asset-Based Approach	January 1992	
	to Business Valuation	Revised January 1994	
BVS-IV	Income Approach to Business	September 1992	
	Valuation	Revised January 1994	
BVS-V	Market Approach to Business	September 1992	
	Valuation	Revised January 1994	
BVS-VI	Reaching a Conclusion of Value	September 1992	
		Revised January 1994	
BVS-VII	Comprehensive, Written	June 1991	
	Business Valuation Report	Revised January 1994	
DEFINITIONS		January 1980	
		Revised September 1992	
		Revised June 1993	
		Revised January 1994	
STATEMENTS ON BUSINESS VALUATION STANDARDS			
SBVS-1	The Guideline Company	January 1992	
	Valuation Method	Revised January 1994	
PROCEDURAL GUIDELINES AND/OR ADVISORY OPINIONS			
(To be issued when appropriate)			

AMERICAN SOCIETY OF APPRAISERS
Business Valuation Standards

Preamble©

Approved by the ASA Board of Governors, September, 1992

I.   To enhance and maintain the quality of business valuations for the benefit of the business valuation profession and users of business valuations, the American Society of Appraisers, through its Business Valuation Committee, has adopted these standards.

II. The American Society of Appraisers (in its Principles of Appraisal Practice and Code of Ethics) and the Appraisal Foundation (in its Uniform Standards of Professional Appraisal Practice) have established authoritative principles and a code of professional ethics. These standards include these requirements, either explicitly or by reference, and are designed to clarify and provide additional requirements specifically applicable to the valuation of businesses, business ownership interests or securities.

III. These standards incorporate, where appropriate, all relevant business valuation standards adopted by the American Society of Appraisers through its Business Valuation Committee.

IV. These standards provide minimum criteria to be followed by business appraisers in the valuation of businesses, business ownership interests or securities.

V.   If, in the opinion of the appraiser, circumstances of a specific business valuation assignment dictate a departure from any provisions of any Standard, such departure must be disclosed and will apply only to the specific departure.

VI. These Standards are designed to provide guidance to ASA Appraisers conducting business valuations and to provide a structure for regulating conduct of members of the ASA through Uniform Practices and Procedures. Deviations from the Standards are not designed or intended to be the basis of any civil liability; and should not create any presumption or evidence that a legal duty has been breached; or create any special relationship between the appraiser and any other person.

AMERICAN SOCIETY OF APPRAISERS
Business Valuation Standards

BVS-I General Requirements For Developing A Business Valuation©

I. **Preamble**

    A. This standard is required to be followed in all valuations of businesses, business ownership interests, and securities by all members of the American Society of Appraisers, be they Candidates, Accredited Members (AM), Accredited Senior Appraisers (ASA), or Fellows (FASA).

    B. The purpose of this standard is to define and describe the general requirements for developing the valuation of businesses, business ownership interests, or securities.

    C. This standard incorporates the general preamble to the Business Valuation Standards of the American Society of Appraisers.

II. **The Valuation Assignment shall be Appropriately Defined**

    A. In developing a business valuation, an appraiser must identify and define the following:

        1. The business, business ownership interest, or security to be valued

        2. The effective date of the appraisal

        3. The standard of value

        4. The purpose and use of the valuation

    B. The nature and scope of the assignment must be defined. Acceptable scopes of work would generally be of three types as delineated below. Other scopes of work should be explained and described.

        1. Appraisal

           a. The objective of an appraisal is to express an unambiguous opinion as to the value of the business, business ownership interest, or security, which is supported by all procedures that the appraiser deems to be relevant to the valuation.

           b. An appraisal has the following qualities:

              (1) It is expressed as a single dollar amount or as a range.

              (2) It considers all relevant information as of the appraisal date available to the appraiser at the time of performance of the valuation.

              (3) The appraiser conducts appropriate procedures to collect and analyze all information expected to be relevant to the valuation.

              (4) The valuation is based upon consideration of all conceptual approaches deemed to be relevant by the appraiser.

2. Limited Appraisal
   a. The objective of a limited appraisal is to express an estimate as to the value of a business, business ownership interest, or security, which lacks the performance of additional procedures that are required in an appraisal.
   b. A limited appraisal has the following qualities:
      (1) It is expressed as a single dollar amount or as a range.
      (2) It is based upon consideration of limited relevant information.
      (3) The appraiser conducts only limited procedures to collect and analyze the information which such appraiser considers necessary to support the conclusion presented.
      (4) The valuation is based upon the conceptual approach(es) deemed by the appraiser to be most appropriate.

3. Calculations
   a. The objective of calculations is to provide an approximate indication of value based upon the performance of limited procedures agreed upon by the appraiser and the client.
   b. Calculations have the following qualities:
      (1) They may be expressed as a single dollar amount or as a range.
      (2) They may be based upon consideration of only limited relevant information.
      (3) The appraiser performs limited information collection and analysis procedures.
      (4) The calculations may be based upon conceptual approaches as agreed upon with the client.

III. **Information Collection and Analysis**
The appraiser shall gather, analyze, and adjust relevant information to perform the valuation as appropriate to the scope of work. Such information shall include the following:
A. Characteristics of the business, business ownership interest or security to be valued including rights, privileges and conditions, quantity, factors affecting control and agreements restricting sale or transfer.
B. Nature, history and outlook of the business.
C. Historical financial information for the business.
D. Assets and liabilities of the business.
E. Nature and conditions of the relevant industries which have an impact on the business.
F. Economic factors affecting the business.
G. Capital markets providing relevant information, e.g. available rates of return on alternative investments, relevant public stock transactions, and relevant mergers and acquisitions.

H. Prior transactions involving subject business, interest in the subject business, or its securities.

I. Other information deemed by the appraiser to be relevant.

IV. Approaches, Methods, and Procedures

A. The appraiser shall select and apply appropriate valuation approaches, methods, and procedures.

B. The appraiser shall develop a conclusion of value pursuant to the valuation assignment as defined, considering the relevant valuation approaches, methods, and procedures, and appropriate premiums and discounts, if any.

V. Documentation and Retention

The appraiser shall appropriately document and retain all information and work product that were relied on in reaching the conclusion.

VI. Reporting

The appraiser shall report to the client the conclusion of value in an appropriate written or oral format. The report must meet the requirements of Standard 10 of The Uniform Standards of Professional Appraisal Practice. In the event the assignment results in a comprehensive written report, the report shall meet the requirements of BVS-VII.

AMERICAN SOCIETY OF APPRAISERS
Business Valuation Standards

BVS-II Financial Statement Adjustments©

I. Preamble

A. This standard is required to be followed in all valuations of businesses, business ownership interests, and securities by all members of the American Society of Appraisers, be they Candidates, Accredited Members (AM), Accredited Senior Appraisers (ASA), or Fellows (FASA).

B. The purpose of this standard is to define and describe the requirements for making financial statement adjustments in valuation of businesses, business ownership interests, and securities.

C. This present standard is applicable to appraisals and may not necessarily be applicable to limited appraisals and calculations as defined in BVS-I, Section II.B.

D. This standard incorporates the general preamble to the Business Valuation Standards of the American Society of Appraisers.

II. **Conceptual Framework**

    A. Financial statements should be analyzed and, if appropriate, adjusted as a procedure in the valuation process. Financial statements to be analyzed include those of the subject entity and any entities used as guideline companies.

    B. Financial statement adjustments are modifications to reported financial information that are relevant and significant to the appraisal process. Adjustments may be necessary in order to make the financial statements more meaningful for the appraisal process. Adjustments may be appropriate for the following reasons, among others: (1) To present financial data of the subject and guideline companies on a consistent basis; (2) To adjust from reported values to current values; (3) To adjust revenues and expenses to levels which are reasonably representative of continuing results; and (4) To adjust for non-operating assets and liabilities and the related revenue and expenses.

    C. Financial statement adjustments are made for the purpose of assisting the appraiser in reaching a valuation conclusion and for no other purpose.

III. **Documentation of Adjustments**

Adjustments made should be fully described and supported.

AMERICAN SOCIETY OF APPRAISERS
Business Valuation Standards

BVS-III Asset Based Approach to Business Valuation©

I. **Preamble**

    A. This standard is required to be followed in all valuations of businesses, business ownership interests, and securities by all members of the American Society of Appraisers, be they candidates, Accredited Members (AM), Accredited Senior Appraisers (ASA), or Fellows (FASA).

    B. The purpose of this standard is to define and describe the requirements for the use of the Asset Based Approach to business valuation and the circumstances in which it is appropriate.

    C. This present standard is applicable to appraisals and may not necessarily be applicable to limited appraisals and calculations as defined in BVS-I, Section II.B.

    D. This standard incorporates the general preamble to the Business Valuation Standards of the American Society of Appraisers.

II. The Asset Based Approach

A. In business valuation the Asset Based Approach may be analogous to the Cost Approach of other disciplines.

B. Assets, liabilities and equity relate to a business that is an operating company, a holding company, or a combination thereof (mixed business).

1. An operating company is a business which conducts an economic activity by generating and selling, or trading, in a product or service.

2. A holding company is a business which derives its revenues by receiving returns on its assets which may include operating companies and/or other businesses.

C. The Asset Based Approach should be considered in valuations conducted at the *total entity level* and involving the following:

1. An investment or real estate holding company

2. A business appraised on a basis other than as a going concern. Valuations of *particular ownership interests* in an entity may or may not require the use of the Asset Based Approach.

D. The Asset Based Approach should not be the sole appraisal approach used in assignments relating to operating companies appraised as going concerns unless it is customarily used by sellers and buyers. In such cases, the appraiser must support the selection of this approach.

AMERICAN SOCIETY OF APPRAISERS
Business Valuation Standards

BVS-IV Income Approach to Business Valuation©

I. Preamble

A. This standard is required to be followed in all valuations of businesses, business ownership interests, and securities by all members of the American Society of Appraisers, be they Candidates, Accredited Members (AM), Accredited Senior Appraisers (ASA), or Fellows (FASA).

B. The purpose of this standard is to define and describe the requirements for the use of the income approach in valuation of businesses, business ownership interests, and securities, but not the reporting therefor.

C. This present standard is applicable to appraisals and may not necessarily be applicable to limited appraisals and calculations as defined in BVS-I, Section II.B.

D. This standard incorporates the general preamble to the Business Valuation Standards of the American Society of Appraisers.

II. The Income Approach

A. The income approach is a general way of determining a value indication of a business, business ownership interest or security using one or more methods wherein a value is determined by converting anticipated benefits.

B. Both capitalization of benefits methods and discounted future benefits methods are acceptable. In capitalization of benefits methods, a representative benefit level is divided or multiplied by a capitalization factor to convert the benefit to value. In discounted future benefits methods, benefits are estimated for each of several future periods. These benefits are converted to value by the application of a discount rate using present value techniques.

III. Anticipated Benefits

A. Anticipated benefits, as used in the income approach, are expressed in monetary terms. Depending on the nature of the business, business ownership interest or security being appraised and other relevant factors, anticipated benefits may be reasonably represented by such items as net cash flow, dividends, and various forms of earnings.

B. Anticipated benefits should be estimated considering such items as the nature, capital structure, and historical performance of the related business entity, expected future outlook for the business entity and relevant industries, and relevant economic factors.

IV. Conversion of Anticipated Benefit

A. Anticipated benefits are converted to value using procedures which consider the expected growth and timing of the benefits, the risk profile of the benefits stream and the time value of money.

B. The conversion of anticipated benefits to value normally requires the determination of a capitalization rate or discount rate. In determining the appropriate rate, the appraiser should consider such factors as the level of interest rates, rates of return expected by investors on relevant investments, and the risk characteristics of the anticipated benefits.

C. In discounted future benefits methods, expected growth is considered in estimating the future stream of benefits. In capitalization of benefits methods, expected growth is incorporated in the capitalization rate.

D. The rate of return used (capitalization rate or discount rate) should be consistent with the type of anticipated benefits used. For example, pre-tax rates of return should be used with pre-tax benefits; common equity rates of return should be used with common equity benefits; and net cash flow rates should be used with net cash flow benefits

---

AMERICAN SOCIETY OF APPRAISERS
Business Valuation Standards

BVS-V Market Approach to Business Valuation©

I. **Preamble**
  A. This standard is required to be followed in all valuations of businesses, business ownership interests, and securities by all members of the American Society of Appraisers, be they Candidates, Accredited Members (AM), Accredited Senior Appraisers (ASA), or Fellows (FASA).
  B. The purpose of this standard is to define and describe the requirements for the use of the market approach in valuation of businesses, business ownership interests, and securities, but not the reporting therefor.
  C. This present standard is applicable to appraisals and may not necessarily be applicable to limited appraisals and calculations as defined in BVS-I, Section II.B.
  D. This standard incorporates the general preamble to the Business Valuation Standards of the American Society of Appraisers.

II. **The Market Approach**
  A. The market approach is a general way of determining a value indication of a business, business ownership interest or security using one or more methods that compare the subject to similar businesses, business ownership interests and securities that have been sold.
  B. Examples of market approach methods include the Guideline Company method and analysis of prior transactions in the ownership of the subject company.

III. **Reasonable Basis for Comparison**
  A. The investment used for comparison must provide a reasonable basis for the comparison.
  B. Factors to be considered in judging whether a reasonable basis for comparison exists include:
    1. Sufficient similarity of qualitative and quantitative investment characteristics.
    2. Amount and verifiability of data known about the similar investment.
    3. Whether or not the price of the similar investment was obtained in an arms length transaction, or a forced or distress sale.

IV. **Manner of Comparison**
  A. The comparison must be made in a meaningful manner and must not be misleading. Such comparisons are normally made through the use of valuation raitos. The computation and use of such ratios should provide meaningful insight about the pricing of the subject considering all relevant factors. Accordingly, care should be exercised in the following:

1. Selection of underlying data used for the ratio.
2. Selection of the time period and/or averaging method used for the underlying data.
3. Manner of computing and comparing the subject's underlying data.
4. The timing of the price data used in the ratio.

B. In general, comparisons should be made using comparable definitions of the components of the valuation ratios. However, where appropriate, valuation ratios based on components which are reasonably representative of continuing results may be used.

V. Rules of Thumb

A. Rules of thumb may provide insight on the value of a business, business ownership interest or security. However, value indications derived from the use of rules of thumb should not be given substantial weight unless supported by other valuation methods and it can be established that knowledgeable buyers and sellers place substantial reliance on them.

AMERICAN SOCIETY OF APPRAISERS
Business Valuation Standards

BVS-VI Reaching a Conclusion of Value©

I. Preamble

A. This standard is required to be followed in all valuations of businesses, business ownership interests, and securities by all members of the American Society of Appraisers, be they Candidates, Accredited Members (AM), Accredited Senior Appraisers (ASA), or Fellows (FASA).

B. The purpose of this standard is to define and describe the requirements for reaching a final conclusion of value in valuation of businesses, business ownership interests, or securities.

C. This present standard is applicable to appraisals and may not necessarily be applicable to limited appraisals and calculations as defined in BVS-I, Section II.B.

D. This standard incorporates the general preamble to the Business Valuation Standards of the American Society of Appraisers.

II. General

A. The conclusion of value reached by the appraiser shall be based upon the applicable standard of value, the purpose and intended use of the valuation, and all relevant information obtained as of the appraisal date in carrying out the scope of the assignment.

B. The conclusion of value reached by the appraiser will be based on value indications resulting from one or more methods performed under one or more appraisal approaches.

III. Selection and Weighing of Methods

A. The selection of and reliance on the appropriate method and procedures depends on the judgment of the appraiser and not on the basis of any prescribed formula. One or more approaches may not be relevant to the particular situation. More than one method under an approach may be relevant to a particular situation.

B. The appraiser must use informed judgment when determining the relative weight to be accorded to indications of value reached on the basis of various methods or whether an indication of value from a single method should dominate. The appraiser's judgment may be presented either in general terms or in terms of mathematical weighting of the indicated values reflected in the conclusion. In any case, the appraiser should provide the rationale for the selection or weighting of the method or methods relied on in reaching the conclusion.

C. In formulating a judgment about the relative weights to be accorded to indications of value determined under each method or whether an indication of value from a single method should dominate, the appraiser should consider factors such as:

1. The applicable standard of value;
2. The purpose and intended use of the valuation;
3. Whether the subject is an operating company, a real estate or investment holding company, or a company with substantial non-operating or excess assets;
4. Quality and reliability of data underlying the indication of value;
5. Such other factors which, in the opinion of the appraiser, are appropriate for consideration.

IV. Additional Factors to Consider

As appropriate for the valuation assignment as defined, and if not considered in the process of determining and weighting the indications of value provided by various procedures, the appraiser should separately consider the following factors in reaching a final conclusion of value:

A. Marketability, or lack thereof, considering the nature of the business, business ownership interest or security, the effect of relevant contractual and legal restrictions, and the condition of the markets.

B. Ability of the appraised interest to control the operation, sale, or liquidation of the relevant business.

C. Such other factors which, in the opinion of the appraiser, are appropriate for consideration.

AMERICAN SOCIETY OF APPRAISERS
Business Valuation Standards

BVS-VII Comprehensive, Written Business Valuation Report ©

I. Preamble

A. This standard is required to be followed in the preparation of comprehensive, written business valuation reports by all members of the American Society of Appraisers, be they Candidates, Accredited Members (AM), Accredited Senior Appraisers (ASA), or Fellows (FASA).

B. The purpose of this standard is to define and describe the requirements for the written communication of the results of a business valuation, analysis or opinion, but not the conduct thereof.

C. This standard incorporates the general preamble to the Business Valuation Standards of the American Society of Appraisers.

II. Signature and Certification

A. An appraiser assumes responsibility for the statements made in the comprehensive, written report and indicates the acceptance of that responsibility by signing the report. To comply with this standard, a comprehensive, written report must be signed by the appraiser. For the purpose of this standard, the appraiser is the individual or entity undertaking the appraisal assignment under a contract with the client.

B. Clearly, at least one individual is responsible for the valuation conclusion(s) expressed in the report. A report must contain a certification, as required by Standard 10 of the *Uniform Standards of Professional Appraisal Practice* of The Appraisal Foundation, in which the individuals responsible for the valuation conclusion(s) must be identified.

III. Assumptions and Limiting Conditions

The following assumptions and/or limiting conditions must be stated:

1. Pertaining to bias—a report must contain a statement that the appraiser has no interest in the asset appraised, or other conflict, which could cause a question as to the appraiser's independence or objectivity or if such an interest or conflict exists, it must be disclosed.

2. Pertaining to data used—where appropriate, a report must indicate that an appraiser relied on data supplied by others, without further verification by the appraiser, as well as the sources which were relied on.

3. Pertaining to validity of the valuation—a report must contain a statement that a valuation is valid only for the valuation date indicated and for the purpose stated.

IV. **Definition of the Valuation Assignment**

The precise definition of the valuation assignment is a key aspect of communication with users of the report. The following are key components of such a definition and must be included in the report:

1. The business interest valued must be clearly defined, such as "100 shares of the Class A common stock of the XYZ Corporation" or "a 20% limited partnership interest in the ABC Limited Partnership." The existence, rights and/or restrictions of other classes of ownership in the business appraised must also be adequately described if they are relevant to the conclusion of value.

2. The purpose and use of the valuation must be clearly stated, such as "a determination of fair market value for ESOP purposes" or "a determination of fair value for dissenter's rights purposes." If a valuation is being done pursuant to a particular statute, the particular statute must be referenced.

3. The standard of value used in the valuation must be stated and defined. The premise of value, such as a valuation on a minority interest or a control basis, must be stated.

4. The appraisal date must be clearly defined. The date of the preparation of the report must be indicated.

V. **Business Description**

A comprehensive, written business valuation report must include a business depreciation which covers all relevant factual areas, such as:

1. Form of organization (corporation, partnership, etc.)
2. History
3. Products and/or services and markets and customers
4. Management
5. Major assets, both tangible and intangible
6. Outlook for the economy, industry and company
7. Past transactional evidence of value
8. Sensitivity to seasonal or cyclical factors
9. Competition
10. Sources of information used.

VI. **Financial Analysis**

A. An analysis and discussion of a firm's financial statements is an integral part of a business valuation and must be included. Exhibits summarizing balance sheets and income statements for a period of years sufficient to the purpose of the valuation and the nature of the subject company must be included in the valuation report.

B. Any adjustments made to the reported financial data must be fully explained.

   C. If projections of balance sheets or income statements were utilized in the valuation, key assumptions underlying the projections must be included and discussed.

   D. If appropriate, the company's financial results relative to those of its industry must be discussed.

VII. Valuation Methodology

   A. The valuation method or methods selected, and the reasons for their selection, must be discussed. The steps followed in the application of the method or methods selected must be described and must lead to the valuation conclusion.

   B. The report must include an explanation of how any variables such as discount rates, capitalization rates or valuation multiples were determined and used. The rationale and/or supporting data for any premiums or discounts must be clearly presented.

VIII. Comprehensive, Written Report Format

The comprehensive, written report format must provide a logical progression for clear communication of pertinent information, valuation methods and conclusions and must incorporate the other specific requirements of this standard, including the signature and certification provisions.

IX. Confidentiality of Report

No copies of the report will be furnished to persons other than the client without the client's specific permission or direction unless ordered by a court of competent jurisdiction.

AMERICAN SOCIETY OF APPRAISERS
Business Valuation Standards

Definitions©

ADJUSTED BOOK VALUE	—The book value which results after one or more asset or liability amounts are added, deleted or changed from the respective book amounts.
APPRAISAL	—The act or process of determining value. It is synonymous with valuation.
APPRAISAL APPROACH	—A general way of determining value using one or more specific appraisal methods. (See Asset Based Approach, Market Approach and Income Approach definitions.)

APPRAISAL METHOD	—Within approaches, a specific way to determine value.
APPRAISAL PROCEDURE	—The act, manner and technique of performing the steps of an appraisal method.
APPRAISED VALUE	—The appraiser's opinion or determination of value.
ASSET BASED APPROACH	—A general way of determining a value indication of a business's assets and/or equity interest using one or more methods based directly on the value of the assets of the business less liabilities.
BOOK VALUE	—1. With respect to assets, the capitalized cost of an asset less accumulated depreciation, depletion or amortization as it appears on the books of account of the enterprise.
	2. With respect to a business enterprise, the difference between total assets (net of depreciation, depletion and amortization) and total liabilities of an enterprise as they appear on the balance sheet. It is synonymous with net book value, net worth and shareholder's equity.
BUSINESS APPRAISER	—A person, who by education, training and experience is qualified to make an appraisal of a business enterprise and/or its intangible assets.
BUSINESS ENTERPRISE	—A commercial, industrial or service organization pursuing an economic activity.
BUSINESS VALUATION	—The act or process of arriving at an opinion or determination of the value of a business or enterprise or an interest therein.
CAPITALIZATION	—1. The conversion of income into value.
	2. The capital structure of a business enterprise.
	3. The recognition of an expenditure as a capital asset rather than a period expense.
CAPITALIZATION FACTOR	—Any multiple or divisor used to convert income into value.
CAPITALIZATION RATE	—Any divisor (usually expressed as a percentage) that is used to convert income into value.
CAPITAL STRUCTURE	—The composition of the invested capital.
CASH FLOW	—Net income plus depreciation and other non-cash charges.
CONTROL	—The power to direct the management and policies of an enterprise.
CONTROL PREMIUM	—The additional value inherent in the control interest as contrasted to a minority interest, that reflects its power of control.

DISCOUNT FOR LACK OF CONTROL:	—An amount or percentage deducted from a prorata share of the value of 100 percent of an equity interest in a business, to reflect the absence of some or all of the powers of control.
DISCOUNT RATE	—A rate of return used to convert a monetary sum, payable or receivable in the future, into present value.
ECONOMIC LIFE	—The period over which property may be profitably used.
EFFECTIVE DATE	—The date as of which the appraiser's opinion of value applies (also referred to as Appraisal Date, Valuation Date and/or As Of Date).
ENTERPRISE	—See BUSINESS ENTERPRISE.
EQUITY	—The owner's interest in property after deduction of all liabilities.
FAIR MARKET VALUE	—The amount at which property would change hands between a willing seller and a willing buyer when neither is under compulsion and when both have reasonable knowledge of the relevant facts.
GOING CONCERN	—An operating business enterprise.
GOING CONCERN VALUE	—1. The value of an enterprise, or an interest therein, as a going concern. 2. Intangible elements of value in a business enterprise resulting from factors such as: having a trained workforce; an operational plant; and the necessary licenses, systems and procedures in place.
GOODWILL	—That intangible asset which arises as a result of name, reputation, customer patronage, location, products and similar factors that have not been separately identified and/or valued but which generate economic benefits.
INCOME APPROACH	—A general way of determining a value indication of a business, business ownership interest or security using one or more methods wherein a value is determined by converting anticipated benefits.
INVESTED CAPITAL	—The sum of the debt and equity in an enterprise on a long term basis.
MAJORITY INTEREST	—Ownership position greater than 50% of the voting interest in an enterprise.
MAJORITY CONTROL	—The degree of control provided by a majority position.

MARKET APPROACH	—A general way of determining a value indication of a business, business ownership interest or security using one or more methods that compare the subject to similar businesses, business ownership interests or securities that have been sold.
MARKETABILITY DISCOUNT	—An amount or percentage deducted from an equity interest to reflect lack of marketability.
MINORITY INTEREST	—Ownership position less than 50% of the voting interest in an enterprise.
MINORITY DISCOUNT	—A Discount for Lack of Control applicable to a minority interest.
NET ASSETS	—Total assets less total liabilities.
NET INCOME	—Revenue less expenses, including taxes.
RATE OF RETURN	—An amount of income (loss) and/or change in value realized or anticipated on an investment, expressed as a percentage of that investment.
REPLACEMENT COST NEW	—The current cost of a similar new item having the nearest equivalent utility as item being appraised.
REPORT DATE	—The date of the report. May be the same as or different from the APPRAISAL DATE.
REPRODUCTION COST NEW	—The current cost of an identical new item.
RULE OF THUMB	—A mathematical relationship between or among a number of variables based on experience, observation, hearsay or a combination of these, usually applicable to a specific industry.
VALUATION	—See APPRAISAL.
VALUATION RATIO	—A factor wherein a value or price serves as the numerator and financial, operating or physical data serve as the denominator.
WORKING CAPITAL	—The amount by which current assets exceed current liabilities.

AMERICAN SOCIETY OF APPRAISERS
Business Valuation Statements

SBVS-1 The Guideline Company Valuation Method©

I. **Preamble**
   A. This statement is required to be followed in all valuations of businesses, business ownership interests, and securities by all members of the American Society of Appraisers, be they Candidates, Accredited Members (AM), Accredited Senior Appraisers (ASA), or Fellows (FASA).
   B. The purpose of this statement is to define and describe the requirements for the use of guideline companies in the valuation of businesses, business ownership interests or securities.
   C. This statement incorporates the general preamble to the Business Valuation Standards of the American Society of Appraisers.

II. **Conceptual Framework**
   A. Market transactions in businesses, business ownership interests or securities can provide objective, empirical data for developing valuation ratios to apply in business valuation.
   B. The development of valuation ratios from guideline companies should be considered for use in the valuation of businesses, business ownership interests or securities, to the extent that adequate information is available.
   C. Guideline companies are companies that provide a reasonable basis for comparison to the investment characteristics of the company being valued. Ideal guideline companies are in the same industry as the company being valued; but if there is insufficient transaction evidence available in the same industry it may be necessary to select companies with an underlying similarity of relevant investment characteristics such as markets, products, growth, cyclical variability and other salient factors.

III. **Search for and Selection of Guideline Companies**
   A. A thorough, objective search for guideline companies is required to establish the credibility of the valuation analysis. The procedure must include criteria for screening and selecting guideline companies.
   B. Empirical data from guideline companies can be found in transactions involving either minority or controlling interests in either publicly traded or closely held companies.

IV. **Financial Data of the Guideline Companies**
   A. It is necessary to obtain and analyze financial and operating data on the guideline companies, as available.

B. Consideration should be given to adjustments to the financial data of the subject company and the guideline companies to minimize the difference in accounting treatments when such differences are significant. Unusual or nonrecurring items should be analyzed and adjusted as appropriate.

V. **Comparative Analysis of Qualitative and Quantitative Factors**
A comparative analysis of qualitative and quantitative similarities and differences between guideline companies and the subject company must be made to assess the investment attributes of the guideline companies relative to the subject company.

VI. **Valuation Ratios Derived From Guideline Companies**
A. Price information of the guideline companies must be related to the appropriate underlying financial data of each guideline company in order to compute appropriate valuation ratios.
B. The valuation ratios for the guideline companies and comparative analysis of qualitative and quantitative factors should be used together to determine appropriate valuation ratios for application to the subject company.
C. Several valuation ratios may be selected for application to the subject company and several value indications may be obtained. The appraiser should consider the relative importance accorded to each of the value indications utilized in arriving at the valuation conclusion.
D. To the extent that adjustments for dissimilarities with respect to minority and control, or marketability, have not been made earlier, appropriate adjustments for these factors must be made, if applicable.

AMERICAN SOCIETY OF APPRAISERS
Business Valuation Standards

BVS-VII Valuation Discounts and Premiums©

Adopted by the ASA Business Valuation Committee, November 1, 1995
Approved by the ASA Board of Governors, January 21, 1996

I. **Preamble**
A. This standard is required to be followed in all valuations of businesses, business ownership interests, and securities by all members of the American Society of Appraisers, be they Candidates, Accredited Members (AM), Accredited Senior Appraisers (ASA), or Fellows (FASA).

B. The purpose of this standard is to define and describe the requirements for use of discounts and premiums in the valuation of businesses, business ownership interests, or securities whenever they are applied.

C. This standard incorporates the general preamble to the Business Valuation Standards of the American Society of Appraisers.

D. This standard is applicable to appraisals and may not necessarily be applicable to limited appraisals and calculations as defined in BVS-I, Section II.B.

E. This standard applies at any time in the valuation process, whether within a method, to the value indicated by a valuation method, or to the result of weighing or correlating methods.

II. The Concept of Discounts and Premiums

A. A discount has no meaning until the conceptual basis underlying the value to which it is applied is defined.

B. A premium has no meaning until the conceptual basis underlying the value to which it is applied is defined.

C. A discount or premium is warranted when characteristics affecting the value of the subject interest differ sufficiently from those inherent in the base value to which it is applied.

D. A premium or discount quantifies an adjustment to account for differences in characteristics affecting the value of the subject interest relative to the base value to which it is being compared.

III. The Application of Discounts and Premiums

A. The purpose, applicable standard of value, or other circumstances of an appraisal may indicate the need to account for differences between the base value and the value of the subject interest. If so, appropriate discounts or premiums should be applied.

B. The base value to which the discount or premium is applied must be specified and defined.

C. Each discount or premium to be applied to the base value must be defined.

D. The primary reasons why each discount or premium selected applies to the appraised interest must be stated.

E. The evidence considered in deriving the discount or premium must be specified.

F. The appraiser's reasoning in arriving at a conclusion regarding the size of any discount or premium applied must be explained.

Appendix G

BUSINESS VALUATION STANDARDS OF THE INSTITUTE OF BUSINESS APPRAISERS*

*Business Appraisal Standards, The Institute of Business Appraisers, Inc., © 1993. Reprinted with permission.

BUSINESS APPRAISAL STANDARDS

As
Promulgated
by

The Institute Of Business Appraisers, Inc.

July 1, 1993

Publication P-311a

NOTICE

This publication supersedes and replaces the following IBA publications:
P-243 Standards of Business Appraisal Practice
P-244 Standards for Business Appraisal Reports

FOREWORD

Only a small percentage of individuals representing themselves as business appraisers have been tested and certified by a professional business appraisal institute or society.

Those considering employing a business appraiser are undoubtedly doing so in relation to a matter which can have far reaching financial or legal ramifications. Beyond the obvious caution that a proper valuation cannot be done without adequate preparation, competency, and documentation, we suggest verification that the individual is certified as a business appraiser and intends to prepare the appraisal in compliance with these standards.

The Institute of Business Appraisers would like to thank those associated with The Appraisal Foundation and the American Society of Appraisers whose efforts toward developing business appraisal standards and ethics have contributed greatly to the product of this Committee.

FOUNDING STANDARDS COMMITTEE

David M. Bishop, CBA, Chairman
Larry R. Cook, CBA, CPA
James M. Hansen, CBA, CRA
Steven F. Schroeder, CBA, ASA
Raymond C. Miles, CBA, ASA Ex-Officio

PREAMBLE:

1. Certain professions, by their nature, and by the way they are perceived by the public, are capable of exerting substantial influence on the public welfare. It is our firm conviction that the practice of business appraisal falls in a similar category.

2. The performance of business appraisal/valuation requires a high degree of skill, imposes upon the appraiser a duty of non-advocacy to the client and an obligation to the general public as a third party beneficiary of the work. It is our purpose here to articulate standards by which those who aspire to participation, and those already established in business appraisal practice may be guided in the ethical and skillful execution of their tasks, and report the results and conclusions of their work in the most effective manner.

3. It is also our purpose to state these standards in such a clear and unequivocal way that the world at large, and especially those who may engage the services of a business appraiser, will know the parameters by which professional competence is to be measured, and by which its professional practitioners wish to be judged.

4. Each standard is qualified as: (i) should, (ii) must or (iii) shall. Should and must standards are guidelines. While an appraiser may depart from a should standard without a statement of departure, such departure should be made knowingly. In those instances where the appraiser feels a departure from a must standard is warranted, the report shall include a statement of departure. It is the position of the IBA that standards designated shall are those from which departure is not justified.

5. These standards have been developed to provide guidance to appraisers who are members of the Institute of Business Appraisers (IBA) and others performing appraisals of closely held businesses, business ownership interests or securities. They have also been developed to assist in the evaluation and regulation of members of the IBA through creating uniform practices and procedures. Departures from the standards are not intended to provide a basis for civil liability, and should not be presumed to create evidence that any legal duty has been breached, or to imply the creation of any additional relationships or duties other than those specified herein.

FORMAT:

These standards are presented in a naturally progressive format beginning with overall professional conduct and ethics, followed by specific standards applicable to oral reports, expert testimony, letter reports, formal reports, and preliminary reports.

No attempt is made to anticipate every possible scenario or unique circumstance and create standards specific thereto. Conversely, these standards were developed under the premise that the professional business appraiser practicing within the proper standard of care can, on a case-by-case basis, adequately apply these standards in such a manner to result in a competent report while still permitting the flexibility necessary to meet the reasonable requests of the client and the vicissitudes of the assignment.

Within this publication, reference to all individuals has been in the masculine. This is done in the interest of simplicity and is not intended as a gender bias. Terms should be assumed to be in the singular or plural as appropriate to the context in which they are used.

STANDARD ONE

1.0   ## PROFESSIONAL CONDUCT & ETHICS

1.1   Competence. The achievement of certification as a business appraiser (CBA) is a result of specialized training, study, practice, the successful completion of a proctored examination, and a favorable review of the candidate's actual appraisal reports by The Institute of Business Appraisers' Qualifications Review Committee. To maintain certification, a CBA will adhere to continuing education requirements and periodic recertification as required by IBA.

Prior to accepting an engagement to perform a business appraisal, the appraiser must judge his competence to complete the assignment. Should the appraiser have a meaningful lack of knowledge and experience, the appraiser must immediately disclose that fact to the client. If the client desires the appraiser to continue with the assignment, the appraiser shall take those steps necessary to perform the appraisal in a competent manner, or take those steps necessary to complete the assignment under the supervision of an appraiser who has the requisite skill, or with the permission of the client, refer the engagement to a qualified business appraiser.

It is essential that a business appraiser communicate the research and thought processes which led to his opinions and conclusions in a manner that is clear, meaningful and not misleading. Said communication, whether oral or written, shall not be rendered in a careless or negligent manner.

The appraiser as an individual must be competent. Software valuation programs and/or excessive reliance on rules of thumb are not surrogates for individual competence.

The professional business appraiser recognizes and understands that compliance with these standards and ethics is an essential part of competence.

1.2 Confidentiality. The very fact an appraiser has been retained to value all or a portion of a business enterprise, or its securities, is in itself confidential. Consequently, it is considered unethical for a business appraiser to disclose either the assignment itself or any of the reasonably identifiable contents of an appraisal report without the client's express permission.

1.3 Disinterestedness. It is unethical for a business appraiser to accept any assignment when the appraiser has a present or contemplated interest in the property being appraised, or a bias for or against any person associated therewith, either directly or indirectly. Such interests include, but are not limited to, present, contemplated or prospective activity with the business enterprise, its officers, directors, or owners, including possible acquirers or investors.

However, if a prospective client, after full disclosure by the appraiser of said interest or bias, still elects to engage the appraiser, the appraiser may accept the assignment. When accepting such an assignment, the business appraiser <u>shall</u> include a Statement of Departure as required by Standard 1.21(b). The Statement of Departure <u>shall</u> include a complete disclosure of the interest or bias.

1.4 Nonadvocacy v. Advocacy. Nonadvocacy is considered to be a mandatory standard of appraisal.

The appraiser's obligation to serve the public interest assures that the integrity of valuations will be preserved. Hence, the appraiser may only be an advocate for his unbiased process and conclusions. The appraiser <u>must</u> be guided by nothing other than his informed judgment, the dictates of the client (as permitted under these standards), applicable administrative rulings, and the law.

In the event the appraiser is engaged to function not as an appraiser but as an advisor or consultant, he may serve as an advocate. In such instances the appraiser <u>shall</u> include a statement of departure which states, that any positions taken were taken as an advocate for the client.

1.5 Engagement. Prior to performing an appraisal assignment, a business appraiser <u>should</u> obtain a written agreement signed by the client or his agent. At the very least, the engagement agreement <u>should</u> specify what the appraiser is being engaged to appraise, the function (use) of the appraisal, the purpose (standard of value) including the definition thereof, the effective date of the appraisal, the scope of the appraisal, that the appraisal will be performed on a nonadvocacy basis (see Standard 1.4), the amount of or method for calculating the appraiser's fee, together with the method for payment of same, and an indication of when the client may expect the report.

1.6   Coherence and Production. Appraisal reports must have logical organization. Readers' questions that can reasonably be anticipated should be answered. Data in one part of the report should not contradict other portions without reconciliation.

The appraiser should develop contributing conclusions from the various components of the appraisal process drawing them together in a cross-supporting manner that logically brings the reader to the appraiser's conclusion.

The report should be produced in a manner and style which brings credit to the appraiser and the profession. Typographical errors and the like <u>shall</u> be eliminated. In formal reports, page and exhibit numbers <u>should</u> be used together with a table of contents or index to enhance readability.

1.7   Supportable Opinion. The essence of business appraisal is a supportable opinion.

While it is intuitively logical that on a case-by-case basis certain opinions will be based on the informed, but subjective, judgment of the appraiser to a greater degree than others, the appraiser's goal is to have a supportable opinion. The reader should not be expected to accept critical elements such as adjustments to financial statements, the selected capitalization or discount rates or weightings, without support—even in those instances where the vicissitudes of the assignment dictate that support be primarily based on the informed judgment of the appraiser.

1.8   Replicability. The appraiser's procedures and conclusions in the formal report <u>must</u> be presented in sufficient detail to permit the reader to replicate the appraisal process.

1.9   Appropriateness. The standard of value, the type of report and the valuation approaches/methods utilized should be appropriate to the assignment. The material included in the report should be relevant, clear and cogent.

1.10   Jurisdictional Exception. If any part of these standards is contrary to the law or public policy of any jurisdiction, only that part shall be void and of no force and effect in that jurisdiction.

1.11   Fiduciary Duty to Clients, and Other Duties.

<u>Client</u> The one employing the business appraiser.

<u>Third Parties</u> Others who could be expected to review the report, e.g., attorneys, accountants, lenders, buyers, investors, regulatory agencies, courts, etc.

<u>Public</u> Society at large.

(a)   <u>Specialized Character of Business Appraisal.</u> Seldom are others intimately familiar with the process of business appraisal. Therefore, it is anticipated the business appraiser will use his professional abilities properly, as more fully described throughout these standards.

(b)   <u>Loyalty, Obedience and Reasonable Skill and Care.</u> Agents have such duties to clients. While no fiduciary or other affirmative duty is owed to others, services provided in accordance with these standards should be clear as to meaning and not be misleading to others.

1.12 Duty to Profession.

(a)   <u>Professional Cooperation and Courtesy.</u> It is unethical to damage or attempt to damage the professional reputations or interfere with the performance of other business appraisers practicing within the scope of these standards through false or malicious statement or innuendo.

(b)   <u>Conduct.</u> Every member is reminded that his demeanor and general conduct represents his profession and fellow practitioners, and unprofessional conduct damages more than his individual reputation.

(c)   <u>Cooperation.</u> Each member <u>shall</u> cooperate fully with the efforts of the Institute and/or its Ethics and Discipline Committee when investigating possible activities which are contrary to these standards.

1.13 Substance v. Form. The form of an appraisal report can be oral or written with variations of each. However, it is only the form of the report that varies. The appraiser's responsibilities to gather data, analyze the data, and draw supportable conclusions as applicable to the type of assignment undertaken does not change. Regardless of whether the final valuation is reported orally, in a summarizing letter report or a formal report, the appraiser <u>must</u> have first completed an appropriate valuation determination process.

A preliminary report is an exception to the above requirement for a thorough, complete work process. By its nature, a preliminary report results from a more cursory evaluation. (See Standard Six, Preliminary Reports.)

1.14 Professional Fees. The fees charged for the services of an appraiser are a product of the marketplace; however, a business appraiser is ethically denied the selection of a fee that could in itself call to question the objectivity of the appraiser.

(a)   Finder's Fees. No appraiser will pay fees, or offer gain in any form, to others to promote the appraiser's work in such a way, or under any circumstances, that will diminish the dignity of, or reflect discredit or disrepute upon, the appraisal profession.

(b)   Referral Fees. It is the right of an appraiser and, therefore, not unethical to pay a referral fee to another professional for the referral of appraisal assignments.

(c)   Percentage Fees. To accept any engagement for which the compensation is based on a percentage of the valuation conclusion impairs independence and is thus unethical.

1.15 Access to Requisite Data. The business appraiser, <u>must</u> decide what documents and/or information are requisite to a competent appraisal.

(a)   Reliability of Data. An appraiser may rely upon documents and/or information provided by the client and/or his agents without further corroboration; provided, the report clearly states he has done so. This right, however, does not abrogate the appraiser's duty to ask or otherwise inquire regarding information which on its surface clearly appears to be incomplete or otherwise inaccurate.

(b)   Pertinent Data. In situations where access to "pertinent" data is denied to the appraiser, the appraiser may, at his option, withdraw from completing the assignment. However, should the appraiser elect to complete the assignment, the report <u>must</u> include a Statement of Departure as required under Standard 1.21(b). Such Statement of Departure <u>must</u> describe the limitation and/or restriction and its potential effect on the appraiser's conclusion.

(c)   Essential Data. When the business appraiser is denied access to data considered essential to a proper appraisal, the business appraiser <u>should</u> not proceed with the assignment.

1.16 Valuation Approaches/Methods. The approaches/methods used within a given assignment are a matter that must be determined by the business appraiser's professional judgment. The task is generally decided through consideration of the approaches/methods that are conceptually most appropriate and those for which the most reliable data is available.

1.17 Definitions.

(a)   Terms. The appraiser should be careful in the use of ambiguous or esoteric terms. Such terms require definition to prevent the reader from applying a different definition.

(b) Computations. All computations, particularly those used to compute ratios and weightings should be clearly defined.

1.18 Principal Sources and References.

(a) Formal Report. A formal report must include a list of the principal sources of nonconfidential information and references whenever their inclusion will materially contribute to the clarity and understanding of the report.

(b) Oral and Informal Reports. The appraiser's workpapers must include a general description of the principal sources of information and references.

1.19 Site Tours and Interviews.

(a) Tour. Familiarity with an appraisal subject is a compelling necessity to a credible valuation. For this reason, it is desirable that a business appraiser make personal inspections or tours of appraisal subject sites whenever possible. When such activities are not performed, the appraiser's report shall disclose that the appraisal process did not include a site tour.

(b) Interview. An appraiser should not perform an appraisal without interviewing the management and other parties considered appropriate in the circumstances.

1.20 Eligibility of Data. An appraisal shall be based upon what a reasonably informed person would have knowledge of as of a certain date. This shall be known as the appraisal's "date of valuation" or "effective date" and accordingly reflect the appraiser's supportable conclusion as of that date. Information unavailable or unknown on the date of valuation must not influence the appraiser or contribute to the concluding opinion of value.

(a) Imminent Change. The appraiser is sometimes faced with the knowledge of a material imminent change in the business; a change not known of on the "date of valuation," but known as of the appraisal's "report" date. In such an event, the imminent change (positive or negative) should not affect the valuation conclusion, unless a reasonably informed person could have anticipated the imminent change. However, it is not uncommon for an appraiser to disclose such a change within the narrative portion of the report.

(b) Data on Guideline Companies. When an appraiser selects guideline companies, the data on the companies judged sufficiently similar should be information knowable, although perhaps not yet compiled, on or before the appraisal's date of valuation. Additionally, the data on the guideline companies should be for the same accounting period; however, if it is as of a different period, said different period <u>must</u> be on or before the appraisal's date of valuation.

This restriction should apply whether the guideline companies are specific companies or aggregate industry statistics or ratios.

1.21   Departure. A business appraiser may be engaged to perform an appraisal assignment that calls for something different from the work that would routinely result from the appraiser's compliance with all <u>must</u> standards; provided, that prior to entering into an agreement to perform such an assignment:

(a)   The appraiser is of the opinion that the assignment is not so limited in scope that the resulting report would tend to mislead or confuse the client or other anticipated readers; and

(b)   The appraiser has advised the client that the assignment calls for something different than that which would normally result from compliance with applicable standards and, therefore, the report <u>shall</u> include a statement of departure.

1.22   Hypothetical Reports. An analysis or appraisal may be prepared under a hypothetical assumption, or series thereof, even though they may appear improbable. However, such a report <u>must</u> clearly state (i) the hypothetical assumption and (ii) the purpose of the analysis or appraisal, and any opinion of value <u>must</u> clearly be identified as resulting from a hypothetical assumption.

1.23   Dissenting Opinion.

(a)   <u>Dissenting Opinion With Other Appraisers.</u> Collaborating appraisers, and review appraisers <u>must</u> sign the report. When a signing appraiser disagrees in whole or in part with any or all of the findings of other appraisers, said dissenting opinion <u>must</u> be included in the report, signed by the dissenting appraiser.

(b)   <u>Dissenting Opinion With Case Law and/or Administrative Regulation.</u> As any other member of society, appraisers are required to comply with statutory law and statutory definitions as they may exist from time to time and from jurisdiction to jurisdiction. However, case law and/or administrative regulations do not have the same force as statutory law. Therefore, the business appraiser may, when he believes it is warranted, express within the appraisal report a dissenting opinion to case law and/or an administrative regulation.

1.24   Membership Designations. It is considered unethical conduct for any individual to explicitly or implicitly indicate he is a Certified Business Appraiser (CBA) when he has not been awarded the designation.

(a)   <u>Certified Business Appraisal Reports.</u> An appraisal report may be considered a "Certified Report" when it is signed by a Certified Business Appraiser who is taking technical responsibility for its content.

(b)   <u>Certification of Firms.</u> The designation Certified Business Appraiser (CBA) is awarded to individuals, not business enterprises; therefore, it is unethical for an appraiser to explicitly or implicitly indicate that the firm is certified.

(c)   <u>Misuse of Certification.</u> Each Certified Business Appraiser is honor-bound to refrain from any use of his professional designation in connection with any form of activity that may reflect discredit upon his designation, or the organization that conferred it, or deceive his client, or the public. As with actual appraisal conclusions, this has been left as a matter of individual judgment and conscience; those who abuse this privilege could be subject to disciplinary action by IBA's Ethics and Discipline Committee.

1.25 Certification. Each written report <u>must</u> contain a certification signed by the appraiser. Additional appraisers signing the report <u>must</u> accept responsibility for the full contents of the report. [In the event of a dissenting opinion, see Standard 1.23(a).] The certificate must be similar in content to the following:

(a)   That to the best of the appraiser's knowledge, the statements of fact contained in the report are true and correct.

(b)   That the reported analyses, opinions, and conclusions are limited only by the reported assumptions and limiting conditions, and are the appraiser's personal, unbiased professional analyses, opinions and conclusions.

(c)   That the appraisal was performed on a basis of nonadvocacy, including a statement that the appraiser has no present or contemplated interest in the property appraised and has no personal bias with respect to the parties involved, or a complete disclosure of any such interest or bias.

(d)   That the appraiser's compensation is not contingent on an action or event resulting from the analyses, opinions, or conclusions in, or the use of, the report.

(e)   That the appraiser's analyses, opinions, and conclusions were developed and that the report has been prepared in conformity with the Business Appraisal Standards of The Institute of Business Appraisers.

(f)   That no one provided significant professional assistance to the person signing the report. However, if there are exceptions to this, then the name of each individual providing significant professional assistance must be disclosed.

1.26   Qualifications of the Appraiser. The reader cannot fully judge the quality of the appraisal report without being given the opportunity to judge the appraiser's qualifications. Therefore, each appraisal report <u>must</u> include the appraiser's qualifications in a manner the appraiser believes accurately presents his appraisal experience, certification, professional activities, and other qualifications.

1.27   Force and Effect. These standards shall be in full force and effect on the date of their issuance. (Earlier compliance is encouraged.) Any and all prior standards regarding business appraisal practices, reports, conduct, or ethics are superseded. Future amendments, to be effective, <u>shall</u> be initiated and passed in accordance with Standard 1.29.

1.28   Enforcement. The enforcement of these standards, including amendments or modifications as may occur in accordance with Standard 1.29, <u>shall</u> be the responsibility and duty of all members as to their own performance, and otherwise by the standing Ethics and Discipline Committee of The Institute of Business Appraisers and/or such other individuals or committees as are designated from time to time by the governing body of The Institute of Business Appraisers.

1.29   Amendments to Standards. The Standards Committee of The Institute of Business Appraisers is a standing committee. Certified members desiring to propose amendments, additions, or deletions to these standards should submit a clear expression of the proposed change to The Institute of Business Appraisers, Attention: Chairperson, Standards Committee. The chairperson reserves the right to return any submitted change for further clarification as to the precise change proposed. The chairperson shall distribute copies of the proposed change to the members of the Standards Committee for their opinions on the proposed change. Should two-thirds or more of the Committee support the change, it shall be endorsed by the Committee and an exposure draft will be provided to all CBAs. The exposure draft shall provide for a thirty-day period for the vote of all CBAs. In the event that those certified members who vote "No" exceeds 50% of all CBAs (those voting plus those not voting), the Committee's vote will be overruled and the proposed change will die for lack of support. Otherwise, the change will be adopted as of the first day of the month following the date copies of the amendments are provided to all members.

(a)   <u>Automatic Amendment.</u> It is the intent of the Business Appraisal Standards Committee (BASC) of The Institute of Business Appraisers (IBA) that these standards not conflict with standards nine and ten of the Uniform Standards of Professional Appraisal Practice as promulgated by The Appraisal Foundation. In the event of such a conflict, these standards will be amended as necessary. Pending said amendment, the conflicting portion of these standards will be temporarily suspended. However, nothing contained herein is intended to imply that these Business Appraisal Standards, promulgated by the IBA cannot restrict or require standards in excess of the restrictions or requirements of The Appraisal Foundation.

1.30   Signing Reports. Each written report <u>must</u> be signed by the appraiser and any other appraisers, including those signing as a "Review Appraiser" or "Collaborating Appraiser," <u>shall</u> accept responsibility for the full content of the report. [In the event of a dissenting opinion, see Standard 1.23(a).]

(a)   <u>Exception.</u> Should the policy of a given firm be that all reports are to be signed by a person authorized to sign reports on behalf of the firm, an exception to Standards 1.30 and 1.25 is permitted. However, in this event:

(i)   The designated signer <u>shall</u> take technical responsibility for the full content of the report; and

(ii)   The report may not be considered a "Certified Appraisal Report" unless a Certified Business Appraiser taking technical responsibility signs the report.

(iii)   The fact that a given appraisal report is signed under 1.30(a) is not intended in any way to justify or excuse deviation from any standard that would otherwise apply.

STANDARD TWO

2.0   **ORAL APPRAISAL REPORTS**

2.1   Usage. In general written reports are preferred; however, oral appraisal reports are permitted when ordered by the client.

2.2   Mandatory Content. When presenting an oral report, the business appraiser <u>shall</u> in a manner that is clear and not misleading communicate the following:

(a)   <u>Introduction.</u> Identify the client, and set forth the property being appraised, the purpose and function of the appraisal, the definition of the standard of value, and the effective date of the appraisal.

(b)   <u>Assumptions and Limiting Conditions.</u> Disclose any extraordinary assumptions or limiting conditions that in the appraiser's judgment affected the value.

(c)   <u>Disinterestedness.</u> That the appraisal was performed on a basis of nonadvocacy, including a statement that the appraiser has no present or contemplated interest in the property appraised and has no personal bias with respect to the parties involved, or a complete disclosure of any such interest or bias. [See Standard 1.3]

    (d)   <u>Valuation Conclusion.</u> Represents a concluding opinion of value expressed as:

        (i)   a statement of a specific opinion of value; or

        (ii)   a range of values; or

        (iii)   a preliminary estimate which <u>must</u> include a statement that an opinion of value resulting from a formal report might be different and that difference might be material. (See also Standard Six, Preliminary Reports)

2.3   Conformity. Oral appraisal reports should comply with all applicable sections of Standard One, Professional Conduct and Ethics.

2.4   Written Follow-up. By its nature, the oral report is less detailed than the written report. Therefore, whenever feasible, it is suggested that oral reports be followed by a written presentation of the salient features of the oral report. In general, the written follow-up <u>should</u> include:

    (a)   <u>Assumptions and Limiting Conditions.</u> All applicable assumptions and limiting conditions.

    (b)   <u>Support.</u> In general, a brief presentation of the information considered, the appraisal approaches used and the research and thought processes that support the appraiser's analyses, opinions and conclusions.

    (c)   <u>Appraiser's Certification</u> as specified in Section 1.25.

2.5   Recordkeeping. An appraiser <u>should</u> retain written records of appraisal reports for a period of at least five (5) years after preparation or at least two (2) years after final disposition of any judicial proceeding in which the appraiser gave testimony, whichever period expires last.

STANDARD THREE

3.0 ## EXPERT TESTIMONY

3.1 **Definition.** Expert testimony is an oral report given in the form of testimony in a deposition and/or on the witness stand before a court of proper jurisdiction or other trier of fact.

3.2 **Mandatory Content.** The appraiser shall answer all questions put to him in a manner that is clear and not misleading. When giving testimony, the appraiser shall not advocate any position that is incompatible with the appraiser's obligation of non-advocacy; i.e., it is unethical for the appraiser to suppress any facts, data, or opinions which are adverse to the case his client is trying to establish, or to over-emphasize any facts, data, or opinions which are favorable to his client's case, or in any other particulars become an advocate. The expert witness must at least comply in a manner that is clear and not misleading with the following:

(a)   Introduction. Identify the client, and set forth the property being appraised, the purpose and function of the appraisal, the definition of the standard of value, and the effective date of the appraisal.

(b)   Assumptions and Limiting Conditions. Disclose any extraordinary assumptions or limiting conditions that in the appraiser's judgment affected the value.

(c)   Disinterestedness. That the appraisal was performed on a basis of nonadvocacy, including a statement that the appraiser has no present or contemplated interest in the property appraised and has no personal bias with respect to the parties involved, or a complete disclosure of any such interest or bias. (See Standard 1.3)

(d)   Valuation Conclusion. Any concluding opinion of value may be expressed as:

(i)   a statement of a specific opinion of value; or

(ii)   a range of values; or

(iii)   a preliminary estimate which must include a statement that an opinion of value resulting from a formal report may be different and that difference may be material. (See also Standard Six, Preliminary Reports.)

3.3   Conformity. Expert testimony reports <u>should</u> comply with all applicable sections of Standard One, Professional Conduct and Ethics.

3.4   Recordkeeping. An appraiser <u>should</u> retain written records of appraisal reports for a period of at least five (5) years after preparation or at least two (2) years after final disposition of any judicial proceeding in which the appraiser gave testimony, whichever period expires last.

STANDARD FOUR

4.0   <u>LETTER FORM WRITTEN APPRAISAL REPORTS</u>

4.1   Definition. An appraiser's written report can be in the form of a letter report or a formal report. The letter report, which is shorter than the formal report, presents conclusions together with brief generalized comments. This type of report is often referred to as a short-form report, letter opinion, or an informal report.

By its nature, the letter form report is an instrument of brevity. It should contain at least a summary of the material factors that led to its conclusions, but it is usually intended by the parties to reduce the normal appraisal burden of writing a comprehensive report, and thereby allow the client to realize some economic benefit. However, the appraiser is still required to perform materially the same investigation and analysis as would be required for a comprehensive formal report and maintain in his file the workpapers necessary to support the conclusions stated in the letter report.

4.2   Conformity. The letter form written report <u>must</u> comply with all applicable provisions of Business Appraisal Standards, Standard One, Professional Conduct and Ethics.

4.3   Mandatory Content. All letter form written appraisal reports <u>shall</u> minimally set forth in a manner that is clear and not misleading:

(a)   Identify the client, and set forth a description of the business enterprise, security or other tangible and/or intangible property being appraised.

(b)   Form of the organization and if incorporated, the state of incorporation, together with a description, adequate to the assignment, of all classes of securities outstanding and a list of shareholders whose interest should, in the appraiser's judgment be specified. If a partnership, the type and the state of filing, together with a list of those partners, whether general or limited, whose interest should, in the appraiser's judgment, be specified.

(c)   The purpose (standard of value) of the appraisal.

(d)   The function (use) of the appraisal.

(e)   The definition of the standard of value that is the purpose of the appraisal.

(f)   The effective ("as of") date of the appraisal.

(g)   The date the appraisal report was prepared.

(h)   The report's assumptions and limiting conditions.

(i)   Any special factors that affected the opinion of value. Such factors include, but are not limited to, buy-sell agreements, restrictive stock agreements, corporate articles, bylaws and resolutions, partnership agreements, litigation, regulatory compliance, or environmental hazards.

(j)   Applicable discounts and premiums such as minority interest, control, marketability or lack thereof.

(k)   A certification consistent with the intent of section 1.25.

4.4   Distribution of Report. The letter report <u>should</u> include a clear statement of the expected distribution of the report.

4.5   Valuation Conclusion. The letter report <u>must</u> include a clear statement of the appraiser's concluding opinion of value expressed as appropriate to the assignment:

(a)   a statement of a specific opinion of value; or

(b)   a range of values; or

(c)   a preliminary estimate which <u>must</u> include a statement that an opinion of value resulting from a formal report might be different and that difference might be material. (See also Standard Six, Preliminary Reports.)

4.6   Transmittal Letter. If a transmittal letter is used, it <u>should</u> include a summary of the engagement. It may be structured in the form of a letter, an executive summary, or a similar rendering. However, regardless of the structure used, if a transmittal is used, it <u>shall</u> refer to the report in a manner sufficient to discourage any attempt to remove and use the transmittal without the report.

4.7   Recordkeeping. An appraiser <u>should</u> retain written records of appraisal reports for a period of at least five (5) years after preparation or at least two (2) years after final disposition of any judicial proceeding in which the appraiser gave testimony, whichever period expires last.

STANDARD FIVE

5.0   FORMAL WRITTEN APPRAISAL REPORTS

5.1   Definition. The formal appraisal report is a comprehensive business appraisal report prepared to contain at a minimum, the requirements described within this standard. It is sometimes called the long form, narrative or comprehensive report.

5.2   Conformity. The formal written report <u>must</u> comply with all applicable provisions of Business Appraisal Standards, Standard One, Professional Conduct and Ethics.

5.3   Mandatory Content. All formal appraisal reports <u>shall</u> minimally set forth the following items in a manner that is clear and not misleading, including detail sufficient to permit the reader to reasonably replicate the appraiser's procedures:

(a)   Identify the client, and set forth a description of the business enterprise, security, or other tangible and/or intangible property being appraised.

(b)   Form of the organization and if incorporated, the state of incorporation, together with a description, adequate to the assignment, of all classes of securities outstanding and a list of shareholders whose interest should, in the appraiser's judgment be specified. If a partnership, the type and the state of filing, together with a list of those partners, whether general or limited, whose interest should, in the appraiser's judgment, be specified.

(c)   The purpose (standard of value) of the appraisal.

(d)   The function (use) of the appraisal.

(e)   The definition of the standard of value that is the purpose of the appraisal.

(f)   The effective ("as of") date of the appraisal.

(g)   The date the appraisal report was prepared.

(h)   The report's assumptions and limiting conditions.

(i)   The principal sources and references used by the appraiser.

(j)   The consideration of relevant data regarding:

    (i)   The nature and history of the business.

    (ii)   The present economic conditions and the outlook affecting the business, its industry, and the general economy.

    (iii)   Past results, current operations, and future prospects of the business.

    (iv)   Past sales of interests in the business enterprise being appraised.

    (v)   Sales of similar businesses or interests therein, whether closely-held or publicly-held.

    (vi)   The valuation approaches/methods considered and rejected, the approaches/methods utilized, and the research, sources, computations, and reasoning that supports the appraiser's analyses, opinions and conclusions.

    (vii)   Any special factors that affected the opinion of value. Such factors include, but are not limited to, buy-sell agreements, restrictive stock agreements, corporate articles, bylaws and resolutions, partnership agreements, litigation, regulatory compliance, or environmental hazards.

    (viii) Applicable discounts and premiums such as minority interest, control, marketability or lack thereof.

    (ix)   When valuing a majority interest in a business on a "going concern" basis, consider whether the business' highest value may be achieved on a liquidation basis.

(k)   A Certification consistent with the intent of section 1.25.

5.4   Distribution of Report. The formal report <u>should</u> include a clear statement of the expected distribution of the report.

5.5   Valuation Conclusion. The formal report <u>must</u> include a clear statement of the appraiser's concluding opinion of value expressed as appropriate to the assignment:

(a)   a statement of a specific opinion of value; or

(b)   a range of values.

5.6   Transmittal Letter. If a transmittal letter is used, it <u>should</u> include a summary of the engagement. It may be structured in the form of a letter, an executive summary, or a similar rendering. However, regardless of the structure, if used, the transmittal <u>shall</u> refer to the report in a manner sufficient to discourage any attempt to remove and use the transmittal without the report.

5.7   Recordkeeping. An appraiser <u>should</u> retain written records of appraisal reports for a period of at least five (5) years after preparation or at least two (2) years after final disposition of any judicial proceeding in which the appraiser gave testimony, whichever period expires last.

<u>**STANDARD SIX**</u>

6.0   <u>**PRELIMINARY REPORTS**</u>

6.1   Definition. A brief oral or written report reflecting the appraiser's limited opinion.

A preliminary report <u>must</u> clearly identify any valuation as a "limited" opinion of value as the appraiser has not performed the detailed investigation and analysis essential to a cogent appraisal. [See Standard 6.5]

6.2   Conformity. The preliminary report <u>must</u> comply with all applicable provisions of Business Appraisal Standards, Standard One, Professional Conduct and Ethics.

6.3   Usage. The preliminary report has use when a client desires the appraiser's limited opinion.

6.4   Disclosure. The presentation of a preliminary opinion without disclosing its limitations is unethical.

6.5   Departure. If an appraiser makes a preliminary report without including a clear statement that it is preliminary, there is the possibility a user of the report could accord the report and its limited opinion of value a greater degree of accuracy and reliability than is inherent in the preliminary report process. Therefore, all preliminary reports <u>shall</u> include a Statement of Departure in accordance with Standard 1.21(b). The Statement of Departure <u>shall</u> include a statement that the report is preliminary and the conclusion subject to change following a proper appraisal and that said change could be material.

6.6   Oral v. Written. All preliminary reports whether oral or written are subject to Standard Six.

6.7   Recordkeeping. An appraiser <u>should</u> retain written records of appraisal reports for a period of at least five (5) years after preparation or at least two (2) years after final disposition of any judicial proceeding in which the appraiser gave testimony, whichever period expires last.

COPIES

OF THESE STANDARDS

ARE AVAILABLE FROM

THE INSTITUTE OF BUSINESS APPRAISERS, INC.
P.O. BOX 1447
BOYNTON BEACH, FLORIDA 33425

Telephone: (407) 732-3202

Ask for publication P-311a

Appendix H

BUSINESS VALUATION STANDARDS OF THE NATIONAL ASSOCIATION OF CERTIFIED VALUATION ANALYSTS*

PROFESSIONAL STANDARDS

INTRODUCTION

NACVA being an association of CPAs who perform valuation services, are bound by the standards and definitions of the AICPA's Standards on Consulting Services (SSCS), issued on October 1, 1991. This new standard replaced all Statements on Standards for Management Advisory Services (SSMAS) effective January 1, 1992.

Under the statement on Standards for Consulting Services, litigation support and valuation services are considered "transaction" consulting services, when the practitioner's function is to provide services related to a specific client transaction, generally in conjunction with a third party.

In February, 1992, the Management Consulting Services Executive Committee (MCS) proposed that separate standards on business valuations be written, but such standards have not yet been issued.

NACVA members will be bound by the forthcoming standards as promulgated by the Management Consulting Services Executive Committee. NACVA will adopt the standards when they are made available. However, in the interim, the CPA when performing either litigation support or valuation services is governed by the general standards contained in Rule 201 of the AICPA's Code of Professional Conduct.

GENERAL STANDARDS

The following general standards are extracted from Rule 201 of the AICPA's Code of Professional Conduct. They are as follows:

*Business Valuation Standards of the National Association of Certified Valuation Analysts, Salt Lake City: National Association of Certified Business Analysts, ©1995. Reprinted with permission.

— Professional Competence
— Due Professional Care
— Planning and Supervision
— Sufficient Relevant Data

Professional Competence: A member of NACVA shall: "undertake only those professional services that the member or the member's firm can reasonable expect to be completed with professional competence."

Due Professional Care: A member of NACVA shall: "exercise due professional care in the performance of professional services."

Planning and Supervision: A member of NACVA shall: "adequately plan and supervise the performance of professional services," particularly when non-NACVA members are involved in the performance of such services.

Sufficient Relevant Data: A member of NACVA shall: "obtain sufficient relevant data to afford a reasonable basis for conclusions or recommendations in relation to any professional services performed."

REPORT WRITING STANDARDS

OVERVIEW

The final stage in the valuation process is the communication of the results of the valuation to the client or other user of the report. Reports may differ in nature, but, in all cases, they must inform the parties of the degree of correspondence between quantifiable information and established criteria. Reports may also differ in form and can vary from highly technical, fully documented and extensive reports to less technical and less extensive oral reports. The form and content of any particular report will depend on the nature of the engagement, its purpose, its findings, and the needs of the decision makers who receive and rely upon it.

The business valuation profession has categorized the communication of the results into four modes or formats of reporting. They are as follows:

— Full (Formal) Written Reports
— Summary Written Reports
— Letter (Informal) Written Reports, and
— Oral (Verbal) Reports

The Board of Directors, of the National Association of Certified Valuation Analysts, has adopted the following standards for each of the above methods of reporting. The purpose of these standards is to establish minimum reporting criteria as they pertain to each form of communication. The objective of these standards is to ensure consistency and quality of valuation reports that are issued by members of the Association. The following standards will not only benefit the member, by giving him or her direction on issuing reports, but they will also benefit the client and those individuals or institutions that use and rely upon valuation reports in various decision making situations.

The intent of these standards is not to establish or attempt to define valuation engagement procedures. For purposes of this standard, the valuation analyst is the individual ultimately responsible for the valuation engagement.

STANDARDS FOR FULL (FORMAL) WRITTEN REPORTS

General: The Board of Directors has established the following minimum reporting requirements that pertain specifically to full (formal) written reports.

A full (formal) written report must be organized, well written and communicate the results and identify the information relied upon in the valuation process. The wording used in the report should not be overly technical and complicated, but should effectively communicate important thoughts, methods, reasoning and identify the supporting documentation in a simple and concise manner.

Often, circumstances arise where the analyst is confronted with issues that may require the analyst to depart from certain criteria established by this standard. If this is the case, the analyst must fully disclose the departure.

Format: The format of full (formal) written reports is as follows:

- Identification/Cover Page
- Table of Contents
- Opinion Letter
- Body of Report
- Appendix

Identification/Cover Page. The identification/cover page must indicate the following:

- Identification or name of the enterprise that is the subject of the report.
- Effective date of the valuation conclusion.
- Identification of the analyst and/or his or her firm.
- Date that the report is issued.

Table of Contents. Due to the extensive amount of material that is typically included in a full (formal) written report, a table of contents should be included. Any item referenced in the table of contents must also be included in the report.

Opinion Letter. For the purposes of this standard, an opinion letter must be presented that sets forth minimum information concerning the valuation engagement and its results. The opinion letter must include:

— The identification of the entity being valued.
— The effective date of the valuation and date of issuance.
— The purpose of the valuation.
— Identification of the standard and premise of value.
— Description of the equity interest being valued.
— Conclusion as to valuation results.
— Limitation on use of report.
— Signature of the valuation analyst.

Body of Report. In addition to the opinion letter's minimum reporting requirements, a full written report must also include sufficient information that clearly communicates the thoughts, reasoning, methods and information or data used and relied upon to reach the estimate of value conclusion. The following are items of information that are necessary to clearly communicate the determination of value reached and the description of information used and relied upon to support the value conclusion.

Purpose of Valuation: The purpose of the valuation is a critical aspect of the engagement. Although the purpose is stated in the opinion letter of the report, it must be restated in the body of the report. The purpose of the valuation must be clearly communicated in a manner that will not lead to any confusion on the part of the user of the report.

Approach to Valuation: A discussion describing your general or overall approach to the valuation must be included. An example of this discussion is as follows:

Our approach has been to determine an estimate of value which would provide a fair and reasonable return on investment to an investor or owner, in view of the facts available to use at the time. Our opinion is based on, among other things, our estimate of the risks facing the Company and the return on investment which would be required on alternative investments with similar levels of risk.

Both internal and external factors which influence the value of (subject company) are reviewed, analyzed and interpreted. Internal factors include the Company's financial position, results of operations and the size and marketability of the interest being valued. External factors include, among other things, the status of the industry and the position of the Company relative to the industry.

Identification of sources of information utilized and the degree of reliance on such information should be disclosed.

Statement of Limiting Conditions. Each valuation engagement requires the valuation analyst to identify (in the body of the full written report) any material qualifying matters regarding the analyst's estimate of value. Since all valuation cases will vary as to their specific limiting conditions, the following are provided to assist the analyst regarding examples of limiting conditions that are often encountered:

We have no present or contemplated financial interest in the (subject company). Our fees, for this valuation, are based upon our normal hourly billing rates, and in no way are contingent upon the results of our findings. We have no responsibility to update this report for events and circumstances occurring subsequent to the date of this report.

This report has been prepared for the specific purpose of valuing the subject company's (describe equity interest) as of (effective date of valuation) (describe purpose of the valuation) and is intended for no other purpose. This report is not to be copied or made available to any persons without the express written consent of (your company).

Our report is based on historical and prospective financial information provided to us by management and other third parties. Had we audited or reviewed the underlying data, matters may have come to our attention which would have resulted in our using amounts which differ from those provided, accordingly, we take no responsibility for the underlying data presented or relied upon in this report.

Users of this business valuation report should be aware that business valuations are based on future earnings potential that may or may not materialize. Therefore, the actual results achieved during the projection period will vary from the projections utilized in this valuation, and the variations may be material.

We have relied upon the representations of the owners, management and other third parties concerning the value and useful condition of all equipment, real estate, investments used in the business, and any other assets or liabilities except as specifically stated to the contrary in this report. We have not attempted to confirm whether or not all assets of the business are free and clear of liens and encumbrances, or that the company has good title to all assets.

The estimate of value included in this report assumes that the existing company will maintain the character and integrity of the company through any sale, reorganization or reduction of any owner's/manager's participation in the existing activities of the company.

(Your company) does not purport to be a guarantor of value. Valuation of closely held companies is an imprecise science, with value being a question of fact, and reasonable people can differ in their estimates of value. (Your company) has, however, performed conceptually sound and commonly accepted methods and procedures of valuation in determining the estimate of value included in this report.

The valuation analyst, by reason of performing this valuation and preparing this report, is not to be required to give expert testimony nor to be in attendance in court or at any government hearing with reference to the matters contained herein, unless prior arrangements have been made with (your company) regarding such additional engagement.

Enterprise Background and Description. Individuals and institutions that rely on valuation reports are often not intimately or even generally informed about the business' organization or its structure, background, products and markets. Therefore, it is necessary to adequately describe the company in order to assist the user of the report. The following are examples of items that must be included to adequately describe the enterprise:

— Nature of the enterprise
— Type of enterprise (i.e., wholesaler, distribution, retailer, etc.)
— History of the enterprise
— Organization form (i.e., corporation, partnership, etc.)
— Description of service or products
— Competition, when appropriate
— Location of operations
— Markets
— Discussion of managements' ability and depth, when appropriate
— Other items of information the analyst believes necessary to adequately describe the enterprise, the industry and the economic climate in which the enterprise operates.

Ownership and Structure. The business structure and ownership interests of the entity being valued has significant impact on the estimate of value conclusion, and should be described in the report. Any restrictions on the transferability of the subject equity interest must be fully described.

Financial Review. A comprehensive financial analysis of the subject company's financial history is an essential procedure in the valuation process. Therefore, the results of the financial analysis must be included in the report. The financial review must include an adequate description of the financial data included in the analysis, the period it covers, and the degree to which the analyst has relied on such data. The financial review must also include the discussion of key factors that lead the analyst to his or her conclusions regarding management performance, financial position and results of operations.

The source of the financial data must be disclosed and whether or not the data was adjusted by the analyst. If the analyst has made adjustments to the data, the adjustment and reasoning for the adjustment must be adequately disclosed.

If the analyst has performed a comparative analysis between the subject company's data and data of comparative public or private companies, or if he or she has based the comparison on industry averages, the source of the data and the results of the comparative analysis must be adequately communicated.

Nature of the Security. The nature of the security interest being valued must be discussed. The discussion must include the identification of the security and the percentage of ownership which it represents. Issues involving control, marketability, minority interest and restrictions (if any) must also be adequately communicated.

Valuation Methodology. A discussion of the valuation methodology must be included in the report. The method(s) of valuation must be identified and adequately explained. The reasoning for selecting certain methods must be provided. The source, method and/or basis for determining key variables utilized in the valuation method must be clearly described.

The progression of the valuation methodology must flow in a logical and straight forward manner and must result in the estimate of value conclusion.

If third party appraisers of tangible assets were involved, their identity and conclusions must be incorporated in the report.

All methods or sources of determining tangible asset values, estimated projected earnings, capitalization/discount rates, discounts or premiums or any other material factors utilized in the valuation methodology must be fully described.

Other Statements. Other comments that address concerns of confidentiality of the report itself and descriptions of the level of independence and the method of compensation should also be included in the full written report. The analyst may decide where in the report to include these comments either in the opinion letter or the body of the full written report.

Appendix. Various items of financial or other information should be included in the appendix of the report. Certain detailed information should not be included in the body of the report, but rather in its appendix. Items of information which may be included in the appendix are:

— Historical financial statement summaries
— Adjustments to historical financial statements
— Adjusted financial statement summaries
— Common size analysis summaries
— Ratio analysis summaries
— Comparative analysis data
— Independent appraisals on tangible assets

STANDARDS OF SUMMARY WRITTEN REPORTS

Overview: The Board of Directors has established an intermediate level report writing standard. This standard pertains to Summary Written Reports. The Valuation Analyst may be engaged to perform a valuation and issue a report where an intermediate level of assurance opinion is adequate for the purpose of the valuation. Summary Written Reports (at a minimum) must meet all Letter (Informal) Report Writing requirements and must:

- Clearly be identified as a Summary Written Report.
- Be substantially in the form of a full (formal) written report, and
- Not fail to disclose any fact which would materially affect the valuation conclusion.

STANDARDS OF LETTER (INFORMAL) REPORTS

Overview: The Board of Directors has established the following reporting requirements that pertain specifically to letter (informal) written reports. A valuation analyst may be engaged to perform a valuation and issue a report where a limited assurance opinion is adequate for the purpose of the valuation.

The limitation on the report can result from the primary situations as follows:

1. Where the analyst has performed the necessary valuation procedures that would enable him or her to issue a full (formal) written report, but, has only been engaged to issue a letter (informal) report, or

2. Where the analyst has been engaged to perform a valuation where the scope of his or her procedures have been limited, and where limited procedures and consequently a limited report is adequate for the purpose of the valuation.

Opinion Letter: The opinion letter of a Letter Report should contain at a minimum the following information:

- The identification of the entity being valued.
- The effective date of the valuation and date of report.
- The purpose of the valuation.
- Identification of the standard and premise of value.
- Description of the equity interest being valued.
- Conclusion as to valuation results.
- Limitation on use of report.
- Signature of the valuation analyst.

Including (if applicable) a scope and/or report limitation statement. Examples of which are as follows:

<u>Scope Limitation:</u>

The scope of this valuation engagement and valuation report was limited. We were engaged to perform a valuation for (subject company) with the intent of ascertain-

ing an approximate estimate of value. If (your company) was engaged to perform a more detailed analysis, matters may have come to our attention that could have a material impact on the estimate of value contained in this report. Accordingly, our level of assurance on the estimate of value is reduced. This report is not intended to serve as a basis for expert testimony in a court of law or other governmental agency without further analysis and resulting documentation.

Report Limitation:

The valuation report is limited in its discussion regarding information utilized in the valuation process. We were engaged to perform a valuation of (subject company) where the scope of the valuation procedures was not limited. However, we were limited in the amount of discussion made in this report. The discussion omitted include (identify discussions omitted). If the omitted discussions were included in this report, they might influence the users level of understanding regarding the estimate of value contained in this report. Accordingly, this report is not designed for those who are not informed about such matters.

Body of Letter Report: In addition to the minimum requirements of the opinion letter of the letter (informal) written report, other minimum information must also be included in the body of the letter (informal) written report. The items that must be included in the body of a letter (informal) written report are as follows:

— Purpose of the valuation.
— Approach to the valuation.
— Statement of limiting conditions (in addition to scope or report limitations).
— Business description (including form of organization, brief history of subject company, products or services described, description of sources of information used and level of reliance on such information).
— Ownership and structure.
— Valuation methodology.
— Other.

STANDARD OF ORAL REPORTS

Overview: Valuation analysts are often requested to report their estimate of value, on a particular business, by means of an oral presentation.

Oral reports made by a valuation analyst must comply with the professional standards of the AICPA except to the extent that they are inconsistent with standards adopted by NACVA.

An oral report must be carefully worded, particularly as it leaves no written documentation and may result in insufficient comprehension of the estimate of value being communicated.

A written outline of the analyst's oral presentation is required. This will help to ensure that an adequate communication occurs.

Adequate Communication: It is recommended that an oral report adequately communicate the following:

— Identification of entity being valued.
— Effective date of the valuation.
— Purpose of the valuation.
— Identification of the standard and premise of value.
— Description of the equity interest being valued.
— Conclusion as to estimate of value results.
— Limitation on use of the oral report.
— Description of any limiting conditions, including any scope limitations.

STANDARD OF INTERNAL REPORTS

An internal report should be prepared and documented in the same manner as any other report or communication of an estimate of value conclusion. No part or parts of the content of the report should be conveyed to any third parties without the written consent of the valuation analyst. A valuation analyst who consents to third party communications must clearly state that there was a lack of independence and such lack of independence must be fully described.

OTHER GUIDELINES

Besides professional guidelines, valuation analysts will also find it necessary to consider report writing requirements established by the users of the valuation report, such as:

— Internal Revenue Service (IRS) requirements
— Department of Labor (DOL) requirements
— State laws and other legal requirements.

IRS Requirements: The IRS has guidelines regarding business valuations. Revenue Ruling 59-60 identifies certain factors that should be considered in valuing a business for gift and estate tax purposes. Accordingly a report for a tax-related valuation should discuss how it meets applicable IRS requirements. If the report relates to a valuation of donated stock, the valuation analyst also may need to consult Revenue Procedure 66-49, which provides general report requirements for those types of valuations.

DOL Requirements: DOL regulations apply to business valuations for ESOPs. In 1988, the DOL proposed a regulation that prescribed procedures and reporting rules for valuations relating to ESOPs. Although the proposed regulation is not yet final, many valuation analysts have conformed their reports to the proposed new rules.

INDEX